American Dress Pattern Catalogs, 1873–1909

Four Complete Reprints

Edited by

Nancy Villa Bryk

Published for
HENRY FORD MUSEUM & GREENFIELD VILLAGE
DEARBORN, MICHIGAN
by
DOVER PUBLICATIONS, INC.
NEW YORK

For Lawrence and Maria

Published in Canada by General Publishing Company, Ltd.,
30 Lesmill Road, Don Mills, Toronto, Ontario.
Published in the United Kingdom by Constable and Company, Ltd.,
10 Orange Street, London WC2H 7EG.

This Dover edition, first published in 1988 in association with Henry Ford Museum &
Greenfield Village, Dearborn, Michigan, is a republication in one volume of *E. Butterick & Co.'s
Catalogue for Summer, 1873*, published by E. Butterick & Co., New York; *E. Butterick & Co.'s
Summer Catalogue 1882*, published by The Butterick Publishing Co. (Limited), New York;
Spring & Summer 1909 Ready Reference Catalogue of McCall Patterns, published by The McCall
Company; and the complete fashion pages of *The Ladies' Standard Magazine, April, 1894, Vol.
XI, No. 2*, published by the Standard Fashion Co., New York. A new introduction has been
written for this edition.

Manufactured in the United States of America
Dover Publications, Inc.
31 East 2nd Street
Mineola, N.Y. 11501

Library of Congress Cataloging-in-Publication Data

American dress pattern catalogs, 1873–1909.

Reprint of works originally published 1873–1909. Contents:
E. Butterick & Co.'s Catalogue for summer, 1873—
E. Butterick & Co.'s Summer catalogue, 1882—The Ladies
standard magazine, April, 1894—[etc.]
1. Dressmaking—United States—Patterns—Catalogs.
2. Costume—United States—History.   I. Bryk, Nancy Villa.
II. Henry Ford Museum and Greenfield Village.
TT556.A54   1988   646.4′07   88-10873
ISBN 0-486-25654-5

Table of Contents

Introduction

THIS PUBLICATION CONTAINS three American dress pattern catalogs and one pattern fashion periodical, ranging in date from 1873 to 1909. It includes *E. Butterick & Co.'s Catalogue for Summer, 1873*, their *Summer Catalogue 1882*, the April 1894 "Special Bicycle Number" of *The Ladies' Standard Magazine* and the *Spring & Summer 1909 Ready Reference Catalogue of McCall Patterns*. All four feature ordinary clothing that was worn on farms as well as on bustling city streets. Viewed separately, each catalog documents middle-class fashions that have not commonly survived in museum collections. When examined together, they chronicle the periodic change in the woman's fashionable silhouette, document the introduction of some new activities and hint at differences in the way the wearer was perceived during this era.

The garments illustrated in these publications could be constructed from mass-produced, pre-cut paper patterns of standard sizes. The manufacturers promoted their stock patterns in seasonal catalogs, and some companies founded their own fashion periodicals, like *The Ladies' Standard Magazine*, which introduced styles and showcased new patterns. While dozens of pattern companies issued catalogs each season of every year, few such publications are found in archives today. They were published for short-term use; thus, merchants and housewives discarded them as seasons changed and styles faded. The reprinting of these catalogs, now in the collections of the Research Library of the Henry Ford Museum & Greenfield Village, reveal some of the clothing choices available to the American seamstress about a century ago.

The moneyed could always commission a tailor or seamstress to produce custom clothing based on the latest European fashion; however, families of limited means found the acquisition of fashionable dress difficult throughout most of the nineteenth century. Although men's and boys' items were available ready-to-wear by 1850, women's ready-made goods lagged behind—few ladies' items, except undergarments and outergarments, were available before 1880. Thus, home construction of clothing was the only practical alternative for many housewives during this period.

The home seamstress recognized that an attractive garment of good fit required a well-drafted clothing pattern. Those who could spare the funds could have a custom pattern drafted, but many more labored over patterns of their own devising. Some ripped apart older garments and used the individual pieces as pattern templates, reconstructing curves and adding seam allowances. While ladies' periodicals often included small pattern diagrams that could be enlarged, tedious re-drafting was required to fit a specific figure. Other periodicals contained full-size patterns, but they were "one-size" and they, too, needed adjustment. Although the availability of an affordable domestic sewing machine lightened her burden after mid-century, the home seamstress still looked for an easily acquired, dependable clothing pattern. The needs of many were met by the mass-produced paper pattern.

In 1864, *Demorest's Monthly Magazine*, a fashion periodical, offered paper patterns "custom fit" to a specific figure if the client mailed in 25 cents and her measurements. It was Ebenezer Butterick, however, who first developed the mass-produced tissue-paper pattern sized according to a system of proportional grading. Although the first Butterick patterns, published in 1863, were for boys' clothing, ladies' fashions, added to the line in 1866, soon made up the majority of the designs. By 1868, E. Butterick & Co. offered fifteen standard pattern sizes in a variety of styles. The pattern envelope contained a cut and notched tissue-paper pattern, cutting and sewing instructions and an illustration of the completed garment.

Butterick provided the consumer with a dependable pattern of the newest fashion by devising careful workroom procedures. A female artist sketched the styles, keeping an eye on European modes. After the designs were approved for production, the fashions were cut in muslin, sewn together as garments and fitted on human models. These mock-ups were taken apart and proportionally sized. The original muslin pieces were used as templates from which the tissue patterns were cut. Envelopes were then packed and ready for purchase, and the style was promoted in the company's catalog or ladies' magazine.

By 1870 James McCall offered mass-produced "Bazar Cut Patterns," featuring them first in his magazine *The Queen*, and then in *McCall's*, founded in 1897. These graded patterns were tremendously successful—Butterick alone was reported to have sold six million in 1871—and by 1900, Butterick and McCall had many competitors. The commercial pattern rendered a fairly well-fitting garment and was cheap and easy to use.

Shrewd entrepreneurs like Butterick and McCall ensured that the consumer could easily purchase the product by mail from the company's main office or from one of their agents, usually a small-town shopkeeper, and the seamstress who yearned to wear the latest fashion constantly purchased new patterns as the mode changed.

The catalogs reprinted here feature middle-class fashions distributed from Boston to Sacramento. They present the products of three different pattern manufacturers, including Butterick and McCall, the two earliest and largest. The two Butterick catalogs are similar in the type of garments they feature because they show the goods of a single manufacturer and are close in date. *The Ladies' Standard Magazine* showcases bicycling dress and is a fine representative of the fashion periodical in which pattern companies aggressively marketed their product. The McCall catalog includes summer wear for housewives and working women in an era when pattern companies were competing with a fully developed ready-to-wear industry. Ladies' fashions predominate for a variety of reasons: Fewer ready-made items were available to ladies during the first half of this period; some women's garments were easier to construct at home than were carefully tailored men's goods; and women's fashions changed constantly, allowing the pattern manufacturer to sell new styles at a rapid pace.

Fashions in both of the Butterick catalogs appealed to the middle-class housewife whose duties were primarily domestic. Wrappers for informal house wear appear next to dresses that could be used for visiting or promenade. No formal evening wear is offered. Varied terms given to the different forms of garments (polonaise, basque and waist were all names for types of bodices in the 1873 catalog) suggest that the lady examining these pages was likely to be concerned with wearing the correct garment for each particular occasion. Babies' long robes, worn by infants until they could crawl, are seen. Girls' and misses' dresses (for young ladies under age 18) mirror their mothers'. Clothes for boys of various ages are also illustrated—boys wore short frocks until about age 3, then knickers, and were buttoned into trousers at about age 8. Few gentlemen's fashions are featured, primarily because many men's items were available ready-made. The later Butterick catalog is expanded to include patterns for doll clothes, stuffed toys and home furnishings such as mantel and window lambrequins. This catalog shows evidence of the hard wear pattern catalogs received; a portion of pages 31 and 32 (Dover pages 69 and 70) has been cut out, perhaps by a seamstress who wanted a reminder of a particular style.

These two Butterick catalogs illustrate some common garments that have not survived in quantity. Both contain men's overalls, drawers (long-legged underpants), bathing costumes, long-sleeve and high-necked corset covers and ladies' walking skirts. The 1882 catalog shows a pattern for a tournure or bustle for the heavily trained skirt, and two illustrations of men's working blouses, one to be tucked into the trousers, one worn as a smock.

The Ladies' Standard Magazine, the fashion periodical of the Standard Fashion Co., was published from 1889 to about 1897; however, the production dates of the pattern company are unknown. In many ways it resembles other fashion magazines in which stylish goods and garments are noted and new fashions introduced. This particular issue features bicycling clothing, including bloomers, an item that revolutionized women's fashion. Many people were horrified by their "objectionable exposure of the figure," but the female bicyclist scoffed, describing bloomers as "serviceable and sensible" as well as "safe, elegant, and comfortable beyond compare," according to *The Ladies' Standard Magazine*. Most skeptics soon acknowledged that this garb could be modest, feminine and practical and the bloomers became acceptable garments for women. As the above quotes indicate, this "Special Bicycle Number" is a treasure for delineating the controversy over the new sports styles as well as depicting the garments themselves.

The 1909 McCall's catalog features casual fashions for women and children. Plain blouses and skirts, work clothes for typewriter girls and stenographers, are offered. In fact, some models are depicted as working women, leaning against desks and holding pen and paper. Also shown are common house dresses, wrappers, dressing gowns and practical suits for "outings" (anything from summer visiting to "automobiling"). Outfits for bicycling and gymnastics are not included although both were acceptable activities for ladies at this time. Likewise, no patterns for dusters, used by both the buggy rider and the modern "automobilist," are shown, possibly because they were more likely to be purchased ready-made. Also, it is likely that the McCall patterns were targeted at the woman with minimal leisure and money.

Women's fashions changed as rapidly one hundred years ago as they do today, and each catalog features a fashionable silhouette. Undergarments rearranged flesh to render the desired figure type throughout these decades by constricting the waist and recontouring the bosom. Bustles or numerous petticoats weighed on the body as they supported skirts. Dresses in 1873 consisted of draped and puffed overskirts, flowing sleeves and skirts laden with rows of machine-applied trim. By 1882, corsets and bodices were very tight; heavy skirts of rich fabric hugged the knees in front, while bustles pushed heavily trained skirts out behind. While the mannish "tailor made" suits of the mid-1890s, with their gored skirts, were easier to move in than skirts of previous decades, waists continued to be tiny. Blouses and skirts shown in 1909 were of lightweight fabrics, but the corset pushed the body beneath into a peculiar S shape, with breasts pushed up and together and the buttocks shoved out in back. Clearly, it was fashion before ease for the wearer of these dresses.

Women's clothing changed more than superficially during this era. Women's activities changed dramatically and the fashions designed for them reflect these changes. An increasing interest in exercise, a commitment to more healthful underclothing for women and children and increasing employment opportunities outside the home all influenced women's costume.

Some writers and physicians began advocating exercise in the 1860s. Sport walking soon gained acceptance and women's walking clubs were organized. The short walking skirt depicted in the 1873 Butterick catalog may well have been used by a sport walker. Walking skirts without trains are shown in the 1882 catalog. Bathing costumes for ladies, misses and children, shown in both Butterick catalogs, reflect the wide appeal of this activity. By 1894, 40,000 Americans had taken to the safety bike, which permitted them to move beyond the front yard with grace and speed. *The Ladies' Standard Magazine* speaks primarily of bicycling, but it also mentions mountain climbing and cross-saddle riding.

Physicians and social reformers had long been concerned with the debilitating aspects of women's dress, particularly undergarments. They objected to scanty undergarments, deforming corsets and layers of petticoats that reduced circulation and restricted movement. Items of "improved dress" were produced in quantity beginning in the 1870s. The 1882 Butterick catalog includes a few such garments. Flannel vests that provided warmth and absorbed perspiration are shown. A pattern is given for a corset-waist that offered a lightly structured alternative to the corset. Ladies' "combinations," single garments consisting of joined corset cover and drawers or petticoat (thus eliminating a constricting waistband), are seen in both the later Butterick catalog and the McCall catalog. And *The Ladies' Standard Magazine* speaks of the absence of the corset for the bicyclist who wanted "the height of comfort."

By 1890, as more and more single and widowed women worked outside the home, they required attractive, practical garments for their new jobs. Previously, many women had worked as boardinghouse keepers or domestics. As women left the home environment and moved into the business office or the department store,

their business "uniform" necessarily differed from their casual home wrappers. Periodicals urged typewriter girls, stenographers and store clerks to adopt pretty garments that permitted movement and could withstand foul weather. The simple shirtwaist and skirt, as well as the mannish wool suit, served them well. The McCall catalog shows a shirtwaist and skirt that have softened in form and fabric. Models in office settings wear frilly blouses and flounced skirts. This clothing appealed to frugal female office workers.

The end of the nineteenth century witnessed a revolution in children's clothing. Physicians, social reformers, educators and mothers began to grasp the fact that children's minds and bodies had needs very different from those of adults. Among other things, clothing was constructed that presented middle-class children not as parlor statues, but as active, growing beings.

The 1873 and 1882 Butterick catalogs show girls' dresses that mirrored their mothers' fashions. Girls were burdened with many petticoats, heavy fabrics and restrictive "waists" or corsets. Boys resembled little dolls, dressed first in frocks, then in colorful knicker suits, before they received their long trousers. The 1882 catalog hints at changes in their dress, however, as more healthful undergarments for children appear. Included are a child's "union dress" that kept perspiration from the skin and eliminated layers at the waist, as well as unrestrictive underwaists and a flannel vest. *The Ladies' Standard Magazine* shows "Mother Hubbard" dresses that flow loosely from the shoulder and permit activity. The McCall catalog includes only comfortable, simple fashions for both sexes, showing bloomers for girls, and most significant, "rompers" for both sexes. This one-piece bloomer playsuit was unrestrictive, durable and easy to clean. It remains virtually unchanged to this day.

These four pattern fashion publications present ordinary clothing familiar to the vast majority of Americans a century ago. They reveal vast differences in the textures of the lives of those who carefully pulled the tissue-paper patterns from envelopes. Despite their different experiences and expectations, seamstresses of 1873, 1882, 1894 and 1909 were most likely amused, appalled or entranced by the fashions in these catalogs. And for the price of a pattern (the company paid postage), a stylish clothing pattern the home sewer spotted while thumbing through the catalog could be brought to her door.

NANCY VILLA BRYK
Curator
Division of Domestic Life
Henry Ford Museum & Greenfield Village

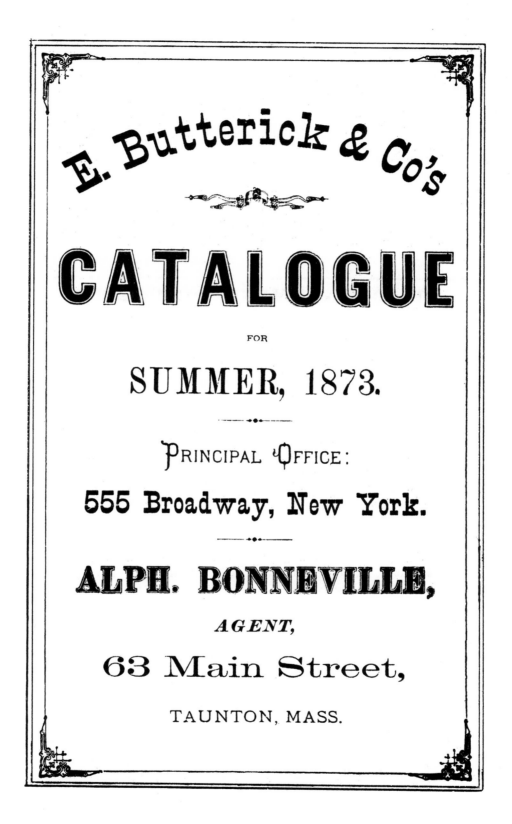

E. Butterick & Co's

CATALOGUE

FOR

SUMMER, 1873.

PRINCIPAL OFFICE:

555 Broadway, New York.

ALPH. BONNEVILLE,

AGENT,

63 Main Street,

TAUNTON, MASS.

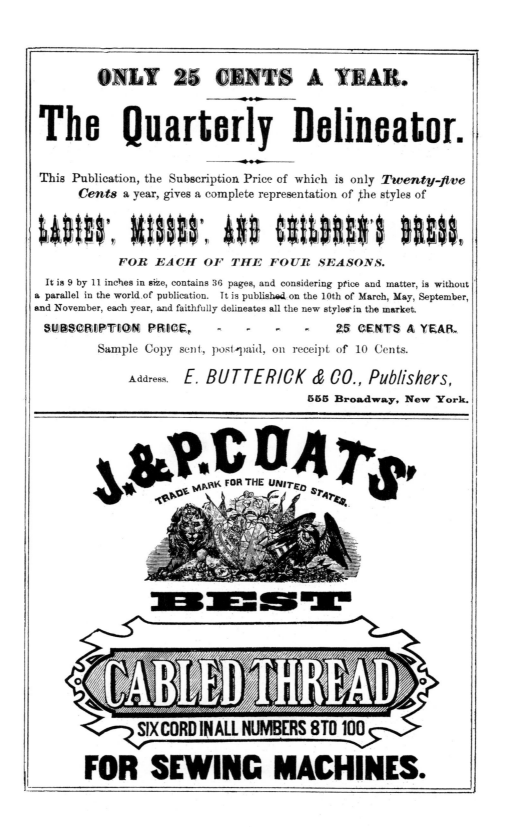
3

HOW TO OBTAIN CORRECT PATTERNS.

In buying our patterns, see for yourselves that the measures are taken correctly, and that the size printed on the label corresponds with the measure as taken. It is immaterial whether the party taking the measure stands before or behind the individual being measured; both ways of taking the measures are represented in the cuts below. If properly observed, the following rules will in all cases insure a satisfactory result.

To Measure for a Lady's Polonaise, Basque, Sack, Cloak, Dress, Waist, or any garment requiring a bust measure to be taken.—Put the measure around the body, over the dress, close under the arms, drawing it closely, *not too tight.*

To Measure for a Skirt.—Put the tape around the waist, over the dress.

☞ *Take the measures for Misses' and Little Girls' Patterns the same as for Ladies. In ordering, give the ages also.*

To Measure for a Boy's Jacket, Coat, Waist, or Vest.—Put the measure around the body under the jacket, close under the arms, drawing it closely, *not too tight.*

For the Overcoat.—Measure the same as for Jacket or Coat—only measure over the Coat or Jacket, or whatever garment the Coat is to be worn over.

To Measure for Pants.—Ascertain the waist measure, by putting the measure around the body. over the Pants, at the waist, drawing it closely, *not too tight.*

To Measure for a Shirt.—For the size of the Neck, measure the exact size where the collar encircles it, allowing one inch, thus:—if the exact size is 14 inches, use a Pattern marked 15 inches. For the Breast, measure the same as for a coat. For length of Sleeve, measure from the socket bone in the back of the neck, over the highest point of the shoulder, down the arm to the lowest point the wrist-band is to extend. *Be careful and not get the sleeve too short.*

NOTICE !

☞ **Any sizes of the Patterns specified in the within Catalogue which cannot be procured of our Agents, will be sent by us post-paid, on receipt of price, to any part of the United States or Canada.**

E. BUTTERICK & CO.

555 Broadway, New York.

LADIES' PATTERNS.

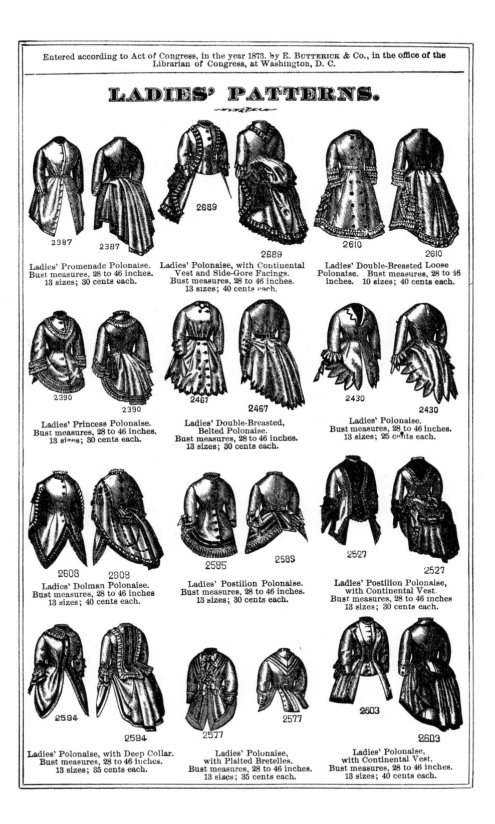

Ladies' Promenade Polonaise.
Bust measures, 28 to 46 inches.
13 sizes; 30 cents each.

Ladies' Polonaise, with Continental Vest and Side-Gore Facings.
Bust measures, 28 to 46 inches.
13 sizes; 40 cents each.

Ladies' Double-Breasted Loose Polonaise. Bust measures, 28 to 46 inches. 10 sizes; 40 cents each.

Ladies' Princess Polonaise.
Bust measures, 28 to 46 inches.
13 sizes; 30 cents each.

Ladies' Double-Breasted,
Belted Polonaise.
Bust measures, 28 to 46 inches.
13 sizes; 30 cents each.

Ladies' Polonaise.
Bust measures, 28 to 46 inches.
13 sizes; 25 cents each.

Ladies' Dolman Polonaise.
Bust measures, 28 to 46 inches
13 sizes; 40 cents each.

Ladies' Postilion Polonaise.
Bust measures, 28 to 46 inches.
13 sizes; 30 cents each.

Ladies' Postilion Polonaise,
with Continental Vest.
Bust measures, 28 to 46 inches
13 sizes; 30 cents each.

Ladies' Polonaise, with Deep Collar.
Bust measures, 28 to 46 inches.
13 sizes; 35 cents each.

Ladies' Polonaise,
with Plaited Bretelles.
Bust measures, 28 to 46 inches.
13 sizes; 35 cents each.

Ladies' Polonaise,
with Continental Vest.
Bust measures, 28 to 46 inches.
13 sizes; 40 cents each.

2738

Ladies' Princess Polonaise.
Bust measures, 28 to 46 inches.
13 sizes; 35 cents each.

2573   **2578**

Ladies' Redingote.
Bust measures, 28 to 46 inches.
13 sizes; 40 cents each.

2751

Ladies' Double-Breasted Redingote.
Bust measures, 28 to 46 inches.
13 sizes; 35 cents each.

2741

Ladies' Redingote.
Bust measures, 28 to 46 inches.
13 sizes; 30 cents each.

2579

Ladies' Redingote, with Vest Front.
Bust measures, 28 to 46 inches.
13 sizes; 35 cents each.

2739

Ladies' Sleeveless Redingote,
with a Cape.
Bust measures, 28 to 46 inches
13 sizes; 30 cents each.

2652

Ladies' Dolman Cloak, with
Lapels and Collar.
Bust measures, 28 to 46 inches.
10 sizes; 35 cents each.

2703

Ladies' Sack Waterproof, with
a Cape and Hood.
Bust measures, 28 to 46 inches.
13 sizes; 40 cents each.

2595

Ladies' Dolman Traveling Cloak.
Bust measures, 28 to 46 inches.
10 sizes; 40 cents each.

2691

Ladies' Sleeveless Waterproof Cloak.
Bust measures, 28 to 46 inches.
10 sizes; 40 cents each.

2604

Ladies' Dolman Cloak, with
Coat Sleeves.
Bust measures, 28 to 46 inches.
13 sizes; 35 cents each.

1887

Ladies' Waterproof Cloak.
Bust measures, 28 to 46 inches,
10 sizes; 40 cents each,

1298   1298
Ladies' Circular Waterproof
Cloak, with Hood.
Bust measures, 28 to 46 inches.
10 sizes; 40 cents each.

2530   2530
Ladies' Gored Waterproof Cloak.
Bust measures, 28 to 46 inches.
10 sizes; 35 cents each.

2525   2525
Ladies' Cloak, with Cape
and Dolman Sleeves.
Bust measures, 28 to 46 inches.
10 sizes; 30 cents each.

2588   2588
Ladies' Gored Cloak.
Bust measures, 28 to 46 inches
13 sizes; 30 cents each.

2526   2526
Ladies Cloak, with Dolman Sleeves.
Bust measures, 28 to 46 inches.
10 sizes; 25 cents each.

2470   2470
Ladies' Gored Cloak, with a Cape.
Bust measures, 28 to 46 inches.
13 sizes; 25 cents each.

2591   2591
Ladies' Talma Dolman.
Bust measures, 28 to 46 inches.
10 sizes; 35 cents each.

2571   2571
Ladies' Dolman.
Bust measures, 28 to 46 inches.
10 sizes; 30 cents each.

2576   2576
Ladies' Dolman.
Bust measures, 28 to 46 inches.
10 sizes; 30 cents each.

2647   2647
Ladies' Talma.
Bust measures, 28 to 46 inches.
10 sizes; 30 cents each.

2581   2581
Ladies' Dolman Talma.
Bust measures, 28 to 46 inches.
10 sizes; 30 cents each.

2726   2726
Ladies' Dolman Mantle.
Bust measures, 28 to 46 inches.
10 sizes; 30 cents each.

2682   2682
Ladies' Dolman Mantle.
Bust measures, 28 to 46 inches.
13 sizes; 35 cents each.

2744   2744
Ladies' Dolman Mantle.
Bust measures, 28 to 46 inches.
10 sizes; 30 cents each.

2509   2509
Ladies' Watteau Mantilla.
Bust measures, 28 to 46 inches.
10 sizes; 25 cents each.

2868   2665

Ladies' Paletot.
Bust measures, 28 to 46 inches.
13 sizes; 35 cents each.

2572   2572

Ladies' Paletot.
Bust measures, 28 to 46 inches.
13 sizes; 30 cents each.

2876   2676

Ladies' Paletot, with Flowing Sleeves.
Bust measures, 28 to 46 inches.
13 sizes; 35 cents each.

2589   2589

Ladies' Paletot.
Bust measures, 28 to 46 inches.
10 sizes; 30 cents each.

2575   2575

Ladies' Gored Paletot.
Bust measures, 28 to 46 inches.
13 sizes; 30 cents each.

2721   2721

Ladies' Half-Fitting Paletot.
Bust measures, 28 to 46 inches
13 sizes; 25 cents each.

2718   2718

Ladies' Half-Fitting Paletot.
Bust measures, 28 to 46 inches.
13 sizes; 30 cents each.

2168   2168

Ladies' Cape.
Bust measures, 28 to 46 inches.
10 sizes; 15 cents each.

2645

2645

Ladies' Fichu, with Belt.
Bust measures, 28 to 46 inches.
10 sizes; 20 cents each.

2401   2401

Ladies' Fichu Cape.
Bust measures, 28 to 46 inches.
10 sizes; 20 cents each.

2731   2731

Ladies' Fichu Cape and Over-Skirt, combined.
Bust measures, 28 to 46 inches.
10 sizes; 25 cents each.

2241

2241

Ladies' Watteau Fichu.
Bust measures, 28 to 46 inches.
10 sizes; 10 cents each.

2764

2164

Ladies' Fichu.
Bust measures, 28 to 46 inches.
10 sizes; 20 cents each.

2531   2531

Ladies' Double-Breasted Walking Coat.
Bust measures, 28 to 46 inches.
13 sizes; 30 cents each.

2377   2377

Ladies' Sleeveless Over-dress.
Bust measures, 28 to 46 inches.
13 sizes; 25 cents each.

2700

2700

Ladies' Tunique Princess Dress.
Bust measures, 28 to 46 inches.
13 sizes; 75 cents each.

2717

2717

Ladies' Princess Gabrielle Dress, with Pointed **Front**.
Bust measures, 28 to 46 inches.
13 sizes; 75 cents each.

2699

2699

Ladies' Princess Dress.
Bust measures, 28 to 46 inches.
13 sizes; 75 cents each.

2714

2714

Ladies' Gabrielle Dress.
Bust measures, 28 to 46 inches.
13 sizes; 75 cents each.

2431

2431

Ladies' Wrapper, with a Full Back.
Bust measures, 28 to 46 inches.
13 sizes; 50 cents each.

2715

2715

Ladies' Wrapper.
Bust measures, 28 to 46 inches.
13 sizes; 50 cents each.

2580

2580

Ladies' Basque, with Vest Front.
Bust measures, 28 to 46 inches.
13 sizes; 30 cents each.

2588

2588

Ladies' Gored Basque.
Bust measures, 28 to 46 inches.
13 sizes; 30 cents each.

2541

2541

Ladies' Basque.
Bust measures, 28 to 46 inches.
13 sizes; 30 cents each.

2524
2524

Ladies' Wrapper. with a Cape.
Bust measures, 28 to 46 inches.
13 sizes; 50 cents each.

2420
2420

Ladies' Sack Wrapper.
Bust measures, 28 to 46 inches.
10 sizes; 50 cents each.

2247
2247

Ladies' Watteau Wrapper.
Bust measures, 28 to 46 inches.
13 sizes; 40 cents each.

2574
2574

Ladies' Wrapper, (only for Dress-makers.)
Bust measures, 28 to 46 inches.
13 sizes; $1.00 each.

2508
2508

Ladies' Gored Wrapper.
Bust measures, 28 to 46 inches.
13 sizes; 50 cents each.

2336
2336

Ladies' Wrapper.
Bust measures, 28 to 46 inches.
13 sizes; 40 cents each.

2592
2592

Ladies' Zouave Postilion Basque.
Bust measures, 28 to 46 inches.
13 sizes; 35 cents each.

2584
2584

Ladies' Pointed Basque Waist.
Bust measures, 28 to 46 inches.
13 sizes; 25 cents each.

2504
2504

Ladies' Short Basque.
Bust measures, 28 to 46 inches.
13 sizes; 25 cents each.

2557   **2557**

Ladies' Box-Plaited Wrapper, with a Yoke.
Bust measures, 28 to 46 inches.
13 sizes; 75 cents each.

2199   **2199**

Ladies' Spanish Wrapper.
Bust measures, 28 to 46 inches.
13 sizes; 40 cents each.

2707   **2707**

Ladies' Gored Wrapper.
Bust measures, 28 to 46 inches.
13 sizes; 50 cents each.

2060   **2060**

Ladies' Circular Wrapper.
Bust measures, 28 to 46 inches.
10 sizes; 50 cents each.

2687   **2687**

Ladies' Basque.
Bust measures, 28 to 46 inches.
13 sizes; 30 cents each.

2690   **2690**

Ladies' Basque.
Bust measures, 28 to 46 inches.
13 sizes; 30 cents each.

2539   **2539**

Ladies' Postilion Basque,
with Vest Front.
Bust measures, 28 to 46 inches.
13 sizes; 25 cents each.

2554   **2554**

Ladies' Basque.
Bust measures, 28 to 46 inches.
13 sizes; 30 cents each.

2666   **2666**

Ladies' Basque, with a Vest.
Bust measures, 28 to 46 inches.
13 sizes; 25 cents each.

2677   **2677**

Ladies' Basque.
Bust measures, 28 to 46 inches.
13 sizes; 30 cents each.

2759   **2759**

Ladies' Basque.
Bust measures, 28 to 46 inches.
13 sizes; 25 cents each.

2166   **2166**

Ladies' Basque.
Bust measures, 28 to 46 inches.
10 sizes; 20 cents each.

2449   **2449**

Ladies' Basque.
Bust measures, 28 to 46 inches.
13 sizes; 20 cents each.

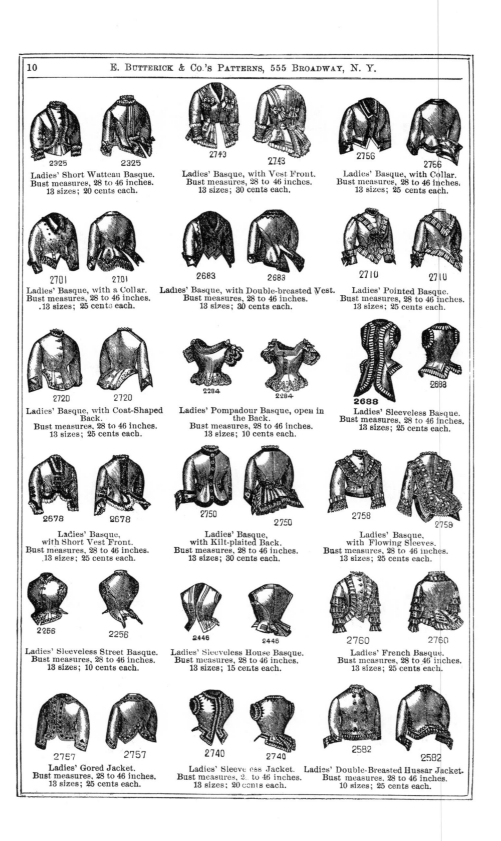

2325   2325

Ladies' Short Watteau Basque.
Bust measures, 28 to 46 inches.
13 sizes; 20 cents each.

2743   2743

Ladies' Basque, with Vest Front.
Bust measures, 28 to 46 inches.
13 sizes; 30 cents each.

2756   2756

Ladies' Basque, with Collar.
Bust measures, 28 to 46 inches.
13 sizes; 25 cents each.

2701   2701

Ladies' Basque, with a Collar.
Bust measures, 28 to 46 inches.
.13 sizes; 25 cents each.

2683   2683

Ladies' Basque, with Double-breasted Vest.
Bust measures, 28 to 46 inches.
13 sizes; 30 cents each.

2710   2710

Ladies' Pointed Basque.
Bust measures, 28 to 46 inches.
13 sizes; 25 cents each.

2720   2720

Ladies' Basque, with Coat-Shaped
Back.
Bust measures, 28 to 46 inches.
13 sizes; 25 cents each.

2284   2284

Ladies' Pompadour Basque, open in
the Back.
Bust measures, 28 to 46 inches.
13 sizes; 10 cents each.

2688   2688

Ladies' Sleeveless Basque.
Bust measures, 28 to 46 inches.
13 sizes; 25 cents each.

2678   2678

Ladies' Basque,
with Short Vest Front.
Bust measures, 28 to 46 inches.
.13 sizes; 25 cents each.

2750   2750

Ladies' Basque,
with Kilt-plaited Back.
Bust measures, 28 to 46 inches.
13 sizes; 30 cents each.

2758   2758

Ladies' Basque,
with Flowing Sleeves.
Bust measures, 28 to 46 inches.
13 sizes; 25 cents each.

2256   2256

Ladies' Sleeveless Street Basque.
Bust measures, 28 to 46 inches.
13 sizes; 10 cents each.

2446   2446

Ladies' Sleeveless House Basque.
Bust measures, 28 to 46 inches.
13 sizes; 15 cents each.

2760   2760

Ladies' French Basque.
Bust measures, 28 to 46 inches.
13 sizes; 25 cents each.

2757   2757

Ladies' Gored Jacket.
Bust measures, 28 to 46 inches.
13 sizes; 25 cents each.

2740   2740

Ladies' Sleeveless Jacket.
Bust measures, 28 to 46 inches.
13 sizes; 20 cents each.

2582   2582

Ladies' Double-Breasted Hussar Jacket.
Bust measures, 28 to 46 inches.
10 sizes; 25 cents each.

2542   2542

Ladies' Double-Breasted Jacket.
Bust measures, 28 to 46 inches.
13 sizes; 25 cents each.

2675   2675

Ladies' Sack Jacket.
Bust measures, 28 to 46 inches.
13 sizes; 25 cents each.

2292   2292

Ladies' Cambridge Jacket.
Bust measures, 28 to 46 inches.
10 sizes; 15 cents each.

2644   2644

Ladies' Street Jacket.
Bust measures, 28 to 46 inches.
13 sizes; 25 cents each.

2492   2492

Ladies' Double-Breasted Jacket.
Bust measures, 28 to 46 inches.
13 sizes; 20 cents each.

2607   2607

Ladies' Gored Sleeveless Jacket.
Bust measures, 28 to 46 inches.
13 sizes; 25 cents each.

2555   2555

Ladies' Gored Sack.
Bust measures, 28 to 46 inches.
10 sizes; 25 cents each.

2578   2578

Ladies' Dolman Sack.
Bust measures, 28 to 46 inches.
10 sizes; 25 cents each.

2646   2646

Ladies' Half-Fitting Sack.
Bust measures, 28 to 46 inches.
13 sizes; 30 cents each.

2742   2742

Ladies' Parisian Sack.
Bust measures, 28 to 46 inches.
10 sizes; 25 cents each.

2227   2227

Ladies' Half-Fitting Slashed Sack.
Bust measures, 28 to 46 inches.
10 sizes; 15 cents each.

2436   2436

Ladies' Dressing Sack.
Bust measures, 28 to 46 inches.
10 sizes; 20 cents each.

2400   2400

Ladies' Blouse.
Bust measures, 28 to 46 inches.
13 sizes; 20 cents each.

1948   1948

Ladies' Box-Plaited Blouse.
Bust measures, 28 to 46 inches.
10 sizes; 20 cents each.

2523   2523

Ladies' Sailor Blouse.
Bust measures, 28 to 46 inches.
13 sizes; 20 cents each.

2725   2725

Ladies' Plaited Waist,
with Yoke and Belt.
Bust measures, 28 to 46 inches.
13 sizes; 20 cents each.

2702   2702

Ladies' Low-Necked Waist.
Bust measures, 28 to 46 inches.
13 sizes; 20 cents each.

2536   2536

Ladies' Postilion Pointed Waist.
Bust measures, 28 to 46 inches.
13 sizes; 20 cents each.

2213   2213

Ladies' Plain Waist.
Bust measures, 28 to 48 inches.
14 sizes; 10 cents each.

2528   2528

Ladies' Basque Waist.
Bust measures, 28 to 46 inches.
13 sizes; 25 cents each.

2716   2716

Ladies' Waist, with
Basque Front and Pointed Back.
Bust measures, 28 to 48 inches.
13 sizes; 25 cents each.

2229   2229

Ladies' Basque Waist,
Open in the Back.
Bust measures, 28 to 46 inches.
13 sizes; 15 cents each.

2513   2513

Ladies' Plaited Blouse Waist.
Bust measures, 28 to 46 inches.
13 sizes; 20 cents each.

1669   1669

Ladies' Pointed Waist.
Bust measures, 28 to 46 inches.
10 sizes; 20 cents each.

1006   1006

Ladies' French or Spencer
Waist.
Bust measures, 28 to 46 inches.
10 sizes; 15 cents each.

2719   2719

Ladies' Low-Necked
Pointed Waist.
Bust measures, 28 to 46 inches.
13 sizes; 10 cents each.

2187   2187

Ladies' Pompadour Waist.
Bust measures, 28 to 46 inches.
13 sizes; 15 cents each.

2329   2329

Ladies' Pointed Waist,
with Half-Long Sleeves.
Bust measures, 28 to 46 inches.
13 sizes; 15 cents each.

2260   2260

Ladies' Spanish Waist.
Bust measures, 28 to 46 inches.
13 sizes; 10 cents each.

2568   2568

Ladies' High-Necked Corset Cover,
with Long Sleeves.
Bust measures, 28 to 46 inches.
13 sizes; 25 cents each.

2704   2704

Ladies' High-Necked
Corset Cover.
Bust measures, 28 to 46 inches.
13 sizes; 25 cents each.

2198   2198

Ladies' Low-Necked
Corset Cover.
Bust measures, 28 to 46 inches.
10 sizes; 15 cents each.

2705   2705

Ladies' Low-Necked
Corset Cover.
Bust measures, 28 to 46 inches.
13 sizes; 25 cents each.

2590   2590

Ladies' Peplum, with a Sash.
Waist measures, 20 to 30 inches.
6 sizes; 25 cents each.

2679   2679

Ladies' Over-Skirt.
Waist measures, 20 to 30 inches.
6 sizes; 25 cents each.

2649   2649

Ladies' Over-Skirt.
Waist measures, 20 to 30 inches.
6 sizes; 25 cents each.

2728

Ladies' Over-Skirt.
Waist measures, 20 to 30 inches.
6 sizes; 30 cents each.

2532

Ladies' Over-Skirt.
Waist measures, 20 to 30 inches.
6 sizes; 25 cents each.

2593

Ladies' Over-Skirt, with Pointed Peplum.
Waist measures, 20 to 30 inches.
6 sizes; 30 cents each.

2737

Ladies' Over-Skirt,
with Spanish Waist.
Waist measures, 20 to 30 inches.
6 sizes; 30 cents each.

2352

Ladies' Over-Skirt, with an
Apron Front, and Sashes at the Back.
Waist measures, 20 to 30 inches.
6 sizes; 25 cents each.

2477

Ladies' Over-Skirt.
Waist measures, 20 to 30 inches.
6 sizes; 25 cents each.

2648

Ladies' Apron Over-Skirt.
with a Sash.
Waist measures, 20 to 30 inches.
6 sizes; 25 cents each.

2506

Ladies' Apron-Shaped
Over-Skirt.
Waist measures, 20 to 30 inches.
6 sizes; 20 cents each.

2560

Ladies' Over-Skirt, with Sash.
(Only for Dress-Makers.)
Waist measures, 20 to 30 inches.
6 sizes; 40 cents each.

2346

Ladies' Flounced Over-Skirt.
Waist measures, 20 to 30 inches.
6 sizes; 25 cents each.

1087

Ladies' Adjustable Train Skirt.
One size; 35 cents.

2208

Ladies' Demi-Trained Skirt.
Waist measures, 20 to 30 inches.
6 sizes; 30 cents each.

1988

Ladies' Trained Skirt.
Waist measures, 20 to 30 inches.
6 sizes; 35 cents each.

2711

Ladies' Tunique Skirt.
Waist measures, 20 to 36 inches.
9 sizes; 50 cents each.

2535   2535

Ladies' Trained Evening Skirt.
Waist measures, 20 to 30 inches.
6 sizes; 50 cents each.

2484   2484

Ladies' Walking Skirt.
Waist measures, 20 to 36 inches.
9 sizes; 30 cents each.

2207   2207

Ladies' Walking Skirt.
Waist measures, 20 to 30 inches.
6 sizes; 30 cents each.

1919

Ladies' Short Walking Skirt.
Waist measures, 20 to 30 inches.
6 sizes; 35 cents each.

2561   2561

Ladies' Petticoat, with Flounces.
Waist measures, 20 to 30 inches.
6 sizes; 40 cents each.

2582   2582

Ladies' Plain Gored Petticoat.
Waist measures, 20 to 30 inches.
6 sizes; 35 cents each.

2766   2766

Ladies' Bathing Costume.
Bust measures, 28 to 46 inches.
10 sizes; 50 cents each.

1714   1714

Ladies' Bathing Costume.
Bust measures, 28 to 46 inches.
10 sizes; 35 cents each.

2765   2033   2033

Ladies' Belt and Chatelaine Pocket.
One size; 10 cents.

Ladies' Apron.
Waist measures, 20 to 30 inches.
6 sizes; 15 cents each.

2275   2275

Ladies' Kitchen Apron.
One size; 10 cents.

2163

Ladies' Apron.
One size; 15 cents.

1717

Ladies' Bathing Cap.
One size; 10 cents.

1827

Ladies' Sun Bonnet.
One size; 20 cents.

1828

Ladies' Sun Bonnet.
One size; 20 cents.

443
Ladies' Flowing Sleeve.
One size; 10 cents.

2736
Ladies' Sleeve.
One size; 10 cents.

2331
Ladies' Sleeve.
One size; 10 cents.

2735
Ladies' Sleeve.
One size; 10 cents.

2332
Ladies' Sleeve.
One size; 10 cents.

1500   1500
Ladies' Circular Night Wrapper.
Bust measures, 28 to 46 inches.
10 sizes; 30 cents each.

1722   1722
Ladies' Short Sack Night Wrapper.
Bust measures, 28 to 46 inches.
10 sizes; 20 cents each.

425   425
Ladies' Sack Night-Dress.
Bust measures, 28 to 46 inches.
10 sizes; 35 cents each.

2050   2050
Ladies' Sack Night-Dress,
with a Plain Yoke.
Bust measures, 28 to 46 inches.
10 sizes; 35 cents each.

2708   2708
Ladies' Night-Dress, with front of
Yoke and Body cut together.
Bust measures, 28 to 46 inches.
13 sizes; 40 cents each.

1741   1741
Ladies' Short-Night Dress,
with Pointed Yoke.
Bust measures, 28 to 46 inches
10 sizes; 25 cents each.

2047   2047
Ladies' Night Dress, with Yoke and
Full Sleeves.
Bust measures, 28 to 46 inches.
10 sizes; 35 cents each.

2713
Ladies' Night-Cap.
One size; 15 cents.

2712
Ladies' Night-Cap.
One size; 15 cents.

1587
Ladies' Chemise.
Bust measures, 28 to 46 inches.
10 sizes; 20 cents each.

2423   2423
Ladies' Chemise.
Bust measures, 28 to 46 inches.
10 sizes; 25 cents each.

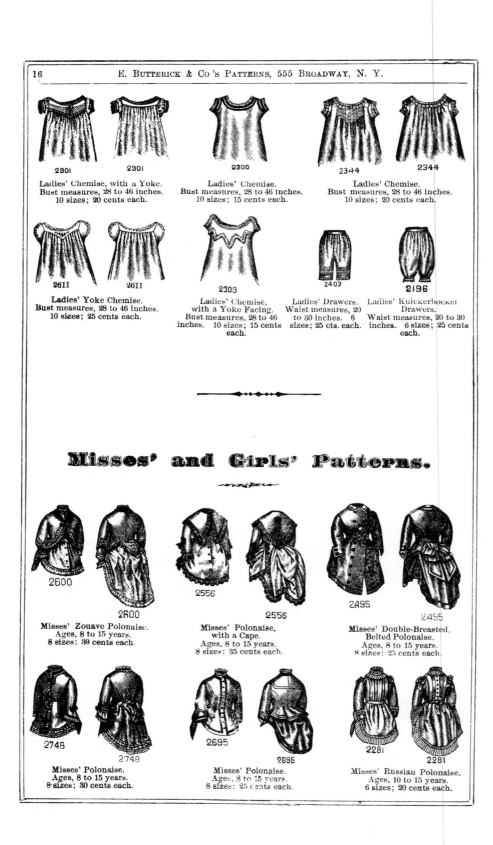

2301   **2301**   **2300**   **2344**   **2344**

Ladies' Chemise, with a Yoke.
Bust measures, 28 to 46 inches.
10 sizes; 20 cents each.

Ladies' Chemise.
Bust measures, 28 to 46 inches.
10 sizes; 15 cents each.

Ladies' Chemise.
Bust measures, 28 to 46 inches.
10 sizes; 20 cents each.

2611   **2611**   **2303**   **2402**   **2196**

Ladies' Yoke Chemise.
Bust measures, 28 to 46 inches.
10 sizes; 25 cents each.

Ladies' Chemise,
with a Yoke Facing.
Bust measures, 28 to 46
inches.   10 sizes; 15 cents
each.

Ladies' Drawers.
Waist measures, 20
to 30 inches.   6
sizes; 25 cts. each.

Ladies' Knickerbocker
Drawers.
Waist measures, 20 to 30
inches.   6 sizes; 25 cents
each.

Misses' and Girls' Patterns.

2600   **2556**   **2495**

2600   **2556**   **2495**

Misses' Zouave Polonaise.
Ages, 8 to 15 years.
8 sizes; 30 cents each.

Misses' Polonaise,
with a Cape.
Ages, 8 to 15 years.
8 sizes; 35 cents each.

Misses' Double-Breasted,
Belted Polonaise.
Ages, 8 to 15 years.
8 sizes; 25 cents each.

2748   **2695**   **2281**

2748   **2695**   **2281**

Misses' Polonaise.
Ages, 8 to 15 years.
8 sizes; 30 cents each.

Misses' Polonaise.
Ages, 8 to 15 years.
8 sizes; 25 cents each.

Misses' Russian Polonaise.
Ages, 10 to 15 years.
6 sizes; 20 cents each.

2749   2749

Misses' Polonaise.
Ages, 8 to 15 years.
8 sizes; 25 cents each.

2596   2596

Misses' Loose Polonaise.
Ages, 8 to 15 years.
8 sizes; 30 cents each.

2684   2684

Misses' Polonaise.
Ages, 8 to 15 years.
8 sizes; 30 cents each.

2613   2613

Girls' Polonaise.
Ages, 3 to 9 years.
7 sizes; 25 cents each.

2685   2685

Girls' Polonaise, with Zouave Front.
Ages, 4 to 9 years.
6 sizes; 25 cents each.

2686   2686

Misses' Polonaise.
Ages, 8 to 15 years.
8 sizes; 30 cents each.

2669   2669

**Girls' Belted Polonaise,
Open in the Back.**
Ages, 3 to 9 years.
7 sizes; 25 cents each.

2621   2621

Girls' Polonaise.
Ages, 4 to 9 years.
6 sizes; 25 cents each.

2627   2627

**Girls' Polonaise, with
Sash Collar.**
Ages, 3 to 9 years.
7 sizes; 25 cents each.

2424   2424

Girls' Polonaise.
Ages, 3 to 9 years.
7 sizes; 25 cents each.

2618   2618

**Girls' Double-Breasted,
Loose Polonaise.**
Ages, 4 to 9 years.
6 sizes; 25 cents each.

2754   2754

**Girls' Double-Breasted
Redingote.**
Ages, 4 to 9 years.
6 sizes; 25 cents each.

2409   2409

**Child's Sack Cloak,
with a Cape.**
Ages, 1 to 7 years.
7 sizes; 20 cents each.

1004   1004

**Misses' Circular
Waterproof Cloak.**
Ages, 10 to 15 years.
6 sizes; 30 cents each.

1589   1589

**Misses' Waterproof Cloak,
with Cape, Sleeve and Hood.**
Ages, 10 to 15 years.
6 sizes; 25 cents each.

1923   1923

**Child's Cloak,
with a Cape.**
Ages, 2 to 5 years.
4 sizes; 20 cents each.

2587 **2587**
Girls' Dolman Cloak.
Ages, 4 to 9 years.
6 sizes; 25 cents each.

1255 **1255**
Girls' Waterproof Cloak,
with Cape and Hood.
Ages. 3 to 9 years.
7 sizes; 25 cents each.

2603 **2609**
Misses' Half Fitting Cloak,
with a Cape.
Ages, 8 to 15 years.
8 sizes; 30 cents each.

1009 **1009**
Girls' Circular Waterproof
Cloak, with Hood.
Ages, 2 to 9 years.
8 sizes; 25 cents each.

2501 **2501**
Misses' Double-Breasted Cloak.
Ages, 8 to 15 years.
8 sizes; 25 cents each.

2503 **2503**
Misses' Dolman, or Sack Cloak,
with Wing Sleeves.
Ages, 8 to 15 years.
8 sizes; 20 cents each.

2464 **2464**
Child's Cloak.
Ages, ½ to 6 years.
7 sizes; 20 cents each.

2615 **2615**
Girls' Cloak, with a Cape.
Ages, 2 to 9 years.
8 sizes; 25 cents each.

816
Infants' Circular,
with Hood.
One size; 35 cents.

2155 **2155**
Infants' Double Circular
with a Hood.
One size; 20 cents.

2681 **2681**
Girls' Mantilla.
Ages, 4 to 9 years.
6 sizes; 25 cents ea

2457 **2457**
Girls' Belted Mantilla.
Ages, 4 to 9 years.
6 sizes; 20 cents each.

2653 **2653**
Girls' Mantilla.
Ages, 3 to 9 years.
7 sizes; 20 cents each.

2680 **2680**
Girls' Belted Mantilla, with a
Cape. Ages, 3 to 9 years.
7 sizes; 25 cents each.

2545 **2545**
Girls' Dolman Mantle.
Ages, 4 to 9 years.
6 sizes; 25 cents each.

2668 **2668**
Girls' Shawl-Shaped Mantle.
Ages, 4 to 9 years.
6 sizes; 25 cents each.

2058 **2058**
Misses' Waterproof Cape.
Ages, 10 to 15 years.
6 sizes; 15 cents each.

2667 **2667**
Misses' Dolman Paletot.
Ages, 8 to 15 years.
8 sizes; 30 cents each.

2599 **2599**
Girls' Slashed Paletot.
Ages, 3 to 9 years.
7 sizes; 25 cents each.

2753 **2753**
Girls' Low-Necked
Over-Dress.
Ages, 2 to 9 years.
8 sizes; 20 cents each.

2761 **2761**
Girls' Low-Necked
Over-Dress.
Ages, 3 to 9 years.
7 sizes; 20 cents each.

2219   2219
Girls' Pompadour Gored Dress.
Ages, 3 to 9 years.
7 sizes; 15 cents each.

2080   2080
Girls' Box-Plaited Over-Dress.
Ages, 4 to 9 years.
6 sizes; 20 cents each.

2252   2252
Girls' Low-Necked Yoke
Dress. Ages, 2 to 9 years.
8 sizes; 20 cents each.

2626   2626
Child's Coat.
Ages, 1 to 5 years.
5 sizes; 20 cents each.

2671   2671
Girls' Low-Necked
Over-Dress.
Ages, 4 to 9 years.
6 sizes; 25 cents each.

2732   2732
Girls' Low-Necked Over-Dress.
Ages, 3 to 9 years.
7 sizes; 20 cents each.

2622   2622
Girls' Low-Necked.
Over-Dress.
Ages, 3 to 9 years.
7 sizes; 20 cents each

2318   2318
Girls' Low-Necked Dress, with
Yoke. Ages, 2 to 9 years.
8 sizes; 20 cents each.

2724   2724
Girls' Low-Necked Over-Dress.
Ages, 3 to 9 years.
7 sizes; 20 cents each.

2747   2747
Misses' Over-Dress.
Ages, 8 to 15 years.
8 sizes; 25 cents each.

2662   2662
Girls' Low-Necked Over-Dress.
Ages, 2 to 9 years.
8 sizes; 25 cents each.

2670   2670
Girls' Over-Dress, with Cape
and Skirt cut together.
Ages, 4 to 9 years.
6 sizes; 25 cents each.

2239
Girls' Dress,
Gored to the Arm-Scye.
Ages, 3 to 9 years.
7 sizes; 20 cents each.

2602   2602
Girls' Gabrielle Dress, with a Cape.
Ages, 3 to 9 years.
7 sizes; 30 cents each.

2612   2612
Misses' Dress, with a Basque Back
and Loose Front. Ages, 8 to 15 years.
8 sizes; 40 cents each.

2620   2620
Girls' Dress, with Loose Front.
Ages, 4 to 9 years.
6 sizes; 30 cents each.

2055   2055

Child's French Yoke Dress.
Ages, 1 to 6 years.
6 sizes; 20 cents each.

1824   1824

Child's Gored Dress.
Ages, ½ to 5 years.
6 sizes; 20 cents each.

2242   2242

Girls' Gabrielle Dress.
Ages, 4 to 9 years.
6 sizes; 15 cents each.

2559   2559

Girls' Gabrielle Dress.
Ages, 3 to 9 years.
7 sizes; 30 cents each.

2723   2723

Misses' Dressing Gown.
Ages, 8 to 15 years.
8 sizes; 40 cents each.

2493   2493

Girls' Box-Plaited Wrapper,
with a Yoke.
Ages, 3 to 9 years.
7 sizes; 25 cents each.

2698   2698

Girls' Dress,
with Basque Front.
Ages, 4 to 9 years.
6 sizes; 30 cents each.

2651   2651

Girls' Morning Wrapper.
Ages, 3 to 9 years.
7 sizes; 35 cents each.

2405   2405

Girls' Circular Wrapper.
Ages, 2 to 9 years.
8 sizes; 30 cents each.

1489   1489

Infants' Wrapper.
One size; 15 cents.

2550   2550

Misses' Watteau Wrapper.
Ages, 8 to 15 years.
8 sizes; 50 cents each.

2209   2209

Misses' Gabrielle Wrapper.
Ages, 10 to 15 years.
6 sizes; 30 cents each.

2650   2650

Misses' Morning Wrapper.
Ages, 8 to 15 years.
8 sizes; 40 cents each.

1805   1805

Child's Wrapper.
Ages, 2 to 9 years.
8 sizes; 20 cents each.

2486   2486

Child's Sack Wrapper.
Ages, 1 to 6 years.
6 sizes; 20 cents each.

2597   2597

Misses' Basquine.
Ages, 8 to 15 years.
8 sizes; 25 cents each.

2872   2672

Girls' Deep Basque.
Ages, 4 to 9 years.
6 sizes; 25 cents each.

2500   2500

Misses' Basque, with Vest Front.
Ages, 8 to 15 years.
8 sizes; 25 cents each.

2133   2133

Misses' Basque, open at the Back.
Ages, 8 to 15 years.
6 sizes; 20 cents each.

2659   2659

Misses' Basque, with a
Cape.
Ages, 8 to 15 years.
8 sizes; 30 cents each.

2696   2696

Misses' Pointed Basque.
Ages, 8 to 15 years.
8 sizes; 25 cents each.

2762   2762

Misses' Loose-Fitting
Square-Necked Basque.
Ages, 8 to 15 years.
8 sizes; 25 cents each.

2697   2697

Girls' Basque, with
Vest Front.
Ages, 4 to 9 years.
6 sizes; 25 cents each.

2706   2706

Misses' Basque.
Ages, 8 to 15 years.
8 sizes; 20 cents each.

2694   2694

Misses' Basque.
Ages, 8 to 15 years.
8 sizes; 25 cents each.

2614   2614

Girls' Zouave Basque,
with a Vest Front.
Ages, 4 to 9 years.
6 sizes; 25 cents each.

2511   2511

Girls' Basque.
Ages, 4 to 9 years.
6 sizes; 20 cents each.

2501   2691

Girls' Gored Basque.
Ages, 5 to 9 years.
5 sizes; 25 cents each.

2693   2693

Girls' Basque.
Ages, 4 to 9 years.
6 sizes; 20 cents each.

2658   2658

Misses' Basque.
Ages, 8 to 15 years.
8 sizes; 25 cents each.

2657   2657

Misses' Basque.
Ages, 8 to 15 years.
8 sizes; 25 cents each.

2606   2606

Girls' Gored Basque.
Ages, 4 to 9 years.
6 sizes; 25 cents each.

2546   2546

Girls' Basque.
Ages, 4 to 9 years.
6 sizes; 20 cents each.

2752   2752

Girls' Basque,
Open in the Back.
Ages, 3 to 9 years.
7 sizes; 20 cents each.

2538   2538

Misses' Double-Breasted
Gored Basque.
Ages, 8 to 15 years.
8 sizes; 20 cents each.

2655   2655

Misses' Sleeveless Jacket.
Ages, 8 to 15 years.
8 sizes; 20 cents each.

2763   2763

Girls' Sleeveless Jacket.
Ages, 3 to 9 years.
7 sizes; 15 cents each.

2673   2673

Girls' Sleeveless Jacket.
Ages, 4 to 9 years.
6 sizes; 20 cents each.

2553   2553

Girls' Dressing Jacket.
Ages, 4 to 9 years.
6 sizes; 25 cents each.

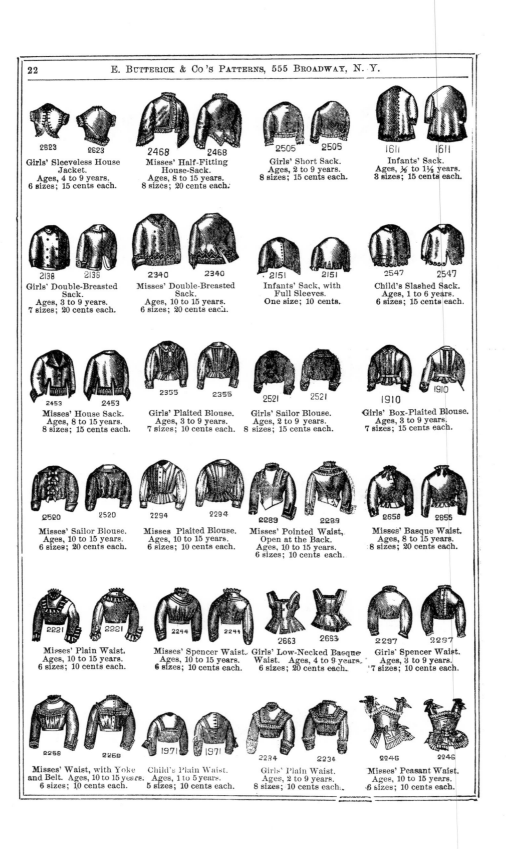

2623   2623
Girls' Sleeveless House
Jacket.
Ages, 4 to 9 years.
6 sizes; 15 cents each.

2468   2468
Misses' Half-Fitting
House-Sack.
Ages, 8 to 15 years.
8 sizes; 20 cents each.

2505   2505
Girls' Short Sack.
Ages, 2 to 9 years.
8 sizes; 15 cents each.

1611   1611
Infants' Sack.
Ages, ½ to 1½ years.
3 sizes; 15 cents each.

2138   2138
Girls' Double-Breasted
Sack.
Ages, 3 to 9 years.
7 sizes; 20 cents each.

2340   2340
Misses' Double-Breasted
Sack.
Ages, 10 to 15 years.
6 sizes; 20 cents each.

2151   2151
Infants' Sack, with
Full Sleeves.
One size; 10 cents.

2547   2547
Child's Slashed Sack.
Ages, 1 to 6 years.
6 sizes; 15 cents each.

2453   2453
Misses' House Sack.
Ages, 8 to 15 years.
8 sizes; 15 cents each.

2355   2355
Girls' Plaited Blouse.
Ages, 3 to 9 years.
7 sizes; 10 cents each.

2521   2521
Girls' Sailor Blouse.
Ages, 2 to 9 years.
8 sizes; 15 cents each.

1910
Girls' Box-Plaited Blouse.
Ages, 3 to 9 years.
7 sizes; 15 cents each.

2520   2520
Misses' Sailor Blouse.
Ages, 10 to 15 years.
6 sizes; 20 cents each.

2294   2294
Misses' Plaited Blouse.
Ages, 10 to 15 years.
6 sizes; 10 cents each.

2289   2289
Misses' Pointed Waist,
Open at the Back.
Ages, 10 to 15 years.
6 sizes; 10 cents each.

2656   2656
Misses' Basque Waist.
Ages, 8 to 15 years.
8 sizes; 20 cents each.

2221   2221
Misses' Plain Waist.
Ages, 10 to 15 years.
6 sizes; 10 cents each.

2244   2244
Misses' Spencer Waist.
Ages, 10 to 15 years.
6 sizes; 10 cents each.

2663   2663
Girls' Low-Necked Basque
Waist. Ages, 4 to 9 years.
6 sizes; 20 cents each.

2297   2297
Girls' Spencer Waist.
Ages, 3 to 9 years.
7 sizes; 10 cents each.

2258   2258
Misses' Waist, with Yoke
and Belt. Ages, 10 to 15 years.
6 sizes; 10 cents each.

1971   1971
Child's Plain Waist.
Ages, 1 to 5 years.
5 sizes; 10 cents each.

2234   2234
Girls' Plain Waist.
Ages, 2 to 9 years.
8 sizes; 10 cents each.

2246   2246
Misses' Peasant Waist.
Ages, 10 to 15 years.
6 sizes; 10 cents each.

2730 2730
Girls' Low-Necked Waist.
Ages, 3 to 9 years.
7 sizes; 10 cents each.

387 387
Child's Under-Waist.
Ages, 3 to 9 years.
7 sizes; 20 cents each.

2425 2425
Girls' Postilion Waist.
Ages, 4 to 9 years.
6 sizes; 20 cents each.

2729 2729
Misses' Low-Necked Waist.
Ages, 10 to 15 years.
6 sizes; 10 cents each.

2543 2543
Girls' Pointed Postilion Waist. Ages, 4 to 9 years.
6 sizes; 20 cents each.

2674 2674
Girls' Bretelle Waist.
Ages, 3 to 9 years.
7 sizes; 20 cents each.

2515 2515
Girls' Jacket Waist.
Ages, 4 to 9 years.
6 sizes; 15 cents each.

2552 2552
Girls' Basque Waist.
Ages, 3 to 9 years.
7 sizes; 25 cents each.

2258 2258
Girls' Waist,
with Yoke and Belt.
Ages, 3 to 9 years.
7 sizes; 10 cents each.

1909 1909
Misses' Low-Necked Corset Cover.
Ages, 10 to 15 years.
6 sizes; 15 cents each.

2755 2755
Girls' Apron.
One size; 15 cents.

2176 2176
Child's Box-Plaited Apron.
Ages, _ to 5 years.
5 sizes; 15 cents each.

2692 2692
Girls' High-Necked Sack Apron.
Ages, 3 to 9 years.
7 sizes; 20 cents each.

2660 2660
Girls' Sack Apron.
Ages, 2 to 9 years.
8 sizes; 20 cents each.

2360 2360
Girls' High-Necked Apron.
Ages, 2 to 9 years.
8 sizes; 15 cents each.

2661 2661
Girls' Apron.
Ages, 3 to 9 years.
7 sizes; 20 cents each.

2624
Misses' Apron.
One size; 15 cents.

2733 2733
Misses' Sack Apron.
Ages, 8 to 15 years.
8 sizes; 20 cents each.

2148 2148
Child's Yoke Apron.
Ages, 2 to 6 years.
5 sizes; 15 cents each.

2428 2428
Child's Bib Apron.
Ages, 1 to 5 years.
5 sizes; 10 cents each.

2411 2411
Child's Apron.
Ages, 2 to 8 years.
7 sizes; 15 cents each.

2463 2463
Girls' Apron.
One size; 10 cents.

2709 2709
Misses' Over-Skirt, with Sashes.
Ages, 8 to 15 years.
8 sizes; 25 cents each.

2598   **2598**

Misses' Over-Skirt, Open in Front.
Ages, 8 to 15 years.
8 sizes; 25 cents each.

2551   **2551**

Misses' Over-Skirt.
Ages, 8 to 15 years.
8 sizes; 25 cents each.

2605   **2605**

Misses' Over-Skirt.
Ages, 8 to 15 years.
8 sizes; 25 cents each

2588   **2588**

Girls' Looped Over-Skirt.
Ages, 4 to 9 years.
6 sizes; 20 cents each.

2619   **2619**

Girls' Over-Skirt.
Ages, 3 to 9 years.
7 sizes; 20 cents each.

2548   **2548**

Girls' Scalloped Over-Skirt.
Ages, 3 to 9 years.
7 sizes; 15 cents each

2540   **2540**

Misses' Over-Skirt.
Ages, 8 to 15 years.
8 sizes; 20 cents each.

2510   **2510**

Girls' Scalloped Over-Skirt.
Ages, 3 to 9 years.
7 sizes; 15 cents each.

2654   **2654**

Misses' Apron Over-Skirt.
Ages, 8 to 15 years.
8 sizes; 20 cents each.

2519   **2519**

Misses' Sailor Skirt.
Ages, 10 to 15 years.
6 sizes; 25 cents each.

2722   **2722**

Girls' Over-Skirt.
Ages, 4 to 9 years.
6 sizes; 20 cents each.

2522   **2522**

Girls' Sailor Skirt.
Ages, 2 to 9 years.
8 sizes; 20 cents each.

2251   **2251**

Misses' Four-Gored Skirt.
Ages, 10 to 15 years.
6 sizes; 20 cents each.

2250   **2250**

Misses' Six-Gored Skirt.
Ages, 10 to 15 years.
6 sizes; 20 cents each.

2253   **2253**

Girls' Four-Gored Skirt.
Ages, 3 to 9 years.
7 sizes; 15 cents each

1922   **1922**

Girls' Six-Gored Skirt.
Ages, 2 to 9 years.
8 sizes; 20 cents each.

2184   **2184**

Child's Petticoat.
Ages, 1 to 4 years.
4 sizes; 15 cents each.

2566   **2566**

Girls' Petticoat, with a Flounce.
Ages, 2 to 9 years.
8 sizes; 25 cents each.

2565   2565
Misses' Petticoat, with Flounces.
Ages, 10 to 15 years.
6 sizes; 30 cents each

2734   2734
Infants' High-Necked Gored Slip.
One size; 20 cents.

2319   2319
Infants' High-Necked Slip.
One size; 15 cents.

761   761
Infants' Slip.
One size; 20 cents.

1713   1713
Misses' Bathing Costume.
Ages, 10 to 15 years.
6 sizes; 25 cents each.

2442   2442
Baby's Pinning Blanket.
One size; 15 cents.

450   450
Infants' Robe.
One size; 20 cents.

423   423
Infants' Robe.
One size; 25 cents.

1752   1752
Infants' Robe.
One size; 20 cents.

446   446
Misses' Sack Night Wrapper.
Ages, 10 to 15 years.
6 sizes; 25 cents each

2617   2617
Misses' Sick, or Night Wrapper.
Ages, 8 to 15 years.
8 sizes; 40 cents each.

2563   2563
Misses' Night-Dress, with a Yoke.
Ages, 8 to 15 years.
8 sizes; 35 cents each.

2516   2516
Girls' Long Sack Night-Dress.
Ages, 3 to 9 years.
7 sizes; 20 cents each.

2414   2414
Child's High-Necked
Night-Dress.
Ages, ½ to 6 years.
7 sizes; 20 cents each.

2569   2569
Girls' Night Dress.
with a Yoke.
Ages, 3 to 9 years.
7 sizes; 25 cents each.

1708
Infants' Flannel
Skirt and Waist.
One size; 15 cents.

2413   2413
Child's Night Drawers.
Ages, 2 to 8 years.
7 sizes; 25 cents each

1880   1880
Child's Night Drawers, with
Stockings.
Ages, 1 to 9 years.
9 sizes; 25 cents each.

1331
Misses' Drawers.
Ages, 10 to 15 years.
6 sizes; 20 cents each.

191
Child's Night Drawers,
with Sleeves. Ages,
2 to 6 years.
5 sizes; 25 cents each.

1947
Girls' Knickerbocker
Drawers.
Ages, 2 to 9 years.
8 sizes; 15 cents each.

2587
Girls' Drawers.
Ages, 2 to 9 years.
8 sizes; 15 cents each.

2465
Baby's Drawers.
One size; 10 cents.

2417
Baby's Drawers.
One size; 15 cents.

2625
Child's Chemise.
Ages, 1 to 6 years.
6 sizes; 20 cents each.

2197
Misses' Chemise.
Ages, 10 to 15 years.
6 sizes; 20 cents each.

1843
Girls' Chemise.
Ages, 3 to 9 years.
7 sizes; 15 cts. each.

2445   2445
Girls' Chemise.
Ages, 2 to 9 years.
8 sizes; 15 cents each.

2664
Girls' Chemise.
Ages, 2 to 9 years.
8 sizes; 20 cents each.

2153   2153
Infants' Bib.
One size; 10 cents.

2154   2154
Infants' Bib.
One size; 10 cents.

434   434
Infants' Shirt, with Square Bib.
One size; 10 cents.

2339   2339
Infants' Shirt.
One size; 10 cents.

2313
Infants' Chemise.
One size; 5 cents.

2564
Girls' Chemise.
Ages, 2 to 9 years.
8 sizes; 20 cents each.

2304
Misses' Chemise,
with Yoke Facing.
Ages, 10 to 15 years.
6 sizes; 15 cents each.

431
Infants' Under-Shirt.
One size; 10 cents.

2441
Child's Shirt.
Ages, 1 to 6 years.
6 sizes; 10 cents each.

2269
Child's Cap.
Ages, ¼ to 4 years.
5 sizes; 10 cents each.

728
Child's Hood, in One Piece.
Ages, 2 to 6 years.
3 sizes; 10 cents each.

820
Child's Sun-Bonnet.
One size; 20 cents.

2019
Misses' Sleeve.
One size; 10 cents.

BOYS' PATTERNS.

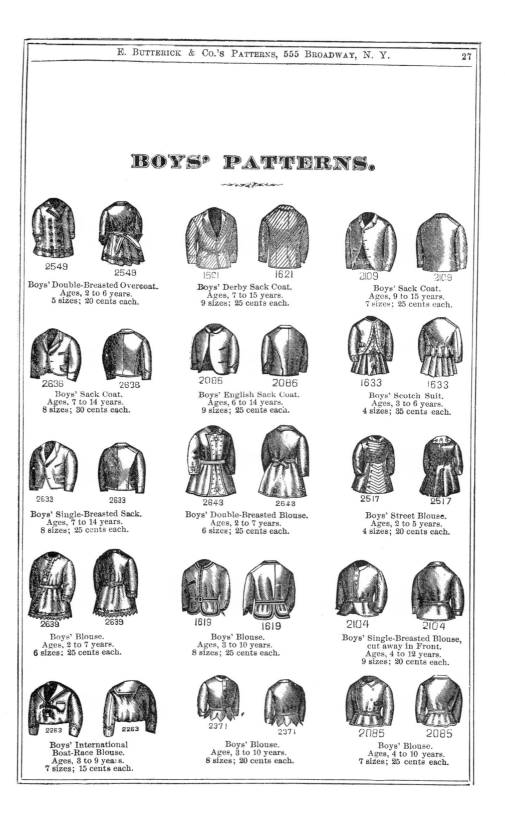

2549   2549
Boys' Double-Breasted Overcoat.
Ages, 2 to 6 years.
5 sizes; 20 cents each.

1621   1621
Boys' Derby Sack Coat.
Ages, 7 to 15 years.
9 sizes; 25 cents each.

2109   2109
Boys' Sack Coat.
Ages, 9 to 15 years.
7 sizes; 25 cents each.

2636   2636
Boys' Sack Coat.
Ages, 7 to 14 years.
8 sizes; 30 cents each.

2086   2086
Boys' English Sack Coat.
Ages, 6 to 14 years.
9 sizes; 25 cents each.

1633   1633
Boys' Scotch Suit.
Ages, 3 to 6 years.
4 sizes; 35 cents each.

2633   2633
Boys' Single-Breasted Sack.
Ages, 7 to 14 years.
8 sizes; 25 cents each.

2643   2643
Boys' Double-Breasted Blouse.
Ages, 2 to 7 years.
6 sizes; 25 cents each.

2517   2517
Boys' Street Blouse.
Ages, 2 to 5 years.
4 sizes; 20 cents each.

2639   2639
Boys' Blouse.
Ages, 2 to 7 years.
6 sizes; 25 cents each.

1619   1619
Boys' Blouse.
Ages, 3 to 10 years.
8 sizes; 25 cents each.

2104   2104
Boys' Single-Breasted Blouse,
cut away in Front.
Ages, 4 to 12 years.
9 sizes; 20 cents each.

2263   2263
Boys' International
Boat-Race Blouse.
Ages, 3 to 9 years.
7 sizes; 15 cents each.

2371   2371
Boys' Blouse.
Ages, 3 to 10 years.
8 sizes; 20 cents each.

2085   2085
Boys' Blouse.
Ages, 4 to 10 years.
7 sizes; 25 cents each.

308
Boys' Double-Breasted Blouse,
with Sash.   Ages, 2 to 5 years.
4 sizes; 25 cents each.

2632   2632
Boys' Sack Jacket.
Ages, 7 to 14 years.
8 sizes; 25 cents each.

2631   2631
Boys' Jacket, with Vest.
Ages, 6 to 10 years.
5 sizes; 25 cents each.

2629   2629
Boys' Jacket, with Shawl Collar.
Ages, 7 to 14 years.
8 sizes; 25 cents each.

2628   2628
Boys' Jacket.
Ages, 6 to 10 years.
5 sizes; 25 cents each.

1617   1617
Boys' Slashed Jacket.
Ages, 4 to 10 years.
7 sizes; 20 cents each.

2368   2368
Boys' Jacket.
Ages, 6 to 12 years.
7 sizes; 25 cents each.

2369   2369
Boys' Slashed Jacket, with a Vest.
Ages, 5 to 10 years.
6 sizes; 25 cents each.

401   401
Boys' Sailor Jacket.
Ages, 3 to 10 years.
8 sizes; 20 cents each.

2074   2074
Boys' Jacket, with Shawl Collar.
Ages, 5 to 12 years.
8 sizes; 25 cents each.

488   488
Boys' Single-Breasted Garibaldi Jacket.
Ages, 3 to 10 years.
8 sizes; 20 cents each.

2638   2638
Boys' Jacket.
Ages, 3 to 6 years.
4 sizes; 20 cents each.

2366   2366
Boys' Jacket.
Ages, 6 to 12 years.
7 sizes; 25 cents each.

2637   2637
Boys' Jacket.
Ages, 5 to 10 years.
6 sizes; 25 cents each.

2634   2634
Boys' Jacket, with Tabs.
Ages, 3 to 6 years.
4 sizes; 20 cents each.

2365   2365
Boys' Jacket.
Ages, 6 to 10 years.
5 sizes; 20 cents each.

2635   2635
Boys' Jacket, with a Vest.
Ages, 6 to 10 years.
5 sizes; 25 cents each.

1895   1895
Boys' Slashed Jacket.
Ages, 3 to 7 years.
5 sizes; 20 cents each.

2156   2156
Boys' Scotch Jacket,
with a Vest.
Ages, 3 to 6 years.
4 sizes; 20 cents each.

557
Boys' Vest.
Ages, 4 to 10 years.
7 sizes; 15 cents each.

1890
Boys' Single-Breasted, High
Rolling Collar Vest.
Ages, 9 to 15 years.
7 sizes; 15 cents each.

2630
Boys' Single-Breasted
Rolling Collar Vest.
Ages, 7 to 15 years.
9 sizes; 15 cents each.

2641
Boys' Double-Breasted Vest,
without Collar.
Ages, 7 to 15 years.
9 sizes; 15 cents each.

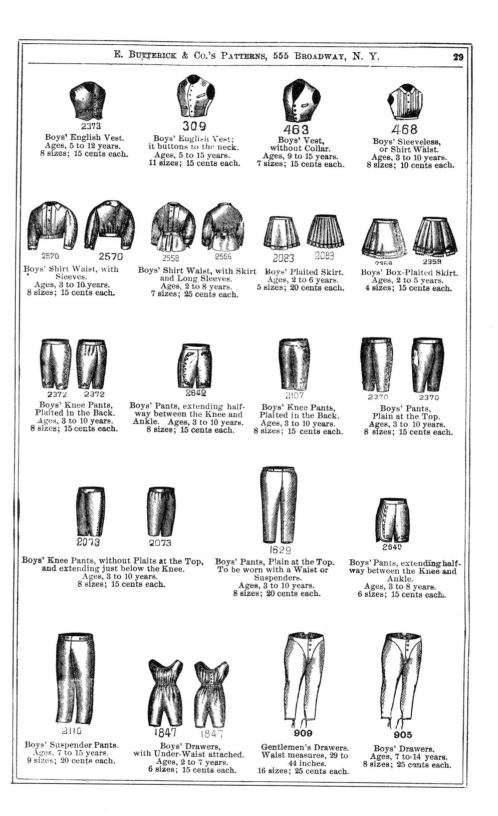

2373
Boys' English Vest.
Ages, 5 to 12 years.
8 sizes; 15 cents each.

309
Boys' English Vest;
it buttons to the neck.
Ages, 5 to 15 years.
11 sizes; 15 cents each.

463
Boys' Vest,
without Collar.
Ages, 9 to 15 years.
7 sizes; 15 cents each.

468
Boys' Sleeveless,
or Shirt Waist.
Ages, 3 to 10 years.
8 sizes; 10 cents each.

2570   **2570**
Boys' Shirt Waist, with
Sleeves.
Ages, 3 to 10 years.
8 sizes; 15 cents each.

2558   2556
Boys' Shirt Waist, with Skirt
and Long Sleeves.
Ages, 2 to 8 years.
7 sizes; 25 cents each.

2083   2083
Boys' Plaited Skirt.
Ages, 2 to 6 years.
5 sizes; 20 cents each.

2359   2359
Boys' Box-Plaited Skirt.
Ages, 2 to 5 years.
4 sizes; 15 cents each.

2372   2372
Boys' Knee Pants,
Plaited in the Back.
Ages, 3 to 10 years.
8 sizes; 15 cents each.

2642
Boys' Pants, extending half-
way between the Knee and
Ankle.   Ages, 3 to 10 years.
8 sizes; 15 cents each.

2107
Boys' Knee Pants,
Plaited in the Back.
Ages, 3 to 10 years.
8 sizes; 15 cents each.

2370   2370
Boys' Pants,
Plain at the Top.
Ages, 3 to 10 years.
8 sizes; 15 cents each.

2073   2073
Boys' Knee Pants, without Plaits at the Top,
and extending just below the Knee.
Ages, 3 to 10 years.
8 sizes; 15 cents each.

1629
Boys' Pants, Plain at the Top.
To be worn with a Waist or
Suspenders.
Ages, 3 to 10 years.
8 sizes; 20 cents each.

2640
Boys' Pants, extending half-
way between the Knee and
Ankle.
Ages, 3 to 8 years.
6 sizes; 15 cents each.

2110
Boys' Suspender Pants.
Ages, 7 to 15 years.
9 sizes; 20 cents each.

1847   1847
Boys' Drawers,
with Under-Waist attached.
Ages, 2 to 7 years.
6 sizes; 15 cents each.

909
Gentlemen's Drawers.
Waist measures, 29 to
44 inches.
16 sizes; 25 cents each.

905
Boys' Drawers.
Ages, 7 to 14 years.
8 sizes; 25 cents each.

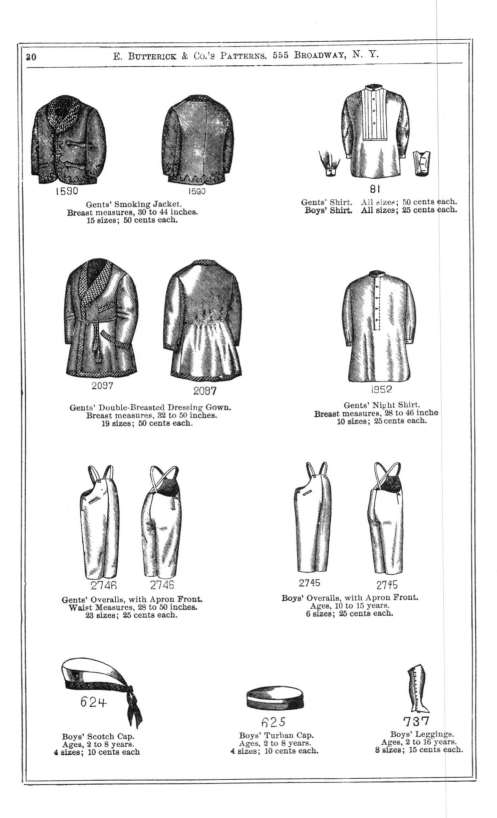

1590   1590

Gents' Smoking Jacket.
Breast measures, 30 to 44 inches.
15 sizes; 50 cents each.

81

Gents' Shirt.   All sizes; 50 cents each.
Boys' Shirt.   All sizes; 25 cents each.

2097   2097

Gents' Double-Breasted Dressing Gown.
Breast measures, 32 to 50 inches.
19 sizes; 50 cents each.

1952

Gents' Night Shirt.
Breast measures, 28 to 46 inche
10 sizes; 25 cents each.

2746   2746

Gents' Overalls, with Apron Front.
Waist Measures, 28 to 50 inches.
23 sizes; 25 cents each.

2745   2745

Boys' Overalls, with Apron Front.
Ages, 10 to 15 years.
6 sizes; 25 cents each.

624

Boys' Scotch Cap.
Ages, 2 to 8 years.
4 sizes; 10 cents each

625

Boys' Turban Cap.
Ages, 2 to 8 years.
4 sizes; 10 cents each.

737

Boys' Leggings.
Ages, 2 to 16 years.
8 sizes; 15 cents each.

Price List of Ladies' Shears and Scissors.

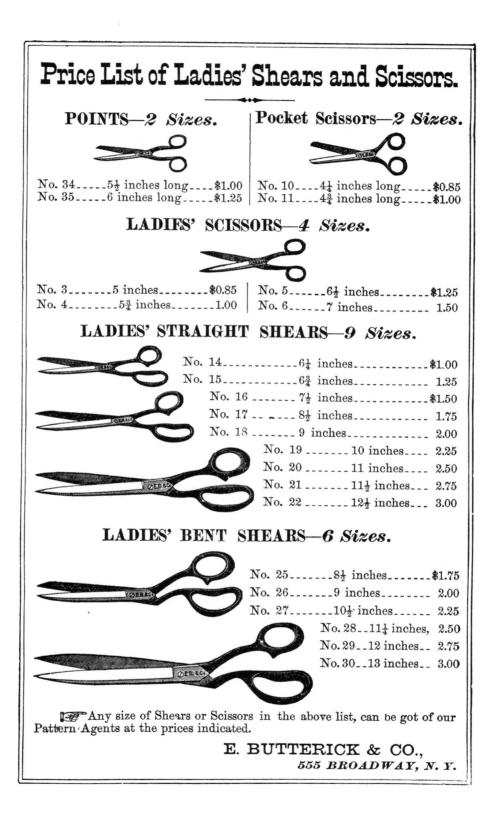

POINTS—*2 Sizes.*

No. 34 _____ 5½ inches long ____ $1.00
No. 35 _____ 6 inches long _____ $1.25

Pocket Scissors—*2 Sizes.*

No. 10 ____ 4¼ inches long ____ $0.85
No. 11 ____ 4¾ inches long ____ $1.00

LADIES' SCISSORS—*4 Sizes.*

No. 3 _____ 5 inches _____ $0.85
No. 4 _____ 5¾ inches _____ 1.00

No. 5 _____ 6½ inches _____ $1.25
No. 6 _____ 7 inches _____ 1.50

LADIES' STRAIGHT SHEARS—*9 Sizes.*

No. 14 _____ 6¼ inches _____ $1.00
No. 15 _____ 6¾ inches _____ 1.25
No. 16 _____ 7½ inches _____ $1.50
No. 17 __ ____ 8¼ inches _____ 1.75
No. 18 _____ 9 inches _____ 2.00
No. 19 _____ 10 inches ____ 2.25
No. 20 _____ 11 inches ____ 2.50
No. 21 _____ 11½ inches ___ 2.75
No. 22 _____ 12½ inches ___ 3.00

LADIES' BENT SHEARS—*6 Sizes.*

No. 25 _____ 8¼ inches _____ $1.75
No. 26 _____ 9 inches _____ 2.00
No. 27 _____ 10½ inches _____ 2.25
No. 28 __ 11¼ inches, 2.50
No. 29 __ 12 inches __ 2.75
No. 30 __ 13 inches __ 3.00

☞ Any size of Shears or Scissors in the above list, can be got of our Pattern Agents at the prices indicated.

E. BUTTERICK & CO.,
555 BROADWAY, N. Y.

SPECIAL PREMIUMS.

To any person sending us after April 1st, 1873, Two Dollars as one years Subscription for "THE METROPOLITAN," we will give a Certificate which will entitle the holder to a selection of *Patterns*, to the value of one dollar, on demand.

To any person sending us Three Dollars we will send THE METROPOLITAN for one year; also THE QUARTERLY REPORT, a Plate, size 24 x 30, printed in chromo, published four times each year, representing the *new styles* for Ladies' Dress, and a certificate entitling the holder to a selection of Patterns on demand, to the value of one dollar.

☞ *The Postage on our Publications is to be Paid by Subscribers.*

CLUB RATES FOR OUR PUBLICATIONS,

TO PARTIES NOT OUR AGENTS.

To any one sending us the names of Six new subscribers for the QUARTERLY DELINEATOR, with $1.50 enclosed in payment for the same, we will allow a gratuitous Selection of Plain Patterns to the amount of $1.00 at regular prices, but the entire amount must be ordered at one time.

To any one sending us the names of Ten new subscribers for THE METROPOLITAN, or THE METROPOLITAN and QUARTERLY REPORT combined, with $20.00 for the Club for ten METROPOLITANS, or $30.00 for the Club for ten METROPOLITANS and QUARTERLY REPORTS combined, we will allow a Selection of Patterns to the value of $15.00, at regular prices.

TERMS OF SUBSCRIPTION.

The QUARTERLY DELINEATOR	25 cents a year.
For Single Copies of THE QUARTERLY DELINEATOR	10 cents.
THE METROPOLITAN (Monthly)	$2.00 a year.
THE METROPOLITAN and QUARTERLY REPORT, combined	3.00 "
For Single Copies of THE METROPOLITAN	25 cents.
For Single Copies of the PLATE and METROPOLITAN	75 cents.

Special Rates for Packages of Patterns.

On orders for PACKAGES of Patterns the following discounts will be allowed, but the entire amount must be ordered at one time. In ordering, specify the Patterns by their numbers.

On receipt of $3.00 we will allow a selection of $4.00, in Patterns.
On receipt of $5.00 we will allow a selection of $7.00, in Patterns.
On receipt of $10.00 we will allow a selection of $15.00, in Patterns.

Patterns, when sent by Mail, are post-paid; but Express charges we cannot pay.

In making Remittances, if possible send by Draft or Post-Office Money Order. Do not risk money in a Letter without Registering it.

☞ A Large **Illustrated Catalogue** of our Patterns will be mailed to any address on receipt of Six Cents in postage stamps.

☞ Our **Catalogue of Patterns**, issued each season, can be had **free** on application at any of our Twelve Hundred Branches and Agencies in principal places in the United States and Canadas.

E. BUTTERICK & CO.,
Publishers, Designers of Fashions and Pattern Manufacturers,
555 BROADWAY, N. Y.

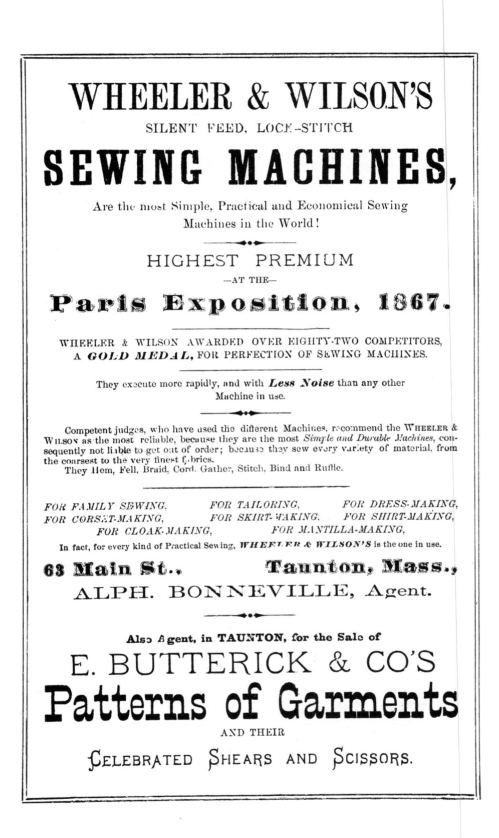

WHEELER & WILSON'S

SILENT FEED, LOCK-STITCH

SEWING MACHINES,

Are the most Simple, Practical and Economical Sewing
Machines in the World!

HIGHEST PREMIUM

—AT THE—

Paris Exposition, 1867.

WHEELER & WILSON AWARDED OVER EIGHTY-TWO COMPETITORS,
A *GOLD MEDAL,* FOR PERFECTION OF SEWING MACHINES.

They execute more rapidly, and with *Less Noise* than any other
Machine in use.

Competent judges, who have used the different Machines, recommend the WHEELER &
WILSON as the most reliable, because they are the most *Simple and Durable Machines,* consequently not liable to get out of order; because they sew every variety of material, from
the coarsest to the very finest fabrics.
They Hem, Fell, Braid, Cord. Gather, Stitch, Bind and Ruffle.

FOR FAMILY SEWING,   *FOR TAILORING,*   *FOR DRESS-MAKING,*
FOR CORSET-MAKING,   *FOR SKIRT-MAKING,*   *FOR SHIRT-MAKING,*
   FOR CLOAK-MAKING,   *FOR MANTILLA-MAKING,*

In fact, for every kind of Practical Sewing, *WHEELER & WILSON'S* is the one in use.

63 Main St.,   Taunton, Mass.,

ALPH. BONNEVILLE, Agent.

Also Agent, in TAUNTON, for the Sale of

E. BUTTERICK & CO'S
Patterns of Garments

AND THEIR

CELEBRATED SHEARS AND SCISSORS.

E. BUTTERICK & CO.'S

Catalogue

SUMMER

1882.

Published by THE BUTTERICK PUBLISHING CO. [Limited].

ANY OF THE PATTERNS ILLUSTRATED IN THIS CATALOGUE, (ALSO HUNDREDS OF OTHERS, COMPRISING EVERY KIND OF GARMENT WORN BY LADIES, MISSES, GIRLS, BOYS, LITTLE CHILDREN AND INFANTS,) CAN BE OBTAINED AT EITHER OF THE

PRINCIPAL OFFICES:

171 to 177 Regent St., 555 Broadway,

LONDON; NEW YORK.

ESTABLISHED 1857.

PRICE, **$1.50.**

BEAUTIFUL WOMEN

Are more frequently known as such by an elegant figure than a pretty face, and many ladies by using an ill-shaped Corset destroy the symmetry of their otherwise shapely figure. All ladies who have any regard for their personal appearance will wear the **DOUBLE HIP, PERFECT-FITTING WOVEN CORSET.**

This being a woven corset, made in one piece, containing **100 Bones** woven diagonally in the body of the corset, **retains its shape under all circumstances,** at the same time yielding to all the motions of the wearer. This is the only corset manufactured that can make good this claim. It is a new invention of **THE NOVELTY CORSET WORKS, N. Y.,** who are its sole manufacturers. Every lady who has ever worn one, or desires a shapely figure, will ask for and insist upon having the **DOUBLE HIP, PERFECT-FITTING WOVEN CORSET.** For sale by all dealers in the U. S. Sent by mail, post-paid, on receipt of price.

SPECIAL NOTICE.

To Correspondents:

When Remittances are sent to us by Mail, Postage Stamps of One or Two Cent Denomination will be accepted as Cash. Do not remit Three-Cent Stamps, if you can conveniently do otherwise.

THE BUTTERICK PUBLISHING CO. [Limited],

555 Broadway, New York.

INSTRUCTIONS
—FOR—
Selecting Patterns

In buying Patterns, see that the measures are taken correctly; that the size printed on the label corresponds with the measure properly observed, the following rules will insure satisfactory results:

TO MEASURE FOR A LADY'S WAIST, OR ANY GARMENT REQUIRING A BUST MEASURE TO BE TAKEN:—Put the measure around the body, OVER the dress, close under the arms, drawing it closely,—NOT TOO TIGHT.

TO MEASURE FOR A SKIRT OR OVERSKIRT:—Put the tape around the waist, OVER the dress.

☞ Take the MEASURES for MISSES' and LITTLE GIRLS' PATTERNS THE SAME AS FOR LADIES'. *In ordering, give the ages also.*

TO MEASURE FOR A BOY'S COAT OR VEST:—Put the measure around the body, UNDER the jacket, close under the arms, drawing it closely,—NOT TOO TIGHT.

FOR THE OVERCOAT:—Measure OVER the garment the coat is to be worn over.

TO MEASURE FOR PANTS:—Put the measure around the body, OVER the pants at the waist, drawing it closely,—NOT TOO TIGHT.

TO MEASURE FOR A SHIRT:—For the size of the Neck, measure the exact size where the collar encircles it, allowing one inch,—thus:—if the exact size be 14 inches, use a pattern marked 15 inches. For the Breast, measure the same as for a Coat.

NOTICE :—Any sizes of the Patterns specified in this Book, which cannot at once be procured of our Agents, will be sent by us, post-paid, on receipt of price, to any part of the World.

☞ Parties writing to us, making enquiries, must enclose a postage stamp for reply, or no notice will be taken.

ADDRESS ORDERS TO

THE BUTTERICK PUBLISHING CO. [Limited],

555 Broadway, New York.

PRICE-LIST OF SHEARS AND SCISSORS.

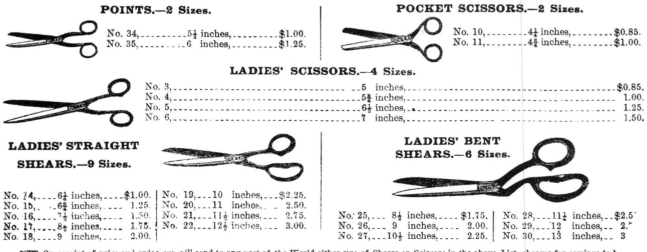

POINTS.—2 Sizes.

No. 34,	5¼ inches,	$1.00.
No. 35,	6 inches,	$1.25.

POCKET SCISSORS.—2 Sizes.

No. 10,	4¼ inches,	$0.85.
No. 11,	4¾ inches,	$1.00.

LADIES' SCISSORS.—4 Sizes.

No. 3,	5 inches,	$0.85.
No. 4,	5¾ inches,	1.00.
No. 5,	6½ inches,	1.25.
No. 6,	7 inches,	1.50.

LADIES' STRAIGHT SHEARS.—9 Sizes.

No. 14,	6¼ inches,	$1.00.	No. 19,	10 inches,	$2.25.
No. 15,	6¾ inches,	1.25.	No. 20,	11 inches,	2.50.
No. 16,	7¼ inches,	1.50.	No. 21,	11½ inches,	2.75.
No. 17,	8¼ inches,	1.75.	No. 22,	12½ inches,	3.00.
No. 18,	9 inches,	2.00.			

LADIES' BENT SHEARS.—6 Sizes.

No. 25,	8½ inches,	$1.75.	No. 28,	11¼ inches,	$2.5
No. 26,	9 inches,	2.00.	No. 29,	12 inches,	2.
No. 27,	10¼ inches,	2.25.	No. 30,	13 inches,	3

☞ On receipt of price and order, we will send to any part of the World either size of Shears or Scissors in the above List, charges for carriage to be by the purchaser. We send out no goods C. O. D.

Address orders to **THE BUTTERICK PUBLISHING CO.** [Limited], 555 Broadway, Ne

STYLES OF GARMENTS:

SUMMER, 1882.

LADIES' PATTERNS.

7942 **7942**

(Issued March, 1882.)
Ladies' Trained Costume: 13 sizes.
Bust measures, 28 to 46 inches.
Any size, 50 cents.

7528 **7528**

(Issued May, 1881.)
Ladies' Trained Costume: 13 sizes.
Bust measures, 28 to 46 inches.
Any size, 50 cents.

7708 **7708**

(Issued September, 1881.)
Ladies' Trained Costume: 13 sizes.
Bust measures, 28 to 46 inches.
Any size, 50 cents.

7846 **7846** **7846**

(Issued November, 1881.)
Ladies' Costume, with Attachable Train:
13 sizes. Bust measures, 28 to 46 inches.
Any size, 50 cents.

7725

(Issued September, 1881.)
Ladies' Costume, with Adjustable Court Train of Full
or Medium Length: 13 sizes. Bust measures, 28 to
46 inches. Any size, 50 cents.

7547 **7547** **7547**

(Issued May, 1881.)
Ladies' Costume, with Removable Train:
13 sizes. Bust measures, 28 to 46 inches.
Any size, 50 cents.

7845 **7845**

(Issued November, 1881.)
Ladies' Trained Costume: 13 sizes.
Bust measures, 28 to 46 inches.
Any size, 50 cents.

7531 **7531**

(Issued May, 1881.)
Ladies' Princess Costume: 13 sizes.
Bust measures, 28 to 46 inches.
Any size, 50 cents.

7546 **7546**

(Issued May, 1881.)
Ladies' Riding Habit: 13 sizes.
Bust measures, 28 to 46 inches.
Any size, 50 cents.

7631 **7631**

(Issued July, 1881.)
Ladies' Costume: 13 sizes.
Bust measures, 28 to 46 inches.
Any size, 50 cents.

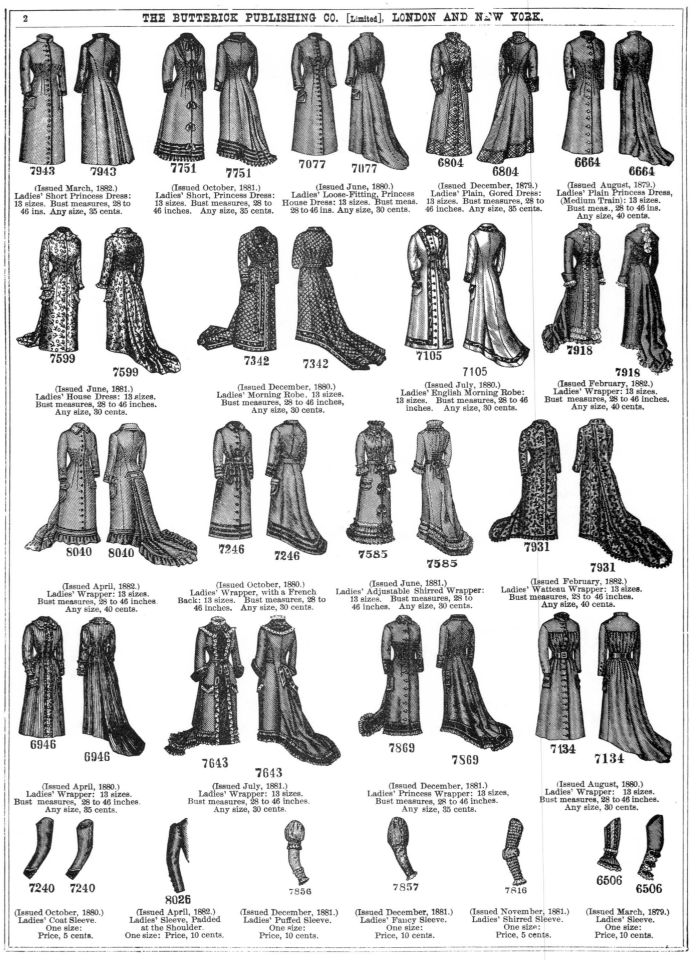

7943　**7943**

(Issued March, 1882.)
Ladies' Short Princess Dress:
13 sizes. Bust measures, 28 to
46 ins. Any size, 35 cents.

7751　**7751**

(Issued October, 1881.)
Ladies' Short, Princess Dress:
13 sizes. Bust measures, 28 to
46 inches. Any size, 35 cents.

7077　**7077**

(Issued June, 1880.)
Ladies' Loose-Fitting, Princess
House Dress: 13 sizes. Bust meas.
28 to 46 ins. Any size, 30 cents.

6804　**6804**

(Issued December, 1879.)
Ladies' Plain, Gored Dress:
13 sizes. Bust measures, 28 to
46 inches. Any size, 35 cents.

6664　**6664**

(Issued August, 1879.)
Ladies' Plain Princess Dress,
(Medium Train): 13 sizes.
Bust meas., 28 to 46 ins.
Any size, 40 cents.

7599　**7599**

(Issued June, 1881.)
Ladies' House Dress: 13 sizes.
Bust measures, 28 to 46 inches.
Any size, 30 cents.

7342　**7342**

(Issued December, 1880.)
Ladies' Morning Robe. 13 sizes.
Bust measures, 28 to 46 inches,
Any size, 30 cents.

7105　**7105**

(Issued July, 1880.)
Ladies' English Morning Robe:
13 sizes. Bust measures, 28 to 46
inches. Any size, 30 cents.

7918　**7918**

(Issued February, 1882.)
Ladies' Wrapper: 13 sizes.
Bust measures, 28 to 46 inches.
Any size, 40 cents.

8040　**8040**

(Issued April, 1882.)
Ladies' Wrapper: 13 sizes.
Bust measures, 28 to 46 inches.
Any size, 40 cents.

7246　**7246**

(Issued October, 1880.)
Ladies' Wrapper, with a French
Back: 13 sizes. Bust measures, 28 to
46 inches. Any size, 30 cents.

7585　**7585**

(Issued June, 1881.)
Ladies' Adjustable Shirred Wrapper:
13 sizes. Bust measures, 28 to
46 inches. Any size, 30 cents.

7931　**7931**

(Issued February, 1882.)
Ladies' Watteau Wrapper: 13 sizes.
Bust measures, 28 to 46 inches.
Any size, 40 cents.

6946　**6946**

(Issued April, 1880.)
Ladies' Wrapper: 13 sizes.
Bust measures, 28 to 46 inches.
Any size, 35 cents.

7643　**7643**

(Issued July, 1881.)
Ladies' Wrapper: 13 sizes.
Bust measures, 28 to 46 inches.
Any size, 30 cents.

7869　**7869**

(Issued December, 1881.)
Ladies' Princess Wrapper: 13 sizes,
Bust measures, 28 to 46 inches.
Any size, 35 cents.

7134　**7134**

(Issued August, 1880.)
Ladies' Wrapper: 13 sizes.
Bust measures, 28 to 46 inches.
Any size, 30 cents.

7240　**7240**

(Issued October, 1880.)
Ladies' Coat Sleeve.
One size:
Price, 5 cents.

8026

(Issued April, 1882.)
Ladies' Sleeve, Padded
at the Shoulder.
One size: Price, 10 cents.

7856

(Issued December, 1881.)
Ladies' Puffed Sleeve.
One size:
Price, 10 cents.

7857

(Issued December, 1881.)
Ladies' Fancy Sleeve.
One size:
Price, 10 cents.

7816

(Issued November, 1881.)
Ladies' Shirred Sleeve.
One size:
Price, 5 cents.

6506　**6506**

(Issued March, 1879.)
Ladies' Sleeve.
One size:
Price, 10 cents.

7474   **7474**

(Issued April, 1881.)
Ladies' Wrapper, with Shirred
Back: 13 sizes. Bust meas.,
28 to 46 ins. Any size, 30 cents.

7184   **7184**

(Issued September, 1880.)
Ladies' Double-Breasted, Adjustable Wrapper: 13 sizes. Bust meas.,
28 to 46 ins. Any size, 30 cents.

6975   **6975**

(Issued April, 1880.)
Ladies' Morning Costume:
13 sizes. Bust measures, 28 to
46 inches. Any size, 30 cents.

6194   **6194**

Ladies' Sack Wrapper:
13 sizes. Bust measures,
28 to 46 inches.
Any size, 40 cents.

6615   **6615**

(Issued June, 1879.)
Ladies' Easy-Fitting, Short
Wrapper: 13 sizes. Bust meas.,
28 to 46 ins. Any size, 30 cents.

8028   **8028**

(Issued April, 1882.)
Ladies' Costume, with Removable Collar: 13 sizes. Bust meas.,
28 to 46 ins. Any size, 40 cents.

8003   **8003**

(Issued April, 1882.)
Ladies' Costume: 13 sizes.
Bust meas., 28 to 46 inches.
Any size, 40 cents.

8007   **8007**

(Issued April, 1882.)
Ladies' Easy-Fitting House Costume: 13 sizes. Bust meas., 28 to
46 inches. Any size, 35 cents.

8006   **8006**

(Issued April, 1882.)
Ladies' Costume: 13 sizes.
Bust meas., 28 to 46 inches.
Any size, 40 cents.

8005   **8005**

(Issued April, 1882.)
Ladies' Costume: 13 sizes.
Bust meas., 28 to 46 inches.
Any size, 40 cents.

7974   **7974**

(Issued March, 1882.)
Ladies' Costume: 13 sizes.
Bust meas., 28 to 46 inches.
Any size, 40 cents.

7965   **7965**

(Issued March, 1882.)
Ladies' Costume, with Adjustable
Cape: 13 sizes. Bust meas., 28 to
46 inches. Any size, 40 cents.

7962   **7962**

(Issued March, 1882.)
Ladies' Costume: 13 sizes.
Bust meas., 28 to 46 inches.
Any size, 40 cents.

7960   **7960**

(Issued March, 1882.)
Ladies' Costume: 13 sizes.
Bust meas., 28 to 46 inches.
Any size, 40 cents.

7959   **7959**

(Issued March, 1882.)
Ladies' Costume: 13 sizes.
Bust meas., 28 to 46 inches.
Any size, 40 cents.

7958   **7958**

(Issued March, 1882.)
Ladies' Costume: 13 sizes.
Bust meas., 28 to 46 inches.
Any size, 40 cents.

7951   **7951**

(Issued March, 1882.)
Ladies' Costume: 13 sizes.
Bust meas., 28 to 46 inches.
Any size, 40 cents.

7946   **7946**

(Issued March, 1882.)
Ladies' Costume: 13 sizes.
Bust meas., 28 to 46 inches
Any size, 35 cents.

7907   **7907**

(Issued January, 1882.)
Ladies' Costume: 13 sizes.
Bust meas., 28 to 46 inches.
Any size, 35 cents.

7899   **7899**

(Issued January, 1882.)
Ladies' Costume: 13 sizes.
Bust meas., 28 to 46 inches.
Any size, 35 cents.

7883   **7883**

(Issued December, 1881.)
Ladies' Costume, with Adjustable
Cape: 13 sizes. Bust meas., 28 to
46 inches. Any size, 35 cents.

7874   **7874**

(Issued December, 1881.)
Ladies' Polonaise Costume:
13 sizes. Bust meas., 28 to
46 inches. Any size, 35 cents.

7852   **7852**

(Issued December, 1881.)
Ladies' Costume: 13 sizes.
Bust meas., 28 to 46 inches.
Any size, 35 cents.

7840   **7840**

(Issued November, 1881.)
Ladies' Costume: 13 sizes.
Bust meas., 28 to 46 inches.
Any size, 35 cents.

7838   **7838**

(Issued November, 1881.)
Ladies' Costume: 13 sizes.
Bust meas., 28 to 46 inches.
Any size, 35 cents.

7837   7837   7835   7835   7836   7836   7834   7834   7822   7822

(Issued November, 1881.)
Ladies' Costume: 13 sizes.
Bust meas., 28 to 46 inches.
Any size, 35 cents.

(Issued November, 1881.)
Ladies' Costume, with Watteau
Plait: 13 sizes. Bust meas., 28 to
46 inches.   Any size, 35 cents.

(Issued November, 1881.)
Ladies' Costume: 13 sizes.
Bust meas., 28 to 46 inches.
Any size, 35 cents.

(Issued November, 1881.)
Ladies' Costume: 13 sizes.
Bust meas., 28 to 46 inches.
Any size, 35 cents.

(Issued November, 1881.)
Ladies' Costume: 13 sizes.
Bust meas., 28 to 46 inches.
Any size, 35 cents.

7820   7820   7891   7891   7796   7796   7778   7778   7722   7722

(Issued November, 1881.)
Ladies' Costume: 13 sizes.
Bust meas., 28 to 46 inches.
Any size, 35 cents.

(Issued January, 1882.)
Ladies' Costume: 13 sizes.
Bust meas., 28 to 46 inches.
Any size, 35 cents.

(Issued October, 1881.)
Ladies' Costume, with Adjustable
Shoulder Collar: 13 sizes. Bust meas.,
28 to 46 inches.   Any size, 35 cents.

(Issued October, 1881.)
Ladies' Costume: 13 sizes.
Bust meas., 28 to 46 inches.
Any size, 35 cents.

(Issued September, 1881.)
Ladies' Costume: 13 sizes.
Bust meas., 28 to 46 inches.
Any size, 30 cents.

7695   7695   7757   7757   7723   7723   7761   7761   7718   7718

(Issued September, 1881.)
Ladies' Costume: 13 sizes.
Bust meas., 28 to 46 inches.
Any size, 30 cents.

(Issued October, 1881.)
Ladies' Costume: 13 sizes.
Bust meas., 28 to 46 inches.
Any size, 30 cents.

(Issued September, 1881.)
Ladies' Costume, with Adjustable
Shoulder Cape: 13 sizes. Bust meas.,
28 to 46 inches.   Any size, 30 cents.

(Issued October, 1881.)
Ladies' Costume: 13 sizes.
Bust meas., 28 to 46 inches.
Any size, 30 cents.

(Issued September, 1881.)
Ladies' Costume: 13 sizes.
Bust meas., 28 to 46 inches.
Any size, 30 cents.

7716   7716   7694   7694   7680   7680   7674   7674   7660   7660

(Issued September, 1881.)
Ladies' Costume: 13 sizes.
Bust meas., 28 to 46 inches.
Any size, 30 cents.

(Issued September, 1881.)
Ladies' Costume, with Adjustable
Collar: 13 sizes. Bust meas., 28 to
46 inches.   Any size, 30 cents.

(Issued September, 1881.)
Ladies' Costume: 13 sizes.
Bust meas., 28 to 46 inches.
Any size, 35 cents.

(Issued August, 1881.)
Ladies' Costume: 13 sizes.
Bust meas., 28 to 46 inches.
Any size, 30 cents.

(Issued August, 1881.)
Ladies' Costume: 13 sizes:
Bust meas., 28 to 46 inches.
Any size, 30 cents.

7623   7623   7621   7621   7610   7610   7602   7602   7581   7581

(Issued July, 1881.)
Ladies' Shirred Costume:
13 sizes. Bust meas., 28 to
46 inches.   Any size, 30 cents.

(Issued July, 1881.)
Ladies' Costume: 13 sizes.
Bust meas., 28 to 46 inches.
Any size, 30 cents.

(Issued June, 1881.)
Ladies' Costume: 13 sizes.
Bust meas., 28 to 46 inches.
Any size, 30 cents.

(Issued June, 1881.)
Ladies' Costume, with Adjustable
Cape: 13 sizes. Bust meas., 28 to
46 inches.   Any size, 30 cents.

(Issued June, 1881.)
Ladies' Shirred Costume:
13 sizes. Bust meas., 28 to
46 inches.   Any size, 30 cents.

7549　　7549　　**7548　　7548**　　**7545　　7545**　　**7532　　7532**　　**7521　　7521**

(Issued May, 1881.)
Ladies' Costume: 13 sizes.
Bust meas., 28 to 46 inches.
Any size, 30 cents.

(Issued May, 1881.)
Ladies' Costume: 13 sizes.
Bust meas., 28 to 46 inches.
Any size, 30 cents.

(Issued May, 1881.)
Ladies' Polonaise Costume:
13 sizes. Bust meas., 28 to
46 inches. Any size, 30 cents.

(Issued May, 1881.)
Ladies' Costume: 13 sizes.
Bust meas., 28 to 46 inches.
Any size, 30 cents.

(Issued May, 1881.)
Ladies' Costume: 13 sizes.
Bust meas., 28 to 46 inches.
Any size, 30 cents.

7510　　7510　　**7421　　7421**　　**7334　　7334**　　**8008　　8008**　　**7894　　7894**

(Issued April, 1881.)
Ladies' Costume, with Adjustable
Cape: 13 sizes. Bust meas., 28 to
46 inches. Any size, 30 cents.

(Issued March, 1881.)
Ladies' Costume: 13 sizes.
Bust meas., 28 to 46 inches.
Any size, 30 cents.

(Issued December, 1880.)
Ladies' Pilgrimage Costume, with
Adjustable Cape and Hood:
13 sizes. Bust meas., 28 to
46 inches. Any size, 30 cents.

(Issued April, 1882.)
Ladies' Wrap: 10 sizes.
Bust meas., 28 to 46 inches.
Any size, 35 cents.

(Issued January, 1882.)
Ladies' Cloak, with Adjust-
able Collar: 10 sizes.
Bust meas., 28 to 46 inches.
Any size, 35 cents.

8017　　8017　　**7764　　7764**　　**8013　　8013**　　**7957　　7957**　　**7916　　7916**

(Issued April, 1882.)
Ladies' Wrap: 10 sizes.
Bust meas., 28 to 46 inches.
Any size, 35 cents.

(Issued October, 1881.)
Ladies' Cloak: 10 sizes.
Bust meas., 28 to 46 inches.
Any size, 30 cents.

(Issued April, 1882.)
Ladies' Wrap: 10 sizes.
Bust meas., 28 to 46 inches.
Any size, 35 cents.

(Issued March, 1882.)
Ladies' Wrap: 10 sizes.
Bust meas., 28 to 46 inches.
Any size, 40 cents.

(Issued February, 1882.)
Ladies' Cloak: 10 sizes.
Bust meas., 28 to 46 inches
Any size, 35 cents.

7900　　7900　　**7769　　7769**　　**7935　　7935**　　**7809　　7809**　　**7535　　7535**

(Issued January, 1882.)
Ladies' Wrap: 10 sizes.
Bust meas., 28 to 46 inches.
Any size, 35 cents.

(Issued October, 1881.)
Ladies' Cloak: 10 sizes.
Bust meas., 28 to 46 inches.
Any size, 35 cents.

(Issued February, 1882.)
Ladies' Circular Wrap: 10 sizes.
Bust meas., 28 to 46 inches.
Any size, 35 cents.

(Issued November, 1881.)
Ladies' Wrap: 10 sizes.
Bust meas., 28 to 46 inches.
Any size, 35 cents.

(Issued May, 1881.)
Ladies' Wrap: 10 sizes.
Bust meas., 28 to 46 inches.
Any size, 30 cents.

7750　　7750　　**7563　　7563**　　**7863　　7863**　　**7386　　7386**　　**7950　　7950**

(Issued October, 1881.)
Ladies' Wrap: 10 sizes.
Bust meas., 28 to 46 inches.
Any size, 35 cents.

(Issued May, 1881.)
Ladies' Travelling Wrap:
10 sizes. Bust meas., 28 to
46 inches. Any size, 30 cents.

(Issued December, 1881.)
Ladies' Wrap: 10 sizes.
Bust meas., 28 to 46 inches.
Any size, 35 cents.

(Issued February, 1881.)
Ladies' Wrap: 10 sizes.
Bust meas., 28 to 46 inches.
Any size, 30 cents.

(Issued March, 1882.)
Ladies' Wrap: 10 sizes.
Bust meas., 28 to 46 inches.
Any size, 35 cents.

7587   **7587**   **7355**   **7855**   **7947**   **7947**   **7911**   **7911**   **7715**   **7715**

(Issued June, 1881.)
Ladies' Shirred Wrap: 10 sizes. Bust Measures, 28 to 46 inches. Any size, 30 cents.

(Issued December, 1881.)
Ladies' Double-Breasted Cloak: 13 sizes. Bust measures, 28 to 46 inches. Any size, 35 cents.

(Issued March, 1882.)
Ladies' Long Coat: 13 sizes. Bust measures, 28 to 46 inches. Any size, 35 cents.

(Issued January, 1882.)
Ladies' Ulster: 10 sizes. Bust measures, 28 to 46 inches. Any size, 35 cents.

(Issued September, 1881.)
Ladies' Ulster: 10 sizes: Bust measures, 28 to 46 inches. Any size, 30 cents.

7608   **7608**   **6897**   **6897**   **6868**   **6868**   **6867**   **6867**   **6866**   **6866**

(Issued June, 1881.)
Ladies' Ulsterette: 13 sizes. Bust measures, 28 to 46 inches. Any size, 30 cents.

(Issued March, 1880.)
Ladies' Ulster: 10 sizes. Bust measures, 28 to 46 inches. Any size, 35 cents.

(Issued February, 1880.)
Ladies' Sack Waterproof: 13 sizes. Bust measures, 28 to 46 inches. Any size, 35 cents.

(Issued February, 1880.)
Ladies' Waterproof Cloak: 13 sizes. Bust measures, 28 to 46 inches. Any size, 35 cents.

(Issued February, 1880.)
Ladies' Circular Waterproof: 13 sizes. Bust measures, 28 to 46 inches Any size, 35 cents.

6343   **6343**   **8024**   **8024**   **7952**   **7952**   **7945**   **7945**   **7864**   **7864**

Ladies' Ulster: 10 sizes. Bust measures, 28 to 46 inches. Any size, 30 cents.

(Issued April, 1882.)
Ladies' Polonaise: 13 sizes. Bust measures, 28 to 46 inches. Any size, 35 cents.

(Issued March, 1882.)
Ladies' Polonaise: 13 sizes. Bust measures, 28 to 46 inches. Any size, 35 cents.

(Issued March, 1882.)
Ladies' Polonaise: 13 sizes. Bust measures, 28 to 46 inches. Any size, 35 cents.

(Issued December, 1881.)
Ladies' Polonaise: 13 sizes. Bust measures, 28 to 46 inches. Any size, 30 cents.

7622   **7622**   **6879**   **6879**   **8014**   **8014**   **7828**   **7828**   **7902**   **7902**

(Issued July, 1881.)
Ladies' Polonaise: 13 sizes. Bust measures, 28 to 46 ins. Any size, 25 cents.

(Issued February, 1880.)
Ladies' Plain Polonaise: 13 sizes. Bust measures, 28 to 46 inches. Any size, 30 cents.

(Issued April, 1882.)
Ladies' Polonaise: 13 sizes. Bust measures, 28 to 46 inches. Any size, 35 cents.

(Issued November, 1881.)
Ladies' Polonaise: 13 sizes. Bust measures, 28 to 46 inches. Any size, 30 cents.

(Issued January, 1882.)
Ladies' Polonaise: 13 sizes. Bust measures, 28 to 46 inches. Any size, 35 cents.

7571   **7571**   **7526**   **7526**   **7659**   **7659**   **7881**   **7881**   **7777**   **7777**

(Issued June, 1881.)
Ladies' Polonaise: 13 sizes. Bust measures, 28 to 46 ins. Any size, 25 cents

(Issued May, 1881.)
Ladies' Polonaise: 13 sizes. Bust measures, 28 to 46 inches. Any size, 30 cents.

(Issued August, 1881.)
Ladies' Polonaise: 13 sizes. Bust measures, 28 to 46 inches. Any size, 30 cents.

(Issued December, 1881.)
Ladies' Polonaise: 13 sizes. Bust measures, 28 to 46 inches. Any size, 30 cents.

(Issued October, 1881.)
Ladies' Polonaise: 13 sizes. Bust measures, 28 to 46 inches. Any size, 30 cents.

7707

7919 **7919**

7956 **7956**

7888 **7888**

7538
7538

(Issued September, 1881.)
Ladies' Polonaise: 13 sizes.
Bust meas., 28 to 46 inches.
Any size, 25 cents.

(Issued February, 1882.)
Ladies' Wrap: 10 sizes.
Bust meas., 28 to 46 inches.
Any size, 30 cents.

(Issued March, 1882.)
Ladies' Wrap: 10 sizes.
Bust meas., 28 to 46 inches.
Any size, 30 cents.

(Issued December, 1881.)
Ladies' Wrap: 10 sizes.
Bust meas., 28 to 46 inches.
Any size, 30 cents.

(Issued May, 1881.)
Ladies' Wrap: 10 sizes,
Bust meas., 28 to 46 inches.
Any size, 25 cents.

8022 **8022**

7228 **7228**

7482 **7482**

7685 **7685**

7763 **7763**

(Issued April, 1882.)
Ladies' Wrap: 10 sizes.
Bust meas., 28 to 46 inches.
Any size. 30 cents.

(Issued October, 1880.)
Ladies' Wrap: 10 sizes.
Bust meas., 28 to 46 inches.
Any size, 25 cents.

(Issued April, 1881.)
Ladies' Wrap: 10 sizes.
Bust meas., 28 to 46 inches.
Any size, 30 cents.

(Issued September, 1881.)
Ladies' Wrap: 13 sizes.
Bust meas., 28 to 46 inches.
Any size, 25 cents.

(Issued October, 1881.)
Ladies' Wrap: 10 sizes.
Bust meas., 28 to 46 inches.
Any size, 30 cents,

7661
7661

7527
7527

7642

7787
7787

7539
7539

(Issued August, 1881.)
Ladies' Mantilla: 10 sizes.
Bust meas., 28 to 46 inches.
Any size, 15 cents.

(Issued May, 1881.)
Ladies' Wrap: 10 sizes.
Bust meas., 28 to 46 inches.
Any size, 15 cents.

(Issued July, 1881.)
Ladies Wrap: 10 sizes.
Bust meas., 28 to 46 inches.
Any size, 20 cents.

(Issued October, 1881.)
Ladies' Wrap: 10 sizes.
Bust meas., 28 to 46 inches.
Any size, 25 cents.

(Issued May, 1881.)
Ladies' Wrap: 10 sizes.
Bust meas., 28 to 46 inches.
Any size, 25 cents.

7699

7699

7700
7700

7810 **7810**

7819 **7819**

7630 **7630**

(Issued September, 1881.)
Ladies' Wrap: 10 sizes.
Bust meas., 28 to 46 inches.
Any size, 25 cents.

(Issued September, 1881.)
Ladies' Mantelet: 10 sizes.
Bust meas., 28 to 46 inches.
Any size, 25 cents.

(Issued November, 1881.)
Ladies' Wrap: 10 sizes.
Bust meas., 28 to 46 inches.
Any size, 30 cents.

(Issued November, 1881.)
Ladies' Wrap: 10 sizes.
Bust meas., 28 to 46 inches.
Any size, 30 cents.

(Issued July, 1881.)
Ladies' Mantelet: 10 sizes.
Bust meas., 28 to 46 inches.
Any size, 20 cents.

7977 **7977**

7533
7533

7677 **7677**

7485 **7485**

7078 **7078**

(Issued March, 1882.)
Ladies' Wrap: 10 sizes.
Bust meas., 28 to 46 inches.
Any size, 30 cents.

(Issued May, 1881.)
Ladies' Cape, with Hood:
10 sizes. Bust meas., 28 to
46 inches. Any size, 15 cents.

(Issued August, 1881.)
Ladies' Pointed Shoulder Cape:
10 sizes. Bust meas., 28 to
46 inches. Any size, 10 cents.

(Issued April, 1881.)
Ladies' Wrap: 10 sizes.
Bust meas., 28 to 46 inches.
Any size, 15 cents.

(Issued, June, 1880.)
Ladies' Cape: 10 sizes.
Bust meas., 28 to 46 inches.
Any size, 15 cents.

7460 **7460**

7583 **7583**

7948 **7948**

7628 **7628**

7798 **7798**

7817 **7817**

(Issued March, 1881.)
Ladies' Shoulder Cape:
10 sizes. Bust meas., 28 to
46 inches. Any size, 10 cents.

(Issued June, 1881.)
Ladies' Cape: 10 sizes.
Bust meas., 28 to 46 inches.
Any size, 15 cents.

(Issued March, 1882.)
Ladies' Adjustable
Collar. One size:
Price, 10 cents.

(Issued July, 1881.)
Ladies' Sailor Collar.
One size:
Price, 5 cents.

(Issued November, 1881.)
Ladies' Shoulder Collar.
One size:
Price, 10 cents.

(Issued Nov., 1881.)
Ladies' Plaited Collar:
10 sizes. Bust meas., 28
to 46 ins. Any size, 10 cents.

7886 7886

(Issued December, 1881.)
Ladies' Cloak: 13 sizes.
Bust measures, 28 to
46 inches.
Any size, 30 cents.

7784 7784

(Issued October, 1881.)
Ladies' Cloak: 10 sizes.
Bust measures, 28 to
46 inches.
Any size, 30 cents.

7347 7347

(Issued December, 1880.)
Ladies' Cloak, with Have-
lock Cape: 10 sizes. Bust
meas., 28 to 46 inches.
Any size, 30 cents.

7901 7901

(Issued January, 1882.)
Ladies' Walking Coat:
13 sizes. Bust measures,
28 to 46 inches.
Any size, 30 cents.

7719 7719

(Issued September, 1881.)
Ladies' Coat: 13 sizes.
Bust measures, 28 to
46 inches.
Any size, 25 cents.

8032 8032

(Issued April, 1882.)
Ladies' Coat: 13 sizes.
Bust measures, 28 to
46 inches.
Any size, 30 cents.

7458 7458

(Issued March, 1881.)
Ladies' Coat: 13 sizes.
Bust measures, 28 to
46 inches.
Any size, 25 cents.

8004 8004

(Issued April, 1882.)
Ladies' Cutaway Coat:
13 sizes. Bust meas-
ures, 28 to 46 inches.
Any size, 30 cents.

7565 7565

(Issued May, 1881.)
Ladies' Coat: 13 sizes.
Bust measures, 28 to
46 inches.
Any size, 25 cents.

7964 7964

(Issued March, 1882.)
Ladies' Coat: 13 sizes.
Bust measures, 28 to
46 inches.
Any size, 30 cents.

7814 7814

(Issued November, 1881.)
Ladies' Double-Breasted Coat:
13 sizes. Bust measures,
28 to 46 inches.
Any size, 30 cents.

7709 7709

(Issued September, 1881.)
Ladies' Coat, with Adjustable Collar: 13 sizes. Bust
meas., 28 to 46 inches.
Any size, 25 cents.

7889 7889

(Issued January, 1882.)
Ladies' Close-Fitting Coat:
13 sizes. Bust measures,
28 to 46 inches
Any size, 30 cents.

7297 7297

(Issued November, 1880.)
Ladies' Double-Breasted
Coat: 13 sizes. Bust
meas., 28 to 46 inches.
Any size, 25 cents.

7512 7512

(Issued April, 1881.)
Ladies' Coat, with Cape:
13 sizes. Bust meas-
ures, 28 to 46 inches.
Any size, 25 cents.

7713 7713

(Issued September, 1881.)
Ladies' Coat: 13 sizes.
Bust measures, 28 to
46 inches.
Any size, 25 cents.

6906 6906

(Issued March, 1880.)
Ladies' Double-Breasted
Coat: 13 sizes. Bust
meas., 28 to 46 inches.
Any size, 30 cents.

7266 7266

(Issued October, 1880.)
Ladies' Double-Breasted
Coat: 13 sizes. Bust
meas., 28 to 46 inches.
Any size, 25 cents.

7975 7975

(Issued March, 1882.)
Ladies' Coat: 13 sizes.
Bust measures, 28 to
46 inches.
Any size, 30 cents.

7779 7779

(Issued October, 1881.)
Ladies' Coat: 13 sizes.
Bust measures, 28 to
46 inches.
Any size, 30 cents.

7842 7842

(Issued November, 1881.)
Ladies' Coat, with Adjustable Cape: 13 sizes. Bust
meas., 28 to 46 inches.
Any size, 30 cents.

7509 7509

(Issued April, 1881.)
Ladies' Coat: 13 sizes.
Bust measures, 28 to
46 inches.
Any size, 25 cents.

7566

7566

(Issued May, 1881.)
Ladies' Coat: 13 sizes.
Bust measures, 28 to
46 inches.
Any size, 25 cents.

7321 7321

(Issued December, 1880.)
Ladies' Double-Breasted
Coat, with French Back:
13 sizes. Bust meas., 28 to
46 ins. Any size, 25 cents.

7768 7768

(Issued October, 1881.)
Ladies' Coat: 13 sizes.
Bust measures, 28 to
46 inches.
Any size, 30 cents.

7770 7770

(Issued October, 1881.)
Ladies' Coat: 13 sizes.
Bust measures, 28 to
46 inches.
Any size, 30 cents.

7711 7711

(Issued September, 1881.)
Ladies' Double-Breasted
Coat: 13 sizes. Bust
meas., 28 to 46 inches.
Any size, 25 cents.

7579 7579

(Issued June, 1881.)
Ladies' Sack: 10 sizes.
Bust measures, 28 to
46 inches.
Any size, 25 cents.

7675 7675

(Issued August, 1881.)
Ladies' Dressing Sack:
13 sizes. Bust meas-
ures, 28 to 46 inches.
Any size, 25 cents.

7811 7811

(Issued November, 1881.)
Ladies' Coat: 13 sizes.
Bust measures, 28 to
46 inches.
Any size, 30 cents,

8036 8036

(Issued April, 1882.)
Ladies' Jacket: 13 sizes.
Bust measures, 28 to
46 inches.
Any size, 30 cents.

7540 7540

(Issued May, 1881.)
Ladies' Jacket: 13 sizes.
Bust measures, 28 to
46 inches.
Any size, 25 cents.

 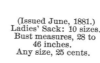

7755 7755

(Issued October, 1881.)
Ladies' Jacket: 13 sizes.
Bust measures, 28 to
46 inches.
Any size, 30 cents.

6878 6878

(Issued February, 1880.)
Ladies' House Jacket:
13 sizes. Bust meas-
ures, 28 to 46 inches.
Any size, 25 cents.

7391 7391

(Issued February, 1881.)
Ladies' Shirred House-
Jacket: 13 sizes. Bust
meas., 28 to 46 inches.
Any size, 25 cents.

6860 6860

(Issued February, 1880.)
Ladies' Dressing Sack:
13 sizes. Bust meas-
ures, 28 to 46 inches.
Any size, 25 cents.

  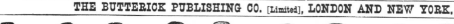

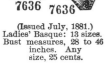  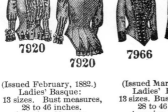 

6177   6177

Ladies' Half-Fitting, Morning Sack: 13 sizes. Bust meas., 28 to 46 inches. Any size, 25 cents.

7928   7928

(Issued February, 1882.) Ladies' Dressing-Sack: 13 sizes. Bust measures, 28 to 46 inches. Any size, 25 cents.

6988   6988

(Issued April, 1880.) Ladies' Sack: 13 sizes. Bust measures, 28 to 46 inches. Any size, 25 cents.

6949   6949

(Issued April, 1880.) Ladies' Easy-Fitting Basque: 13 sizes. Bust measures, 28 to 46 inches. Any size, 25 cents.

7636   7636

(Issued July, 1881.) Ladies' Basque: 13 sizes. Bust measures, 28 to 46 inches. Any size, 25 cents.

7638   7638

(Issued July, 1881.) Ladies' House Basque: 13 sizes. Bust measures, 28 to 46 inches. Any size, 25 cents.

8010   8010

(Issued April, 1882.) Ladies' Basque: 13 sizes. Bust measures, 28 to 46 inches. Any size, 30 cents.

8020   8020

(Issued April, 1882.) Ladies' Basque: 13 sizes. Bust measures, 28 to 46 inches. Any size, 30 cents.

7890   7890

(Issued January, 1882.) Ladies' Basque: 13 sizes. Bust measures, 28 to 46 inches. Any size, 30 cents.

7968   7968

(Issued March, 1882.) Ladies' Street Basque: 13 sizes. Bust measures, 28 to 46 inches. Any size, 30 cents.

7920   7920

(Issued February, 1882.) Ladies' Basque: 13 sizes. Bust measures, 28 to 46 inches. Any size, 30 cents.

7966   7966

(Issued March, 1882.) Ladies' Basque: 13 sizes. Bust measures, 28 to 46 inches. Any size, 30 cents.

8044   8044

(Issued April, 1882.) Ladies' Coat Basque: 13 sizes. Bust measures, 28 to 46 inches. Any size, 30 cents.

8042   8042

(Issued April, 1882.) Ladies' Basque: 13 sizes. Bust measures, 28 to 46 inches. Any size, 30 cents.

8016   8016

(Issued April, 1882.) Ladies' Basque: 13 sizes. Bust measures, 28 to 46 inches. Any size, 30 cents.

7801   7801

(Issued November, 1881.) Ladies' Basque: 13 sizes. Bust measures. 28 to 46 inches. Any size, 30 cents.

7826   7826

(Issued November, 1881.) Ladies' Plaited Basque: 13 sizes. Bust measures, 28 to 46 inches. Any size, 30 cents.

7953   7953

(Issued March, 1882.) Ladies' Shirred Basque: 13 sizes. Bust measures, 28 to 46 inches. Any size, 30 cents.

          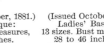 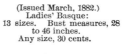

7978   7978

(Issued March, 1882.) Ladies' *Panier* Basque: 13 sizes. Bust measures, 28 to 46 inches. Any size, 30 cents.

7933   7933

(Issued February, 1882.) Ladies' Coat Basque: 13 sizes. Bust measures, 28 to 46 inches. Any size, 30 cents.

7754   7754

(Issued October, 1881.) Ladies' Basque: 13 sizes. Bust measures, 28 to 46 inches. Any size, 30 cents.

7693   7693

(Issued September, 1881.) Ladies' Basque: 13 sizes. Bust measures, 28 to 46 inches. Any size, 25 cents.

7263   7263

(Issued October, 1880.) Ladies' Basque: 13 sizes. Bust measures, 28 to 46 inches. Any size, 25 cents.

7971   7971

(Issued March, 1882.) Ladies' Basque: 13 sizes. Bust measures, 28 to 46 inches. Any size, 30 cents.

 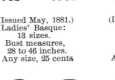

7885   7885

(Issued December, 1881.) Ladies' Basque, with Adjustable Collar: 13 sizes. Bust measures, 28 to 46 inches. Any size, 30 cents.

7574   7574

(Issued June, 1881.) Ladies' Tucked Basque: 13 sizes. Bust measures, 28 to 46 inches. Any size, 25 cents.

7513   7513

(Issued April, 1881.) Ladies' Basque: 13 sizes. Bust measures, 28 to 46 inches. Any size, 25 cents.

7562   7562

(Issued May, 1881.) Ladies' Basque: 13 sizes. Bust measures, 28 to 46 inches. Any size, 25 cents.

7773   7773

(Issued October, 1881.) Ladies' Basque: 13 sizes. Bust measures, 28 to 46 inches. Any size, 30 cents.

7609   7609

(Issued June, 1881.) Ladies' Basque: 13 sizes. Bust measures, 28 to 46 inches. Any size, 25 cents.

7844   7844

(Issued November, 1881.) Ladies' Basque: 13 sizes. Bust measures, 28 to 46 inches. Any size, 30 cents.

7645   7645

(Issued July, 1881.) Ladies' Coat Basque: 13 sizes. Bust measures, 28 to 46 inches. Any size, 25 cents.

7827   7827

(Issued November, 1881.) Ladies' Basque: 13 sizes. Bust meas., 28 to 46 inches. Any size, 30 cents.

7862   7862

(Issued December, 1881.) Ladies' Basque: 13 sizes. Bust measures, 28 to 46 inches. Any size, 30 cents.

7637   7637

(Issued July, 1881.) Ladies' Basque: 13 sizes. Bust measures, 28 to 46 inches. Any size, 25 cents.

7831   7831

(Issued November, 1881.) Ladies' Coat Basque: 13 sizes. Bust meas., 28 to 46 inches. Any size, 30 cents.

7500   **7500**

(Issued April, 1881.)
Ladies' Shirred Basque:
13 sizes. Bust measures,
28 to 46 inches.
Any size, 25 cents.

7591   **7591**

(Issued June, 1881.)
Ladies' Basque:
13 sizes. Bust measures,
28 to 46 inches.
Any size, 25 cents.

7669   **7669**

(Issued August, 1881.)
Ladies' Basque:
13 sizes. Bust measures,
28 to 46 inches.
Any size, 25 cents.

7595   **7595**

(Issued June, 1881.)
Ladies' Shirred Basque:
13 sizes. Bust measures,
28 to 46 inches.
Any size, 25 cents.

7800   **7800**

(Issued November, 1881.)
Ladies' Basque:
13 sizes. Bust measures,
28 to 46 inches.
Any size, 30 cents.

7712
7712

(Issued September, 1881.)
Ladies' Basque:
13 sizes. Bust measures,
28 to 46 inches.
Any size, 25 cents.

7775   **7775**

(Issued October, 1881.)
Ladies' Basque:
13 sizes. Bust measures,
28 to 46 inches.
Any size, 30 cents.

7268   **7268**

(Issued November, 1880.)
Ladies' Basque:
13 sizes. Bust measures,
28 to 46 inches.
Any size, 25 cents.

7597
7597

(Issued June, 1881.)
Ladies' Basque:
13 sizes. Bust measures,
28 to 46 inches.
Any size, 25 cents.

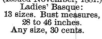

7909   **7909**

(Issued January, 1882.)
Ladies' Basque:
13 sizes. Bust measures,
28 to 46 inches.
Any size, 30 cents.

7525
7525

(Issued May, 1881.)
Ladies' Basque:
13 sizes. Bust measures,
28 to 46 inches.
Any size, 25 cents.

7880   **7880**

(Issued December, 1881.)
Ladies' Basque:
13 sizes. Bust measures,
28 to 46 inches.
Any size, 30 cents.

7640   **7640**

(Issued July, 1881.)
Ladies' Basque:
13 sizes. Bust measures,
28 to 46 inches.
Any size, 25 cents.

7552   **7552**

(Issued May, 1881.)
Ladies' Basque:
13 sizes. Bust measures,
28 to 46 inches.
Any size, 25 cents.

7468   **7468**

(Issued April, 1881.)
Ladies' Pointed Basque:
13 sizes. Bust measures,
28 to 46 inches.
Any size, 25 cents.

7418   **7418**

(Issued March, 1881.)
Ladies' Jersey, without
Darts: 13 sizes. Bust
measures, 28 to 46 inches.
Any size, 25 cents.

7345   **7345**

(Issued December, 1880.)
Ladies' Pointed, Gored
Basque: 13 sizes. Bust
measures, 28 to 46 inches.
Any size, 25 cents.

7776   **7776**

(Issued October, 1881.)
Ladies' Pointed Waist:
13 sizes. Bust measures,
28 to 46 inches.
Any size, 25 cents.

7569   **7569**

(Issued May, 1881.)
Ladies' Basque, with At-
tached Plaits, (also known
as the "Hunting Jacket"):
13 sizes. Bust meas., 28 to
46 inches. Any size, 25 cts.

7523   **7523**

(Issued May, 1881.)
Ladies' Basque, (also
known as the "Shoot-
ing Jacket"): 13 sizes.
Bust meas., 28 to 46
inches. Any size, 25 cts.

7496   **7496**

(Issued April, 1881.)
Ladies' Box-Plaited Blouse,
with Adjustable Hood, (also
known as the Norfolk Jacket): 13 sizes. Bust meas., 28
to 46 ins. Any size, 25 cts.

6968   **6968**

(Issued April, 1880.)
Ladies' Sailor Blouse:
13 sizes.
Bust measures,
28 to 46 inches.
Any size, 15 cents.

7543   **7543**

(Issued May, 1881.)
Ladies' Jacket Blouse,
with Adjustable Collars:
13 sizes. Bust measures,
28 to 46 inches.
Any size, 25 cents.

7629   **7629**

(Issued July, 1881.)
Ladies' Shirred Adjustable
Blouse: 13 sizes,
Bust measures, 28
to 46 inches.
Any size, 20 cents.

7913   **7913**

(Issued February, 1882.)
Ladies' Plain Waist:
13 sizes. Bust measures,
28 to 46 inches.
Any size, 20 cents.

6882   **6882**

(Issued March, 1880.)
Ladies' Surplice Waist:
13 sizes. Bust measures,
28 to 46 inches.
Any size, 15 cents.

7126   **7126**

(Issued July, 1880.)
Ladies' Plaited Waist:
13 sizes. Bust measures,
28 to 46 inches.
Any size, 15 cents.

6959   **6959**

(Issued April, 1880.)
Ladies' Spencer Waist:
13 sizes. Bust measures,
28 to 46 inches.
Any size, 15 cents.

6605   **6605**

(Issued June, 1879.)
Ladies' Corset-Cover:
13 sizes. Bust measures,
28 to 46 inches.
Any size, 25 cents.

4736   **4736**

Ladies' Corset Waist:
13 sizes. Bust measures,
28 to 46 inches.
Any size, 30 cents.

6875   **6875**

(Issued February, 1880.)
Ladies' Corset-Cover:
13 sizes. Bust measures,
28 to 46 inches.
Any size, 20 cents.

6872   **6872**

(Issued February, 1880.)
Ladies' Under-Vest:
10 sizes. Bust measures,
28 to 46 inches.
Any size, 15 cents.

4676   **4676**

Ladies' Flannel Under-
Vest: 10 sizes.
Bust measures,
28 to 46 inches.
Any size, 25 cents.

7925   **7925**

(Issued February, 1882.)
Ladies' Chemise Yoke and
Sleeve: 13 sizes. Bust
measures, 28 to 46 inches.
Any size, 15 cents.

7325   **7325**

(Issued December, 1880.)
Ladies' Skirt Yoke:
9 sizes. Waist measures,
20 to 36 inches.
Any size, 10 cents.

7823

(Issued November,
1881.)
Ladies' Tournure.
One size:
Price 10 cents.

8037 8037 7551 7551 7724 7724 7649 7649 7307 7307 7973 7973

(Issued April, 1882.)
Ladies' Over-Skirt:
9 sizes. Waist meas-
ures, 20 to 36 inches.
Any size, 30 cents.

(Issued May, 1881.)
Ladies' Over-Skirt:
9 sizes. Waist measures,
20 to 36 inches.
Any size, 25 cents.

(Issued September, 1881.)
Ladies' Over-Skirt:
9 sizes. Waist measures,
20 to 36 inches.
Any size, 25 cents.

(Issued July, 1881.)
Ladies' Over-Skirt (Suitable
for Washable Goods): 9 sizes.
Waist meas., 20 to 36 inches.
Any size, 25 cents.

(Issued November, 1880).
Ladies' Over-Skirt:
9 sizes. Waist measures,
20 to 36 inches.
Any size, 25 cents.

(Issued March, 1882.)
Ladies' Over-Skirt:
9 sizes. Waist measures,
20 to 36 inches.
Any size, 30 cents.

7815 7815 7572 7572 7774 7774 8021 8021 8009 8009 8015 8015

(Issued November, 1881.)
Ladies' Over-Skirt:
9 sizes. Waist meas-
ures, 20 to 36 inches.
Any size, 25 cents.

(Issued June, 1881.)
Ladies' Over-Skirt:
9 sizes. Waist measures,
20 to 36 inches.
Any size, 25 cents.

(Issued October, 1881.)
Ladies' Over-Skirt:
9 sizes. Waist measures,
20 to 36 inches.
Any size, 25 cents

(Issued April, 1882.)
Ladies' Walking Skirt:
9 sizes. Waist measures,
20 to 36 inches.
Any size, 35 cents.

(Issued April, 1882.)
Ladies' Walking Skirt:
9 sizes. Waist measures,
20 to 36 inches.
Any size, 35 cents.

(Issued April, 1882.)
Ladies' Walking Skirt:
9 sizes. Waist measures,
20 to 36 inches.
Any size, 35 cents.

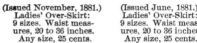 

7934 7934 7972 7972 7944 7944 7884 7884 7910 7910 7875 7875

(Issued February, 1882.)
Ladies' Walking Skirt:
9 sizes. Waist meas-
ures, 20 to 36 inches.
Any size, 35 cents.

(Issued March, 1882.)
Ladies' Walking Skirt:
9 sizes. Waist measures,
20 to 36 inches.
Any size, 35 cents.

(Issued March, 1882.)
Ladies' Walking Skirt:
9 sizes. Waist measures,
20 to 36 inches.
Any size, 35 cents.

(Issued December, 1881.)
Ladies' Walking Skirt:
9 sizes. Waist measures,
20 to 36 inches.
Any size, 30 cents.

(Issued January, 1882.)
Ladies' Walking Skirt:
9 sizes. Waist measures,
20 to 36 inches.
Any size, 30 cents.

(Issued December, 1881.)
Ladies' Walking Skirt:
9 sizes. Waist measures,
20 to 36 inches.
Any size, 30 cents.

7969 7969 7912 7912 7832 7832 7825 7825 7635 7635 7644 7644

(Issued March, 1882.)
Ladies' Walking Skirt:
9 sizes. Waist meas-
ures, 20 to 36 inches.
Any size, 35 cents.

(Issued February, 1882.)
Ladies' Walking Skirt:
9 sizes. Waist meas-
ures, 20 to 36 inches.
Any size, 35 cents.

(Issued November, 1881.)
Ladies' Walking Skirt:
9 sizes. Waist meas-
ures, 20 to 36 inches.
Any size, 30 cents.

(Issued November, 1881.)
Ladies' Walking Skirt:
9 sizes. Waist measures,
20 to 36 inches.
Any size, 30 cents.

(Issued July, 1881.)
Ladies' Walking Skirt:
9 sizes. Waist measures,
20 to 36 inches.
Any size, 30 cents.

(Issued July, 1881.)
Ladies' Walking Skirt:
9 sizes. Waist meas-
ures, 20 to 36 inches.
Any size, 30 cents.

7833 7833 7590 7590 7772 7772 7673 7673 7710 7710 7692 7692

(Issued November, 1881.)
Ladies' Walking Skirt:
9 sizes. Waist meas-
ures, 20 to 36 inches.
Any size, 30 cents.

(Issued June, 1881.)
Ladies' Walking Skirt:
9 sizes. Waist meas-
ures, 20 to 36 inches.
Any size, 30 cents.

(Issued October, 1881.)
Ladies' Walking Skirt:
9 sizes. Waist meas-
ures, 20 to 36 inches.
Any size, 30 cents.

(Issued August, 1881.)
Ladies' Walking Skirt:
9 sizes. Waist measures,
20 to 36 inches.
Any size, 30 cents.

(Issued September, 1881.)
Ladies' Walking Skirt:
9 sizes. Waist measures,
20 to 36 inches.
Any size, 30 cents.

(Issued September, 1881.)
Ladies' Walking Skirt:
9 sizes. Waist meas-
ures, 20 to 36 inches.
Any size, 30 cents.

 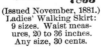       

7803 7803 7804 7804 7714 7714 7753 7753 7542 7542 7771 7771

(Issued November, 1881.)
Ladies' Walking Skirt:
9 sizes. Waist meas-
ures, 20 to 36 inches.
Any size, 30 cents.

(Issued November, 1881.)
Ladies' Walking Skirt:
9 sizes. Waist meas-
ures, 20 to 36 inches.
Any size, 30 cents.

(Issued September, 1881.)
Ladies' Walking Skirt:
9 sizes. Waist meas-
ures, 20 to 36 inches.
Any size, 30 cents.

(Issued October, 1881.)
Ladies' Walking Skirt:
9 sizes. Waist meas-
ures, 20 to 36 inches.
Any size, 30 cents.

(Issued May, 1881.)
Ladies' Walking Skirt:
9 sizes. Waist meas-
ures, 20 to 36 inches.
Any size, 30 cents.

(Issued October, 1881.)
Ladies' Walking Skirt:
9 sizes. Waist meas-
ures, 20 to 36 inches.
Any size, 30 cents.

7799   **7799**

(Issued November, 1881.)
Ladies' Walking Skirt:
9 sizes. Waist meas-
ures, 20 to 36 inches.
Any size, 30 cents.

7706   **7706**

(Issued September, 1881.)
Ladies' Walking Skirt:
9 sizes. Waist meas-
ures, 20 to 36 inches.
Any size, 30 cents.

7639   **7639**

(Issued July, 1881.)
Ladies' Walking Skirt;
9 sizes. Waist meas-
ures, 20 to 36 inches.
Any size, 30 cents.

7524   **7524**

(Issued May, 1881.)
Ladies' Walking Skirt:
9 sizes. Waist meas-
ures, 20 to 36 inches.
Any size, 30 cents.

7267

(Issued November, 1880.)
Ladies' Four-Gored Skirt:
9 sizes. Waist measures,
20 to 36 inches.
Any size, 25 cents.

7522   **7522**

(Issued May, 1881.)
Ladies' Walking Skirt:
9 sizes. Waist meas-
ures, 20 to 36 inches.
Any size, 30 cents.

7573   **7573**

(Issued June, 1881.)
Ladies' Walking Skirt:
9 sizes. Waist measures,
20 to 36 inches.
Any size, 30 cents.

7795

(Issued October, 1881.)
Ladies' Walking Skirt:
9 sizes. Waist meas-
ures, 20 to 36 inches.
Any size, 30 cents.

7544   **7544**

(Issued May, 1881.)
Ladies' Walking Skirt:
9 sizes. Waist measures,
20 to 36 inches.
Any size, 30 cents.

7301   **7036**

(Issued Nov., 1880.)
Ladies' Full Walking
Skirt: 9 sizes. Waist
meas., 20 to 36 inches.
Any size, 25 cents.

(Issued May, 1880.)
Ladies' Full Walking
Skirt: 9 sizes. Waist
meas., 20 to 36 inches.
Any size, 25 cents.

6913   **6913**

(Issued March, 1880.)
Ladies' Walking Skirt, with
Adjustable Train: 9 sizes.
Waist measures, 20 to 36 inches.
Any size, 35 cents.

7967   **7967**   **7967**

(Issued March, 1882.)
Ladies' Walking Skirt, with Adjustable Back
Drapery and Train: 9 sizes.
Waist measures, 20 to 36 inches.
Any size, 40 cents.

6755

(Issued October, 1879.)
Ladies' Demi-Train Skirt:
9 sizes. Waist measures,
20 to 36 inches.
Any size, 30 cents.

7691

(Issued September, 1881.)
Ladies' Trained Skirt:
9 sizes. Waist meas.,
20 to 36 inches.
Any size, 30 cents.

7366   **7366**

(Issued January, 1881.)
Ladies' Adjustable Train:
3 sizes. Waist measures,
20, 28 and 36 inches.
Any size, 15 cents.

6942

(Issued April, 1880.)
Ladies' Petticoat,
with a Yoke: 9 sizes.
Waist meas., 20 to 36
ins. Any size, 25 cts.

6650

(Issued July, 1879.)
Ladies' Plain, Round
Petticoat: 9 sizes.
Waist meas., 20 to 36
ins. Any size, 25 cts.

6018

Ladies' Flannel
Petticoat: 9 sizes.
Waist meas., 20 to
36 inches.
Any size, 30 cents.

4876

Ladies' Under-
Skirt: 9 sizes.
Waist meas.,
20 to 36 inches.
Any size, 30 cts.

7402

(Issued February, 1881.)
Ladies' Flannel Petti-
coat, with Yoke: 9 sizes.
Waist meas., 20 to 36
ins. Any size, 25 cts.

7390   **7390**   **7390**

(Issued February, 1881.)
Ladies' Petticoat, with Adjustable Train:
9 sizes. Waist measures,
20 to 36 inches.
Any size, 25 cents.

7394   **7394**

(Issued February, 1881.)
Ladies' Sack Night-Dress:
10 sizes.
Bust meas., 28 to 46 inches.
Any size, 30 cents.

7582   **7582**

(Issued June, 1881.)
Ladies' Night-Dress, with
Yoke Back: 10 sizes.
Bust meas., 28 to 46 ins.
Any size, 25 cents.

6082   **6082**

Ladies' Night-Dress
with Yoke, (Quite
Narrow): 10 sizes.
Bust meas., 28 to 46 ins.
Any size, 35 cents.

4912   **4912**

Ladies' Circular Night
Wrapper: 13 sizes.
Bust measures, 28 to 46 ins.
Any size, 30 cents.

6553   **6553**

(Issued May, 1879.)
Ladies' Short, Sack Night-
Wrapper: 10 sizes.
Bust meas., 28 to 46 inches.
Any size, 20 cents.

7383   **7383**

(Issued February, 1881.)
Ladies' Night-Dress:
10 sizes.
Bust meas., 28 to 46 inches.
Any size, 30 cents.

7467

(Issued April, 1881.)
Ladies' Chemise:
10 sizes. Bust meas.,
28 to 46 inches.
Any size, 15 cents.

6293

Ladies' Chemise:
10 sizes. Bust
meas., 28 to
46 inches.
Any size, 20 cents.

7131

(Issued Aug., 1880.)
Ladies' Chemise:
10 sizes. Bust meas.,
28 to 46 inches.
Any size, 15 cents.

6665

(Issued Aug., 1879.)
Ladies' Plain Chemise:
10 sizes. Bust meas.,
28 to 46 inches.
Any size, 20 cents.

4894

Ladies' High-Necked
Chemise and Under-
Skirt Combined: 13
sizes. Bust meas., 28 to
46 ins. Any size, 25 cents.

7400   **7400**

(Issued February, 1881.)
Ladies' Princess Chemise:
10 sizes. Bust meas.,
28 to 46 inches.
Any size, 15 cents.

7104

(Issued July, 1880.)
Ladies' Chemise:
10 sizes. Bust meas.,
28 to 46 inches.
Any size, 15 cents.

7586 7586

(Issued June, 1881.)
Ladies' Combination Corset-Cover
and Demi-Trained Skirt: 13 sizes.
Bust measures, 28 to 46 inches.
Any size, 25 cents.

6438 6438

(Issued February, 1879.)
Ladies' Pompadour Chemise:
10 sizes. Bust measures,
28 to 46 inches.
Any size, 25 cents.

7924 7924

(Issued February, 1882.)
Ladies' Chemise, or Corset-Cover
and Under-Skirt Combined: 13 sizes.
Bust measures, 28 to 46 inches.
Any size, 30 cents.

7936 7936

(Issued February, 1882.)
Ladies' Combination Petticoat and Corset-Cover,
with Removable Train and Bustle: 13 sizes.
Bust measures, 28 to 46 inches.
Any size, 40 cents.

7923 7923

(Issued February, 1882.)
Ladies' Chemise and Drawers
Combined: 13 sizes. Bust
measures, 28 to 46 inches.
Any size, 30 cents.

6400 6400

Ladies' Combination
Chemise and Drawers:
13 sizes. Bust measures,
28 to 46 inches.
Any size, 30 cents.

7575 7575

(Issued June, 1881.)
Ladies' Bathing Costume:
10 sizes. Bust meas-
ures, 28 to 46 inches.
Any size, 30 cents.

7765 7765

(Issued October, 1881.)
Ladies' Pinafore: 9 sizes.
Waist measures, 20 to
36 inches.
Any size, 10 cents.

6624 6624

(Issued June, 1879.)
Ladies' Kitchen Apron.
One size: Price, 10 cents.

7550 7550

(Issued May, 1881.)
Ladies' Kitchen Apron:
9 sizes. Waist meas-
ures, 20 to 36 inches.
Any size, 15 cents.

6862 6862

(Issued February, 1880.)
Ladies' Work Apron: 9 sizes.
Waist meas., 20 to 36 inches.
Any size, 10 cents.

7052 7052

(Issued June, 1880.)
Ladies' Apron: 9 sizes.
Waist meas., 20 to 36 inches.
Any size, 10 cents.

4440

Ladies' Apron.
One size:
Price, 15 cents.

7785

(Issued October, 1881.)
Nurses' Apron: 9 sizes.
Waist meas., 20 to 36 inches.
Any size, 15 cents.

7427 7427

(Issued March, 1881.)
Ladies' Apron.
One size:
Price, 10 cents.

7662 7662

(Issued August, 1881.)
Ladies' Pinafore.
One size:
Price, 10 cents.

4738

Ladies' Apron.
One size:
Price, 15 cents.

7378

(Issued January, 1881.)
Ladies' Apron.
One size:
Price, 10 cents.

7379

(Issued Feb., 1881.)
Ladies' Open Drawers:
9 sizes. Waist meas-
ures, 20 to 36 inches.
Any size, 20 cents.

6941

(Issued April, 1880.)
Ladies' Knickerbocker
Drawers: 9 sizes. Waist
meas., 20 to 36 inches.
Any size, 20 cents.

7620

(Issued June, 1881.)
Ladies' Drawers:
9 sizes. Waist meas.,
20 to 36 inches.
Any size, 20 cents.

4697

Ladies' Leggings:
4 sizes, from 13 to 16 ins.
around the largest
part of the leg.
Any size, 20 cents.

7530

(Issued May, 1881.)
Ladies' Shirred
Plastron. One size:
Price, 10 cents.

4557 4557

Ladies' Adjusta-
able Collar, with
Revers. One size:
Price, 10 cents.

7534 7534

(Issued May, 1881.)
Ladies' Adjustable
Collar. One size:
Price, 10 cents.

7157 7157

(Issued Sept., 1880.)
Ladies' Hood.
One size:
Price, 5 cents.

7335

(Issued Dec., 1880.)
Ladies' Shawl
Case. One size:
Price, 10 cents.

7371 7371

(Issued January, 1881.)
Ladies' Jersey
Collar. One size:
Price, 5 cents.

6021

Mitt Pattern; 15 sizes.
Measurement of the
Hand just back of the
knuckles, 4 to 11 inches.
Any size, 10 cents.

4984

Mitten Pattern: 15 sizes.
Measurement of the
Hand just back of the
knuckles, 4 to 11 inches.
Any size, 10 cents.

7611

(Issued June, 1881.)
Ladies' Sun-Bon-
net. One size:
Price, 15 cents.

7062

(Issued June, 1880.)
Ladies' Sun-Bon-
net. One size.
Price, 15 cents.

7065

(Issued June, 1880.)
Ladies' Sun-Bon-
net. One size.
Price, 15 cents.

6636

(Issued July, 1879.)
Ladies' Night-
Cap. One size.
Price, 10 cents.

6659

(Issued August, 1879.)
Ladies' Night-
Cap. One size.
Price, 10 cents.

3392

Ladies' Dusting
Cap. One size.
Price, 10 cents.

7584

(Issued June, 1881.)
Ladies' Morning-
Cap. One size.
Price, 10 cents.

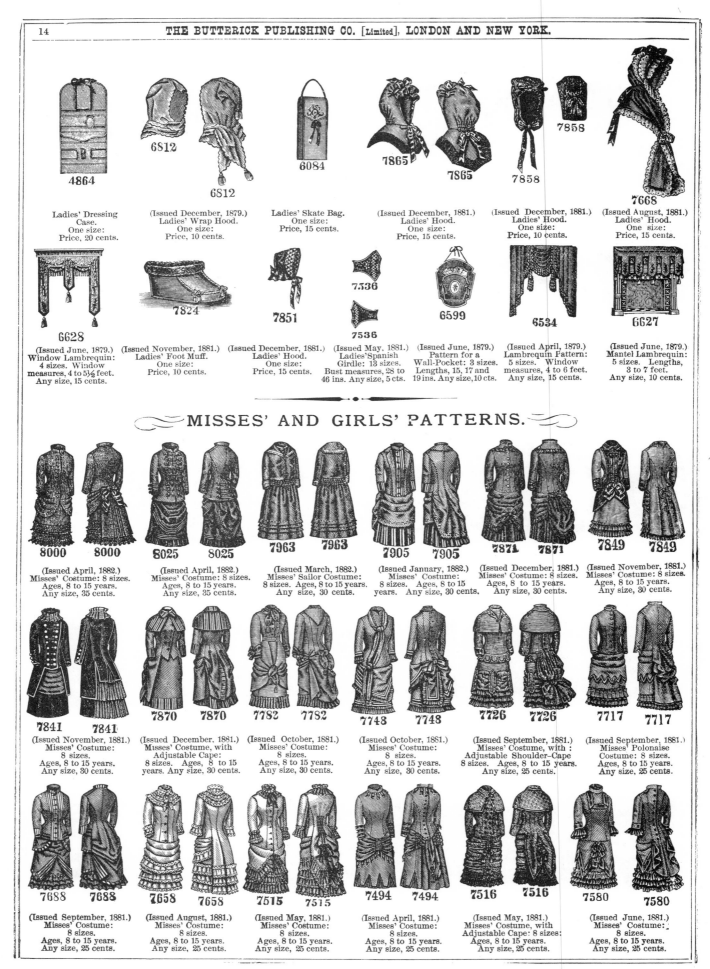

4864

Ladies' Dressing
Case.
One size:
Price, 20 cents.

6812

6812

(Issued December, 1879.)
Ladies' Wrap Hood.
One size:
Price, 10 cents.

6084

Ladies' Skate Bag.
One size:
Price, 15 cents.

7865

7865

(Issued December, 1881.)
Ladies' Hood.
One size:
Price, 15 cents.

7858

7858

(Issued December, 1881.)
Ladies' Hood.
One size:
Price, 10 cents.

7668

(Issued August, 1881.)
Ladies' Hood.
One size:
Price, 15 cents.

6628

(Issued June, 1879.)
Window Lambrequin:
4 sizes. Window
measures, 4 to 5½ feet.
Any size, 15 cents.

7824

(Issued November, 1881.)
Ladies' Foot Muff.
One size:
Price, 10 cents.

7851

(Issued December, 1881.)
Ladies' Hood.
One size:
Price, 15 cents.

7536

7536

(Issued May, 1881.)
Ladies' Spanish
Girdle: 13 sizes.
Bust measures, 28 to
46 ins. Any size, 5 cts.

6599

(Issued June, 1879.)
Pattern for a
Wall-Pocket: 3 sizes.
Lengths, 15, 17 and
19 ins. Any size, 10 cts.

6534

(Issued April, 1879.)
Lambrequin Pattern:
5 sizes. Window
measures, 4 to 6 feet.
Any size, 15 cents.

6627

(Issued June, 1879.)
Mantel Lambrequin:
5 sizes. Lengths,
3 to 7 feet.
Any size, 10 cents.

MISSES' AND GIRLS' PATTERNS.

8000　**8000**

(Issued April, 1882.)
Misses' Costume: 8 sizes.
Ages, 8 to 15 years.
Any size, 35 cents.

8025　**8025**

(Issued April, 1882.)
Misses' Costume: 8 sizes.
Ages, 8 to 15 years.
Any size, 35 cents.

7963　**7963**

(Issued March, 1882.)
Misses' Sailor Costume:
8 sizes. Ages, 8 to 15 years.
Any size, 30 cents.

7905　**7905**

(Issued January, 1882.)
Misses' Costume:
8 sizes. Ages, 8 to 15
years. Any size, 30 cents.

7871　**7871**

(Issued December, 1881.)
Misses' Costume: 8 sizes.
Ages, 8 to 15 years.
Any size, 30 cents.

7849　**7849**

(Issued November, 1881.)
Misses' Costume: 8 sizes.
Ages, 8 to 15 years.
Any size, 30 cents.

7841　**7841**

(Issued November, 1881.)
Misses' Costume:
8 sizes.
Ages, 8 to 15 years.
Any size, 30 cents.

7870　**7870**

(Issued December, 1881.)
Misses' Costume, with
Adjustable Cape:
8 sizes. Ages, 8 to 15
years. Any size, 30 cents.

7782　**7782**

(Issued October, 1881.)
Misses' Costume:
8 sizes.
Ages, 8 to 15 years.
Any size, 30 cents.

7748　**7748**

(Issued October, 1881.)
Misses' Costume:
8 sizes.
Ages, 8 to 15 years.
Any size, 30 cents.

7726　**7726**

(Issued September, 1881.)
Misses' Costume, with
Adjustable Shoulder-Cape
8 sizes. Ages, 8 to 15 years.
Any size, 25 cents.

7717　**7717**

(Issued September, 1881.)
Misses' Polonaise
Costume: 8 sizes.
Ages, 8 to 15 years.
Any size, 25 cents.

7688　**7688**

(Issued September, 1881.)
Misses' Costume:
8 sizes.
Ages, 8 to 15 years.
Any size, 25 cents.

7658　**7658**

(Issued August, 1881.)
Misses' Costume:
8 sizes.
Ages, 8 to 15 years.
Any size, 25 cents.

7515　**7515**

(Issued May, 1881.)
Misses' Costume:
8 sizes.
Ages, 8 to 15 years.
Any size, 25 cents.

7494　**7494**

(Issued April, 1881.)
Misses' Costume:
8 sizes.
Ages, 8 to 15 years.
Any size, 25 cents.

7516　**7516**

(Issued May, 1881.)
Misses' Costume, with
Adjustable Cape: 8 sizes:
Ages, 8 to 15 years.
Any size, 25 cents.

7580　**7580**

(Issued June, 1881.)
Misses' Costume:
8 sizes.
Ages, 8 to 15 years.
Any size, 25 cents.

7655   7655   7338   7338   7624   7624   7408   7408   6822   6822   7606   7606

(Issued August, 1881.) Misses' Costume: 8 sizes. Ages, 8 to 15 years. Any size, 25 cents.

(Issued December, 1880.) Misses' Pilgrimage Costume: with Adjustable Cape and Hood: 8 sizes. Ages, 8 to 15 years. Any size, 25 cents.

(Issued July, 1881.) Misses' Costume: 8 sizes. Ages, 8 to 15 years. Any size, 25 cents

(Issued March, 1881.) Misses' Jersey Costume: 8 sizes. Ages, 8 to 15 yrs. Any size, 25 cents.

(Issued December, 1879.) Misses' English Morning Dress: 8 sizes. Ages, 8 to 15 years. Any size, 30 cents.

(Issued June, 1881.) Misses' Dress; 8 sizes. Ages, 8 to 15 years. Any size, 25 cents.

8031   8031   8019   8019   8023   8023   7867   7867   8012   8012   7922   7922

(Issued April, 1882.) Girls' Costume: 7 sizes. Ages, 3 to 9 years. Any size, 25 cents.

(Issued April, 1882.) Girls' Costume: 7 sizes. Ages, 3 to 9 years. Any size, 25 cents.

(Issued April, 1882.) Girls' Costume: 7 sizes. Ages, 3 to 9 years. Any size, 25 cents.

(Issued December, 1881.) Girls' Costume: 7 sizes. Ages, 3 to 9 years. Any size, 25 cents.

(Issued April, 1882.) Girls' Costume: 7 sizes. Ages, 3 to 9 years. Any size, 25 cents.

(Issued February, 1882.) Girls' Costume: 7 sizes. Ages, 3 to 9 years Any size, 25 cents.

7926   7926   7766   7766   7970   7970   7780   7780   7954   7954   7592   7592

(Issued February, 1882.) Girls' Costume: 7 sizes. Ages, 3 to 9 years. Any size, 25 cents.

(Issued October. 1881.) Girls' Costume, with Adjustable Cape: 7 sizes. Ages, 3 to 9 years, Any size, 25 cents.

(Issued March, 1882.) Girls' Costume, with Adjustable Cape: 7 sizes. Ages, 3 to 9 years. Any size, 25 cents.

(Issued October, 1881.) Girls' Costume: 7 sizes. Ages, 3 to 9 years. Any size, 25 cents.

(Issued March, 1882.) Girls' Costume: 7 sizes. Ages, 3 to 9 years. Any size, 25 cents.

(Issued June, 1881.) Girls' Costume: 7 sizes. Ages, 3 to 9 years. Any size, 20 cents.

7633   7633   7634   7634   7921   7921   7702   7702   7839   7839   7847   7847

(Issued July, 1881.) Girls' Costume: 7 sizes. Ages, 3 to 9 years. Any size, 20 cents.

(Issued July, 1881.) Girls' Costume: 7 sizes. Ages, 3 to 9 years. Any size, 20 cents.

(Issued February, 1882.) Girls' Costume: 7 sizes. Ages, 3 to 9 years. Any size, 25 cents.

(Issued September, 1881.) Girls' Costume; 7 sizes. Ages, 3 to 9 years. Any size, 20 cents.

(Issued November, 1881.) Girls' Costume, with Adjustable Cape: 7 sizes. Ages, 3 to 9 years. Any size, 25 cents.

(Issued November, 1881.) Girls' Costume: 7 sizes. Ages, 3 to 9 years. Any size, 25 cents.

7518   7518   7866   7866   7594   7594   7676   7676   6918   6918   7794   7794

(Issued May, 1881.) Girls' Plaited Costume: 7 sizes. Ages. 3 to 9 yrs. Any size, 20 cents.

(Issued December, 1881.) Girls' Costume: 7 sizes. Ages, 3 to 9 years. Any size, 25 cents.

(Issued June, 1881.) Girls' Costume: 7 sizes. Ages, 3 to 9 years. Any size, 20 cents.

(Issued August, 1881.) Girls' Costume: 7 sizes. Ages, 3 to 9 years. Any size, 20 cents.

(Issued March, 1880.) Girls' Sailor Costume: 8 sizes. Ages, 2 to 9 yrs. Any size, 25 cents.

(Issued October, 1881.) Girls' Costume: 7 sizes. Ages, 3 to 9 years. Any size, 25 cents.

7541   7541   7903   7903   7703   7703   7646   7646   7333   7333   7537   7537

(Issued May, 1881.) Girls' Costume: 7 sizes. Ages, 3 to 9 years. Any size, 20 cents.

(Issued January, 1882.) Girls' Costume: 7 sizes. Ages, 3 to 9 years. Any size, 25 cents.

(Issued September, 1881.) Girls' Costume: 7 sizes. Ages, 3 to 9 years. Any size, 20 cents.

(Issued July, 1881.) Girls' Costume: 7 sizes. Ages, 3 to 9 years. Any size, 20 cents.

(Issued December, 1880.) Girls' Costume: 7 sizes. Ages, 3 to 9 years. Any size, 20 cents.

(Issued May, 1881.) Girls' Costume: 7 sizes. Ages, 3 to 9 years. Any size, 20 cents

7830   **7830**   **7672**   **7672**   **7593**   **7593**   **7336**   **7336**   **7529**   **7529**   **7687**   **7687**

(Issued November, 1881.) Girls' Costume: 7 sizes. Ages, 3 to 9 years. Any size, 25 cents.

(Issued August, 1881.) Girls' Costume: 7 sizes. Ages, 3 to 9 years. Any size, 20 cents.

(Issued June, 1881.) Girls' Costume: 7 sizes. Ages, 3 to 9 years. Any size, 20 cents.

(Issued December, 1880.) Girls' Pilgrimage Costume, with Adjustable Cape and Hood: 7 sizes. Ages, 3 to 9 years. Any size, 20 cents.

(Issued May, 1881.) Girls' Costume: 7 sizes. Ages, 3 to 9 years. Any size, 20 cents.

(Issued September, 1881.) Girls' Costume: 7 sizes. Ages, 3 to 9 years. Any size, 20 cents.

7705   **7705**   **7473**   **7473**   **7859**   **7859**   **7756**   **7756**   **7876**   **7876**   **7781**   **7781**

(Issued September, 1881.) Girls' Costume: 7 sizes. Ages, 3 to 9 years. Any size, 20 cents.

(Issued April, 1881.) Girls' Costume: 7 sizes. Ages, 3 to 9 years. Any size, 20 cents.

(Issued December, 1881.) Girls' Costume: 7 sizes. Ages, 3 to 9 years. Any size, 25 cents.

(Issued October, 1881.) Girls' Costume: 7 sizes. Ages, 3 to 9 years. Any size, 20 cents.

(Issued December, 1881.) Girls' Costume: 7 sizes. Ages, 3 to 9 years. Any size, 25 cents.

(Issued October, 1881.) Girls' "Mother Hubbard" Dress: 7 sizes. Ages, 3 to 9 years. Any size, 25 cents.

6739   **6739**   **7557**   **7557**   **7600**   **7600**   **7116**   **7116**   **7651**   **7651**   **7789**   **7789**

(Issued October, 1879.) Girls' English Morning Dress: 8 sizes. Ages, 2 to 9 years. Any size, 25 cts.

(Issued May, 1881.) Girls' Shirred Dress: 7 sizes. Ages, 3 to 9 years. Any size, 20 cents.

(Issued June, 1881.) Girls' Dress: 7 sizes. Ages, 3 to 9 years. Any size, 20 cents.

(Issued July, 1880.) Girls' Gored Dress: 8 sizes. Ages, 2 to 9 years. Any size, 20 cents.

(Issued July, 1881.) Girls' Gabrielle Dress: 7 sizes. Ages, 3 to 9 years. Any size, 20 cents.

(Issued October, 1881.) Misses' Cloak: 8 sizes. Ages, 8 to 15 years. Any size, 25 cents.

  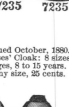 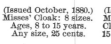

7887   **7887**   **7914**   **7914**   **7806**   **7806**   **7387**   **7387**   **7235**   **7235**   **7292**   **7292**

(Issued December, 1881.) Misses' Double-Breasted Cloak: 8 sizes. Ages, 8 to 15 years. Any size, 25 cts.

(Issued February, 1882.) Misses' Cloak: 8 sizes. Ages, 8 to 15 years. Any size, 30 cents.

(Issued November, 1881.) Misses' Cloak: 8 sizes. Ages, 8 to 15 years. Any size, 25 cents.

(Issued February, 1881.) Misses' Havelock Cloak: 8 sizes. Ages, 8 to 15 years. Any size, 25 cents.

(Issued October, 1880.) Misses' Cloak: 8 sizes. Ages, 8 to 15 years. Any size, 25 cents.

(Issued November, 1880.) Misses' Double-Breasted Cloak: 8 sizes. Ages, 8 to 15 years. Any size, 25 cts.

8011   **8011**   **7759**   **7759**   **7878**   **7878**   **7696**   **7696**   **7690**   **7690**   **7829**   **7829**

(Issued April, 1882.) Girls' Cloak, with Adjustable Cape: 7 sizes. Ages, 3 to 9 yrs. Any size, 25 cts.

(Issued October, 1881.) Girls' Cloak: 7 sizes. Ages, 3 to 9 years. Any size, 20 cents.

(Issued December, 1881.) Girls' Cloak: 7 sizes. Ages, 3 to 9 years. Any size, 25 cents.

(Issued September, 1881.) Girls' Cloak, with Adjustable Cape: 7 sizes. Ages, 3 to 9 years. Any size, 20 cents.

(Issued September, 1881.) Girls' Cloak, with Cape: 7 sizes. Ages, 3 to 9 years. Any size, 20 cents.

(Issued November, 1881.) Girls' Cloak: 7 sizes. Ages, 3 to 9 years. Any size, 25 cents.

7940   **7940**   **7589**   **7589**   **7704**   **7704**   **7877**   **7877**   **7955**   **7955**   **7908**   **7908**

(Issued March, 1882.) Girls' Cloak: 7 sizes. Ages, 3 to 9 years. Any size, 25 cents.

(Issued June, 1881.) Girls' "Mother Hubbard" Cloak: 8 sizes. Ages, 2 to 9 years. Any size, 20 cents.

(Issued September, 1881.) Girls' Cloak, with Shirred Cape: 7 sizes. Ages, 3 to 9 years. Any size, 20 cts.

(Issued December, 1881.) Girls' Cloak, with Cape: 7 sizes. Ages, 3 to 9 cts.

(Issued March, 1882.) Girls' Wrap: 7 sizes. Ages, 3 to 9 years. Any size, 25 cents.

(Issued January, 1882.) Girls' Cloak, with Adjustable Cape: 7 sizes. Ages, 3 to 9 years. Any size, 25 cents.

7752 **7752**

(Issued October, 1881.)
Misses' Ulsterette: 8 sizes.
Ages, 8 to 15 years.
Any size, 30 cents.

7684 **7684**

(Issued September, 1881.)
Misses' Ulster: 8 sizes.
Ages, 8 to 15 years.
Any size, 25 cents.

6441 **6441**

(Issued February, 1879.)
Misses' Circular Wrap:
8 sizes. Ages, 8 to 15 years.
Any size, 30 cents.

6854 **6854**

(Issued January, 1880.)
Misses' Ulster: 8 sizes.
Ages, 8 to 15 years.
Any size, 30 cents.

6874 **6874**

(Issued February, 1880.)
Misses' Circular Waterproof:
8 sizes. Ages, 8 to 15 years.
Any size, 30 cents

6856 **6856**

(Issued February, 1880.)
Misses' Sack Waterproof:
8 sizes. Ages, 8 to 15 years.
Any size, 30 cents.

7749 **7749**

(Issued October, 1881.)
Girls' Cloak, with Cape:
7 sizes. Ages, 3 to 9 years.
Any size, 25 cents.

7927 **7927**

(Issued February, 1882.)
Girls' Cloak, with Cape:
7 sizes. Ages, 3 to 9 years.
Any size, 25 cents.

7941 **7941**

(Issued March, 1882.)
Girls' Ulster, with Adjustable Collar: 7 sizes. Ages, 3 to
9 years. Any size, 25 cents.

7359 **7359**

(Issued Jannary, 1881.)
Girls' Ulster: 7 sizes.
Ages, 3 to 9 years.
Any size, 20 cents.

7598 **7598**

(Issued June, 1881.)
Girls' Ulsterette: 7 sizes.
Ages, 3 to 9 years.
Any size, 20 cents.

6442 **6442**

(Issued February, 1879.)
Girls' Circular Wrap:
8 sizes. Ages, 2 to 9 years.
Any size, 25 cents.

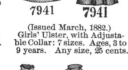

6858 **6858**

(Issued February, 1880.)
Girls' Circular Waterproof:
8 sizes. Ages, 2 to 9 years.
Any size, 25 cents.

6871 **6871**

(Issued February, 1880.)
Girls' Sack Waterproof:
8 sizes. Ages, 2 to 9
years. Any size, 25 cents.

7380 **7380**

(Issued February, 1881.)
Misses' Spanish Wrapper,
Gored to the Shoulder:
8 sizes. Ages, 8 to 15 years.
Any size, 25 cents.

7337 **7337**

(Issued December, 1880.)
Misses' Gored Wrapper:
8 sizes. Ages, 8 to 15 years.
Any size, 25 cents.

8043 **8043**

(Issued April, 1882.)
Misses' Polonaise: 8 sizes.
Ages, 8 to 15 years.
Any size, 30 cents.

7906 **7906**

(Issued January, 1882.)
Misses' Polonaise: 8 sizes.
Ages, 8 to 15 years.
Any size, 25 cents.

7843 **7843**

(Issued November, 1881.)
Misses' Polonaise: 8 sizes.
Ages, 8 to 15 years.
Any size, 25 cents.

7556 **7556**

(Issued May, 1881.)
Misses' Polonaise: 8 sizes:
Ages, 8 to 15 years.
Any size, 25 cents.

7654 **7654**

(Issued July, 1881.)
Misses' Polonaise:
8 sizes. Ages, 8 to
15 yrs. Any size, 25 cts.

6902 **6902**

(Issued March, 1880.)
Misses' *Panier* Polonaise:
8 sizes. Ages, 8 to
15 yrs. Any size, 25 cts.

7783 **7783**

(Issued October, 1881.)
Misses' Polonaise: 8 sizes.
Ages, 8 to 15 years.
Any size, 25 cents.

7601 **7601**

(Issued June, 1881.)
Girls' Over-Dress: 7 sizes.
Ages, 3 to 9 years.
Any size, 20 cents.

 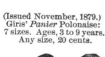    

7850 **7850**

(Issued Nov., 1881.)
Girls' Polonaise: 7 sizes.
Ages, 3 to 9 years.
Any size, 20 cents.

6865 **6865**

(Issued February, 1880.)
Girls' Polonaise: 7 sizes.
Ages, 3 to 9 years
Any size, 20 cents.

6782 **6782**

(Issued November, 1879.)
Girls' *Panier* Polonaise:
7 sizes. Ages, 3 to 9 years.
Any size, 20 cents.

6542 **6542**

(Issued April, 1879.)
Girls' Circular Wrapper:
8 sizes. Ages, 2 to 9 years.
Any size, 20 cents.

7882 **7882**

(Issued December, 1881.)
Misses' Double-Breasted
Coat: 8 sizes. Ages, 8 to
15 years. Any size, 25 cents.

7797 **7797**

(Issued Nov., 1881.)
Misses' Coat, with Vest:
8 sizes. Ages, 8 to 15 years.
Any size, 25 cents.

7689 **7689**

(Issued Sept., 1881.)
Misses' Coat, with Adjustable Cape: 8 sizes. Ages, 8 to
15 years. Any size, 20 cents.

7505 **7505**

(Issued April, 1881.)
Misses' Coat: 8 sizes.
Ages, 8 to 15 years.
Any size, 20 cents.

7686 **7686**

(Issued Sept., 1881.)
Girls' Coat: 7 sizes.
Ages, 3 to 9 years.
Any size, 20 cents.

8018 **8018**

(Issued April, 1882.)
Girls' Coat: 7 sizes.
Ages, 3 to 9 years.
Any size, 25 cents.

7671 **7671**

(Issued August. 1881.)
Girls' Coat: 7 sizes.
Ages, 3 to 9 years.
Any size, 20 cents.

7767 **7767**

(Issued Oct., 1881.)
Girls' Coat: 7 sizes.
Ages, 3 to 9 years.
Any size, 20 cents.

7670   7670
(Issued August, 1881.)
Girls' Coat: 7 sizes.
Ages, 3 to 9 years.
Any size, 20 cents.

7879   7879
(Issued December, 1881.)
Girls' Coat: 7 sizes.
Ages, 3 to 9 years.
Any size, 20 cents.

8035   8035
(Issued April, 1882.)
Misses' Jacket: 8 sizes.
Ages, 8 to 15 years.
Any size, 25 cents.

7892   7892
(Issued January, 1882.)
Misses' Double-Breasted
Jacket: 8 sizes. Ages, 8 to
15 years. Any size, 25 cents.

7788   7788
(Issued October, 1881.)
Misses' Jacket: 8 sizes.
Ages, 8 to 15 years.
Any size, 25 cents.

7961   7961
(Issued March, 1882.)
Misses' Jacket: 8 sizes.
Ages, 8 to 15 years.
Any size, 25 cents.

7501   7501
(Issued April, 1881.)
Misses' Jacket: 8 sizes.
Ages, 8 to 15 years.
Any size, 20 cents.

7653   7653
(Issued July, 1881.)
Misses' Box-Plaited Jacket:
8 sizes. Ages, 8 to 15 years.
Any size, 20 cents.

7555   7555
(Issued May, 1881.)
Misses' Jacket: 8 sizes.
Ages, 8 to 15 years.
Any size, 20 cents.

7812   7812
(Issued November, 1881.)
Girls' Jacket: 7 sizes.
Ages, 3 to 9 years.
Any size, 20 cents.

7568   7568
(Issued May, 1881.)
Girls' Long Dressing Sack:
7 sizes. Ages, 3 to 9 years.
Any size, 15 cents.

8034   8034
(Issued April, 1882.)
Girls' Jacket: 7 sizes.
Ages, 3 to 9 years.
Any size, 20 cents.

6846   6846
(Issued January, 1880.)
Girls' House Sack:
7 sizes.
Ages, 3 to 9 years.
Any size, 15 cents.

7932   7932
(Issued February, 1882.)
Misses' Dressing Sack:
8 sizes.
Ages, 8 to 15 years.
Any size, 25 cents.

7938   7938
(Issued March, 1882.)
Misses' *Panier* Basque:
8 sizes.
Ages, 8 to 15 years.
Any size, 25 cents.

8046   8046
(Issued April, 1882.)
Misses' Basque:
8 sizes.
Ages, 8 to 15 years.
Any size, 25 cents.

8002   8002
(Issued April, 1882.)
Misses' Basque, with Re-
movable Cape: 8 sizes.
Ages, 8 to 15 years.
Any size, 25 cents,

7681   7681
(Issued September, 1881.)
Misses' Basque:
8 sizes.
Ages, 8 to 15 years.
Any size, 20 cents.

7930   7930
(Issued February. 1882.)
Misses' Basque:
8 sizes.
Ages, 8 to 15 years.
Any size, 25 cents.

7745   7745
(Issued October, 1881.)
Misses' Basque, Buttoned
at the Back: 8 sizes.
Ages, 8 to 15 years.
Any size, 20 cents.

7873   7873
(Issued December, 1881.)
Misses' Basque:
8 sizes.
Ages, 8 to 15 years.
Any size, 20 cents.

7807   7807
(Issued November, 1881.)
Misses' Basque:
8 sizes.
Ages, 8 to 15 years,
Any size, 25 cents.

7567   7567
(Issued May, 1881.)
Girls' Basque, Buttoned
at the Back: 7 sizes.
Ages, 3 to 9 years.
Any size, 15 cents.

7607   7607
(Issued June, 1881.)
Misses' Shirred Basque:
8 sizes.
Ages, 8 to 15 years.
Any size, 20 cents.

7554   7554
(Issued May, 1881.)
Misses' Shirred Blouse:
8 sizes. Ages, 8 to 15 years.
Any size, 20 cents.

7793   7793
(Issued October, 1881.)
Misses' Basque: 8 sizes.
Ages, 8 to 15 years.
Any size, 25 cents.

7511   7511
(Issued April, 1881.)
Misses' Basque: 8 sizes.
Ages, 8 to 15 years.
Any size, 20 cents.

6175   6175
Misses' Riding Basque:
6 sizes.
Ages, 10 to 15 years.
Any size, 25 cents.

7470   7470
(Issued April, 1881.)
Girls' Basque: 7 sizes.
Ages, 3 to 9 years.
Any size, 15 cents.

7558   7558
(Issued May, 1881.)
Misses' Basque: 8 sizes.
Ages, 8 to 15 years.
Any size, 20 cents.

7413   7413
(Issued March, 1881.)
Misses' Basque:
8 sizes.
Ages, 8 to 15 years
Any size, 20 cents.

7498   7498
(Issued April, 1881.)
Misses' Box-Plaited Blouse,
with Adjustable Hood, (also
known as the "Norfolk Jacket"):
8 sizes. Ages, 8 to 15 years.
Any size, 20 cents.

7076   7076
(Issued June, 1880.)
Misses' Spencer Waist:
8 sizes.
Ages, 8 to 15 years.
Any size, 15 cents.

7949   7949
(Issued March, 1882.)
Misses' Shirred Waist:
8 sizes. Ages, 8 to 15 years.
Any size, 20 cents.

6397   6397
Misses' Plain Waist:
8 sizes.
Ages, 8 to 15 years.
Any size, 10 cents.

7248   7248
(Issued October, 1880.)
Girls' Spencer Waist:
7 sizes.
Ages, 3 to 9 years.
Any size, 10 cents.

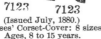

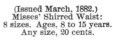

6178   6178
Girls Waist, with Yoke
and Belt: 7 sizes.
Ages, 3 to 9 years.
Any size, 15 cents.

7278   7278
(Issued November. 1880.)
Girls' Plain Waist:
7 sizes. Ages, 3 to 9 yrs.
Any size, 10 cents.

7123   7123
(Issued July, 1880.)
Misses' Corset-Cover: 8 sizes.
Ages, 8 to 15 years.
Any size, 15 cents.

4713   4713
Misses' Corset Waist:
8 sizes.
Ages, 8 to 15 years.
Any size, 25 cents.

7098   7098
(Issued July, 1880.)
Girls' Under-Waist: 7 sizes.
Ages, 3 to 9 years.
Any size, 10 cents.

6199   6199
Girls' Under-Waist:
7 sizes.
Ages, 3 to 9 years.
Any size, 20 cents.

6080 6080   **6005**   **6006**   **7560 7560**   **7872 7872**   **7605 7605**

Girls' Under-Waist or Corset-Cover: 7 sizes. Ages, 3 to 9 years. Any size, 20 cents.

Misses' Under-Flannel: 8 sizes. Ages, 8 to 15 years. Any size, 20 cents.

Girls' Under-Flannel: 8 sizes. Ages, 2 to 9 years. Any size, 15 cents.

(Issued May, 1881.) Misses' Over-Skirt: 8 sizes. Ages, 8 to 15 years. Any size, 20 cents.

(Issued December, 1881.) Misses' Over-Skirt: 8 sizes. Ages, 8 to 15 years. Any size, 20 cents.

(Issued June, 1881.) Misses' Over-Skirt: 8 sizes. Ages, 8 to 15 years. Any size, 20 cents.

6823 6823   **6922 6922**   **8001 8001**   **7929 7929**   **7792 7792**   **7808 7808**

(Issued Dec., 1879.) Girls' Over-Skirt: 7 sizes. Ages, 3 to 9 years. Any size, 20 cents.

(Issued March, 1880.) Girls' Over-Skirt: 7 sizes. Ages, 3 to 9 years. Any size, 20 cents.

(Issued April, 1882.) Misses' Walking Skirt: 8 sizes. Ages, 8 to 15 years. Any size, 30 cents.

(Issued February, 1882.) Misses' Walking Skirt: 8 sizes. Ages, 8 to 15 years. Any size, 30 cents.

(Issued October, 1881.) Misses' Walking Skirt: 8 sizes. Ages, 8 to 15 years. Any size, 25 cents.

(Issued November, 1881.) Misses' Walking Skirt: 8 sizes. Ages, 8 to 15 years. Any size, 25 cents.

7553 7553   **7212**   **7746 7746**   **7937**   **6176**   **7652 7652**   **7682 7682**

(Issued May, 1881.) Misses' Walking Skirt: 8 sizes. Ages, 8 to 15 years. Any size, 25 cents.

(Issued Sept., 1880.) Misses' Skirt: 8 sizes. Ages, 8 to 15 years. Any size, 20 cents.

(Issued October, 1881.) Misses' Walking Skirt: 8 sizes. Ages, 8 to 15 years. Any size, 25 cents.

(Issued March, 1882.) Misses' Walking Skirt: 8 sizes. Ages, 8 to 15 years. Any size, 25 cents.

Misses' Riding Skirt: 6 sizes. Ages, 10 to 15 years. Any size, 30 cts.

(Issued July, 1881.) Misses' Walking Skirt: 8 sizes. Ages, 8 to 15 years. Any size, 25 cents.

(Issued Sept., 1881.) Misses' Walking Skirt: 8 sizes. Ages, 8 to 15 years. Any size, 25 cents.

7314   **7471 7471**   **7570 7570**   **7154**   **7495**   **7059 7059**   **6183**

(Issued Nov., 1880.) Misses' Full Walking Skirt: 8 sizes. Ages, 8 to 15 years. Any size, 20 cents.

(Issued April, 1881.) Girls' Walking Skirt: 7 sizes. Ages, 3 to 9 years. Any size, 20 cents.

(Issued May, 1881.) Girls' Walking Skirt: 7 sizes. Ages, 3 to 9 years. Any size, 20 cents.

(Issued Sept., 1880.) Girls' Skirt: 8 sizes. Ages, 2 to 9 years. Any size, 15 cents.

(Issued April, 1881.) Misses' Petticoat, with Yoke. 8 sizes. Ages, 8 to 15 years. Any size, 20 cents.

(Issued June, 1880.) Girls' Petticoat: 8 sizes. Ages, 2 to 9 years. Any size, 15 cents.

Girls' Night-Dress: 8 sizes. Ages, 2 to 9 years. Any size, 25 cents.

7917 7917   **4900 4900**   **4888 4888**   **4701 4701**   **3089 3089**   **3702 3702**

(Issued February, 1882.) Misses' Night-Dress, with Yoke: 8 sizes. Ages, 8 to 15 years. Any size, 30 cents.

Misses' Circular Night-Wrapper: 8 sizes. Ages, 8 to 15 years. Any size, 30 cents.

Girls' Circular Night-Wrapper: 7 sizes. Ages, 3 to 9 years. Any size, 25 cents.

Misses' Sack Night-Dress, with Yoke: 8 sizes. Ages, 8 to 15 years. Any size, 30 cents.

Misses' Sack Night-Dress: 8 sizes. Ages, 8 to 15 years. Any size, 25 cents.

Girls' Yoke Night-Dress: 7 sizes. Ages, 3 to 9 years. Any size, 15 cents.

4704 4704   **6405 6405**   **7650 7650**   **7576 7576**   **7577 7577**   **4671 4671**

Misses' Chemise and Drawers Combined: 8 sizes. Ages, 8 to 15 years. Any size, 25 cents.

Misses' Combination Chemise, Corset-Cover and Under-Skirt: 8 sizes. Ages, 8 to 15 years. Any size, 25 cents.

(Issued July, 1881.) Misses' Combined Corset-Cover and Under-Skirt: 8 sizes. Ages, 8 to 15 yrs. Any size, 20 cents.

(Issued June, 1881.) Misses' Bathing Costume: 8 sizes. Ages, 8 to 15 years. Any size, 25 cents.

(Issued June, 1881.) Girls' Bathing Costume: 7 sizes. Ages, 3 to 9 years. Any size, 20 cents.

Girls' Drawers and Under-Vest Combined: 8 sizes. Ages, 2 to 9 years. Any size, 25 cents.

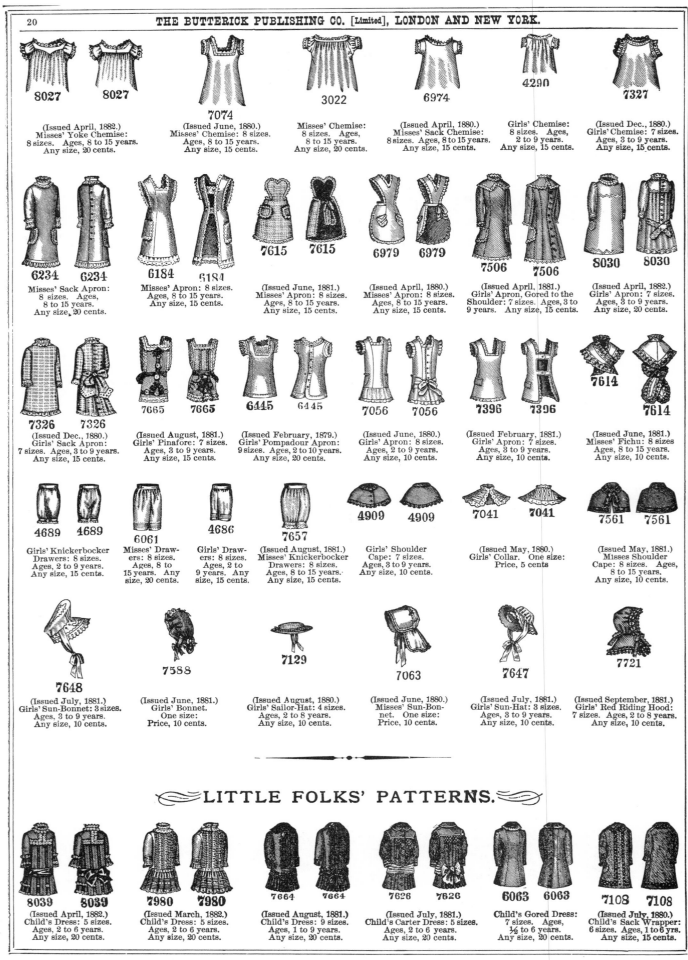

8027   **8027**

(Issued April, 1882.)
Misses' Yoke Chemise:
8 sizes. Ages, 8 to 15 years.
Any size, 20 cents.

7074

(Issued June, 1880.)
Misses' Chemise: 8 sizes.
Ages, 8 to 15 years.
Any size, 15 cents.

3022

Misses' Chemise:
8 sizes. Ages,
8 to 15 years.
Any size, 20 cents.

6974

(Issued April, 1880.)
Misses' Sack Chemise:
8 sizes. Ages, 8 to 15 years.
Any size, 15 cents.

4290

Girls' Chemise:
8 sizes. Ages,
2 to 9 years.
Any size, 15 cents.

7327

(Issued Dec., 1880.)
Girls' Chemise: 7 sizes.
Ages, 3 to 9 years.
Any size, 15 cents.

6234   **6234**

Misses' Sack Apron:
8 sizes. Ages,
8 to 15 years.
Any size, 20 cents.

6184   **6184**

Misses' Apron: 8 sizes.
Ages, 8 to 15 years.
Any size, 15 cents.

7615   **7615**

(Issued June, 1881.)
Misses' Apron: 8 sizes.
Ages, 8 to 15 years.
Any size, 15 cents.

6979   **6979**

(Issued April, 1880.)
Misses' Apron: 8 sizes.
Ages, 8 to 15 years.
Any size, 15 cents.

7506   **7506**

(Issued April, 1881.)
Girls' Apron, Gored to the
Shoulder: 7 sizes. Ages, 3 to
9 years. Any size, 15 cents.

8030   **8030**

(Issued April, 1882.)
Girls' Apron: 7 sizes.
Ages, 3 to 9 years.
Any size, 20 cents.

7326   **7326**

(Issued Dec., 1880.)
Girls' Sack Apron:
7 sizes. Ages, 3 to 9 years.
Any size, 15 cents.

7665   **7665**

(Issued August, 1881.)
Girls' Pinafore: 7 sizes.
Ages, 3 to 9 years.
Any size, 15 cents.

6445   **6445**

(Issued February, 1879.)
Girls' Pompadour Apron:
9 sizes. Ages, 2 to 10 years.
Any size, 20 cents.

7056   **7056**

(Issued June, 1880.)
Girls' Apron: 8 sizes.
Ages, 2 to 9 years.
Any size, 10 cents.

7396   **7396**

(Issued February, 1881.)
Girls' Apron: 7 sizes.
Ages, 3 to 9 years.
Any size, 10 cents.

7614   **7614**

(Issued June, 1881.)
Misses' Fichu: 8 sizes
Ages, 8 to 15 years.
Any size, 10 cents.

4689   **4689**

Girls' Knickerbocker
Drawers: 8 sizes.
Ages, 2 to 9 years.
Any size, 15 cents.

6061

Misses' Draw-
ers: 8 sizes.
Ages, 8 to
15 years. Any
size, 20 cents.

4686

Girls' Draw-
ers: 8 sizes.
Ages, 2 to
9 years. Any
size, 15 cents.

7657

(Issued August, 1881.)
Misses' Knickerbocker
Drawers: 8 sizes.
Ages, 8 to 15 years.
Any size, 15 cents.

4909   **4909**

Girls' Shoulder
Cape: 7 sizes.
Ages, 3 to 9 years.
Any size, 10 cents.

7041   **7041**

(Issued May, 1880.)
Girls' Collar. One size:
Price, 5 cents

7561   **7561**

(Issued May, 1881.)
Misses Shoulder
Cape: 8 sizes. Ages,
8 to 15 years.
Any size, 10 cents.

7648

(Issued July, 1881.)
Girls' Sun-Bonnet: 3 sizes.
Ages, 3 to 9 years.
Any size, 10 cents.

7588

(Issued June, 1881.)
Girls' Bonnet.
One size:
Price, 10 cents.

7129

(Issued August, 1880.)
Girls' Sailor-Hat: 4 sizes.
Ages, 2 to 8 years.
Any size, 10 cents.

7063

(Issued June, 1880.)
Misses' Sun-Bon-
net. One size:
Price, 10 cents.

7647

(Issued July, 1881.)
Girls' Sun-Hat: 3 sizes.
Ages, 3 to 9 years.
Any size, 10 cents.

7721

(Issued September, 1881.)
Girls' Red Riding Hood:
7 sizes. Ages, 2 to 8 years.
Any size, 10 cents.

~LITTLE FOLKS' PATTERNS.~

8039   **8039**

(Issued April, 1882.)
Child's Dress: 5 sizes.
Ages, 2 to 6 years.
Any size, 20 cents.

7980   **7980**

(Issued March, 1882.)
Child's Dress: 5 sizes.
Ages, 2 to 6 years.
Any size, 20 cents.

7664   **7664**

(Issued August, 1881.)
Child's Dress: 9 sizes.
Ages, 1 to 9 years.
Any size, 20 cents.

7626   **7626**

(Issued July, 1881.)
Child's Carter Dress: 5 sizes.
Ages, 2 to 6 years.
Any size, 20 cents.

6063   **6063**

Child's Gored Dress:
7 sizes. Ages,
½ to 6 years.
Any size, 20 cents.

7108   **7108**

(Issued July, 1880.)
Child's Sack Wrapper:
6 sizes. Ages, 1 to 6 yrs.
Any size, 15 cents.

7239　7239 **7060　7060** **7596　7596** **6607　6607** **7667　7667** **7604　7604**

| (Issued October, 1880.) Child's First Short Dress: 4 sizes. Ages, ½ to 3 years. Any size, 15 cents. | (Issued June, 1880.) Child's Circular Dress: 7 sizes. Ages, ½ to 6 yrs. Any size, 15 cents. | (Issued June, 1881.) Child's Dress: 4 sizes. Ages, ½ to 3 years. Any size, 15 cents. | (Issued June, 1879.) Child's Plain Dress: 9 sizes. Ages, 1 to 9 years. Any size, 20 cents. | (Issued August, 1881.) Child's Frock: 6 sizes. Ages, ½ to 5 years. Any size, 15 cents. | (Issued June, 1881.) Child's Low-Necked Dress: 5 sizes. Ages, 2 to 6 years. Any size, 15 cents. |

7818　7818 **8045　8045** **8038　8038** **8033　8033** **7982　7982** **7981　7981**

| (Issued November, 1881.) Child's Low-Necked Dress: 7 sizes. Ages, ½ to 6 years. Any size, 20 cents. | (Issued April, 1882.) Child's Costume: 5 sizes. Ages, 2 to 6 years. Any size, 25 cents. | (Issued April, 1882.) Child's Costume: 5 sizes. Ages, 2 to 6 years. Any size, 25 cents. | (Issued April, 1882.) Child's Costume: 5 sizes. Ages, 2 to 6 years. Any size, 25 cents. | (Issued March, 1882.) Child's Costume: 5 sizes. Ages, 2 to 6 years. Any size, 20 cents. | (Issued March, 1882.) Child's Costume: 5 sizes. Ages, 2 to 6 years Any size, 25 cents. |

7939　7939 **7895　7895** **7860　7860** **7854　7854** **7853　7853** **7813　7813**

| (Issued March, 1882.) Child's Costume: 5 sizes. Ages, 2 to 6 years, Any size, 25 cents. | (Issued January, 1882.) Child's Costume. 5 sizes. Ages, 2 to 6 years. Any size, 20 cents. | (Issued December, 1881.) Child's Costume: 5 sizes. Ages, 2 to 6 years. Any size, 20 cents. | (Issued December, 1881.) Child's Costume: 5 sizes. Ages, 2 to 6 years. Any size, 20 cents. | (Issued December, 1881.) Child's Costume: 5 sizes. Ages, 2 to 6 years. Any size, 20 cents. | (Issued November, 1881.) Child's Costume: 5 sizes. Ages, 2 to 6 years. Any size, 20 cents. |

7802　7802 **7790　7790** **7760　7760** **7758　7758** **7701　7701** **7697　7697**

| (Issued November, 1881.) Child's Costume: 5 sizes. Ages, 2 to 6 years. Any size, 20 cents. | (Issued October, 1881.) Child's Costume: 5 sizes. Ages, 2 to 6 years. Any size, 20 cents. | (Issued October, 1881.) Child's Costume: 5 sizes. Ages, 2 to 6 years. Any size, 20 cents. | (Issued October, 1881.) Child's Sailor Costume: 5 sizes. Ages, 2 to 6 years. Any size, 20 cents. | (Issued September, 1881.) Child's Sailor Costume: 5 sizes. Ages, 2 to 6 years. Any size, 20 cents. | (Issued September, 1881.) Child's Costume: 5 sizes. Ages, 2 to 6 years. Any size, 20 cents. |

 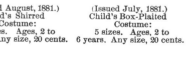

7698　7698 **7683　7683** **7679　7679** **7656　7656** **7641　7641** **7407　7407**

| (Issued September, 1881.) Child's Costume: 5 sizes. Ages, 2 to 6 years. Any size, 20 cents. | (Issued September, 1881.) Child's Costume, with Adjustable Cape: 5 sizes. Ages, 2 to 6 years. Any size, 20 cts. | (Issued September, 1881.) Child's Mother-Hubbard Costume: 6 sizes. Ages, 1 to 6 years. Any size, 20 cts. | (Issued August, 1881.) Child's Shirred Costume: 5 sizes. Ages, 2 to 6 years. Any size, 20 cents. | (Issued July, 1881.) Child's Box-Plaited Costume: 5 sizes. Ages, 2 to 6 years. Any size, 20 cents. | (Issued March, 1881.) Child's Box-Plaited Costume: 5 sizes. Ages, 2 to 6 years. Any size, 20 cts. |

7559　7559 **7489　7489** **7128　7128** **7425　7425** **7517　7517** **7976　7976**

| (Issued May, 1881.) Child's Costume: 5 sizes. Ages, 2 to 6 years. Any size, 20 cents. | (Issued April, 1881.) Child's Costume: 5 sizes. Ages, 2 to 6 years. Any size, 20 cents. | (Issued July, 1880.) Child's Blouse, with Kilt Skirt: 5 sizes. Ages, 2 to 6 years. Any size, 20 cents. | (Issued March, 1881.) Child's Jersey Costume: 5 sizes. Ages, 2 to 6 years. Any size, 20 cents. | (Issued May, 1881.) Child's Slip, with Pointed Yoke: 5 sizes. Ages, 2 to 6 years. Any size, 15 cents. | (Issued March, 1882.) Child's Slip: 5 sizes. Ages, 2 to 6 years. Any size, 20 cents. |

6669 6669
(Issued August, 1879.) Child's Yoke Slip: 6 sizes. Ages, 1 to 6 years. Any size, 15 cents.

6845 6845
(Issued January, 1880.) Child's Loose Slip: 6 sizes. Ages, 1 to 6 years. Any size, 20 cents.

7004 7004
(Issued May, 1880.) Child's Slip: 6 sizes. Ages, 1 to 6 years. Any size, 15 cents.

7678 7678
(Issued September, 1881.) Child's Ulster; 5 sizes. Ages, 2 to 6 years. Any size, 20 cents.

7477 7477
(Issued April, 1881.) Child's Mother-Hubbard Cloak: 8 sizes. Ages, 2 to 9 years. Any size, 20 cents.

7805 7805
(Issued November, 1881.) Child's Cloak, with Cape: 5 sizes. Ages, 2 to 6 years. Any size, 20 cents.

7720 7720
(Issued September, 1881.) Child's Cloak: 6 sizes. Ages, 1 to 6 years. Any size, 15 cents.

7868 7868
(Issued December, 1881.) Child's Cloak, with Cape: 5 sizes. Ages, 2 to 6 years. Any size, 20 cents.

7893 7893
(Issued January, 1882.) Child's Double-Breasted Cloak: 5 sizes. Ages, 2 to 6 years. Any size, 20 cts.

7215 7215
(Issued October, 1880.) Child's Double-Breasted Coat: 6 sizes. Ages, 1 to 6 years. Any size, 15 cents.

7625 7625
(Issued July, 1881.) Child's Pelisse: 7 sizes. Ages, ½ to 6 years. Any size, 20 cents.

6919 6919
(Issued March, 1880.) Child's Sack: 6 sizes. Ages, 1 to 6 years. Any size, 20 cents.

7999 7999
(Issued March, 1882.) Child's Jacket: 5 sizes. Ages, 2 to 6 years. Any size, 20 cents.

7519 7519
(Issued May, 1881.) Child's Jacket: 5 sizes. Ages, 2 to 6 years. Any size, 15 cents.

8041 8041
(Issued April, 1882.) Child's Coat: 5 sizes. Ages, 2 to 6 years. Any size, 20 cents.

6727 6727
(Issued September, 1879.) Child's High-Necked Apron: 6 sizes. Ages, 1 to 6 years. Any size, 20 cents.

6981 6981
(Issued April, 1880.) Child's Sack Apron, with Full Sleeves: 6 sizes. Ages. 1 to 6 yrs. Any size, 15 cents.

6037 6037
Child's Apron: 9 sizes. Ages, 1 to 9 years. Any size, 20 cents.

7627 7627
(Issued July, 1881.) Child's Pinafore: 6 sizes. Ages, 1 to 6 years. Any size, 10 cents.

7663 7663
(Issued August, 1881.) Child's Pinafore: 7 sizes. Ages, ½ to 6 years. Any size, 10 cents.

6071 6071
Child's Circular Apron: 6 sizes. Ages, 1 to 6 years. Any size, 20 cents.

7564 7564
(Issued May, 1881.) Child's Apron: 5 sizes. Ages, 2 to 6 years. Any size, 15 cents.

7897 7897
(Issued January, 1882.) Child's Pinafore: 6 sizes. Ages, 1 to 6 years. Any size, 15 cents.

7821 7821
(Issued November, 1881.) Child's Low-Necked Apron 6 sizes. Ages, 1 to 6 years. Any size, 15 cents.

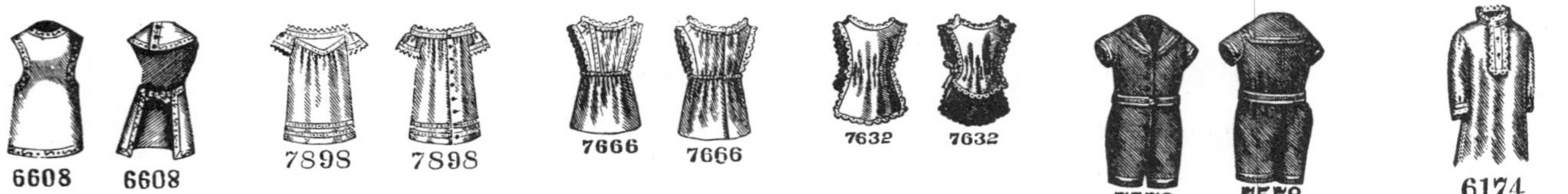

6608 6608
(Issued June, 1879.) Child's Eating Apron: 8 sizes. Ages, 1 to 8 yrs. Any size, 10 cents.

7898 7898
(Issued January, 1882.) Child's Low-Necked Apron: 6 sizes. Ages, 1 to 6 years. Any size, 15 cents.

7666 7666
(Issued August, 1881.) Child's Pinafore: 6 sizes. Ages, ½ to 5 years. Any size, 15 cents.

7632 7632
(Issued July, 1881.) Child's Pinafore: 7 sizes. Ages, ½ to 6 years. Any size, 10 cents.

7578 7578
(Issued June, 1881.) Child's Bathing Costume: 5 sizes. Ages, 2 to 6 years. Any size, 15 cents.

6174
Child's Night-Dress: 7 sizes. Ages, ½ to 6 years. Any size, 20 cents.

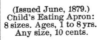

6443 6443
(Issued February, 1879.) Child's Night-Drawers, with Stockings: 9 sizes. Ages, 1 to 9 years. Any size, 25 cents.

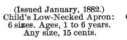

6436 6436
(Issued February, 1879.) Child's Union Dress: 8 sizes. Ages, 2 to 9 years. Any size, 20 cents.

7747 7747
(Issued October, 1881.) Child's Night-Drawers: 5 sizes. Ages, 2 to 6 years. Any size, 20 cents.

3697 3697
Child's Night Drawers: 10 sizes. Ages, 1 to 10 years. Any size, 20 cents.

6294 6294
Child's Petticoat, with Waist extending over the Hip: 6 sizes. Ages, 1 to 6 years. Any size, 15 cents.

6164 6164
Child's Petticoat: 9 sizes. Ages, 1 to 9 years. Any size, 20 cents.

6656 6656
(Issued August, 1879.) Child's Gored Petticoat: 7 sizes. Ages, ½ to 6 yrs. Any size, 15 cents.

6252
Child's Petticoat: 7 sizes. Ages, 2 to 8 years. Any size, 15 cents.

4840
Child's Skirt: 6 sizes. Ages, 1 to 6 yrs. Any size, 15 cents.

6861
(Issued February, 1880.) Child's Shirt: 6 sizes. Ages, 1 to 6 years. Any size, 10 cents.

7603 7603
(Issued June, 1881.) Child's *Guimpe*, (to be worn with Low-Necked Dresses): 5 sizes. Ages, 2 to 6 years. Any size, 10 cents.

7216 7216
(Issued October, 1880.) Child's Under-Waist: 6 sizes. Ages, 1 to 6 years. Any size, 10 cents.

4667 4667
Child's Skirt and Drawers Waist: 7 sizes. Ages, 2 to 8 years. Any size, 15 cents.

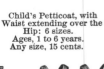

7979　7979

(Issued March, 1882.)
Infants' Dress. One size:
Price, 20 cents.

6517　6517

(Issued April, 1879.)
Infants' Dress. One size:
Price, 20 cents.

6518　6518

(Issued April, 1879.)
Infants' Dress. One size:
Price, 20 cents.

6074　6074

Infants' Gored Dress.
One size:
Price, 20 cents.

6538　6538

(Issued April, 1879.)
Infants' Night-Dress.
One size: Price, 20 cents.

4816　4816

Infants' Dress, with
Seamless, Pointed Yoke.
One size: Price, 20 cts.

7915　7915

(Issued February, 1882.)
Infants' Robe. One size:
Price, 20 cents.

4341　4341

Infants' Low-Necked Robe,
with Yoke and Short Sleeves.
One size: Price, 20 cents.

6989　6989

(Issued April, 1880.)
Infants' High-Necked
Robe. One size:
Price, 20 cents.

7274　7274

(Issued November, 1880.)
Infants' High-Necked
Robe, Gored to the Arms'-Eye.
One size: Price, 20 cents.

6617　6617

(Issued June, 1879.)
Infants' Wrapper.
One size:
Price, 15 cents.

7791　7791

(Issued October, 1881.)
Infants' Night-Wrapper.
One size:
Price, 20 cents.

4815　4815

Infants' Slip.
One size: Price, 20 cents.

7233　7233

(Issued October, 1880.)
Infants' Circular Slip.
One size: Price, 15 cents.

6067　6067

Infants' Double Circular.
One size: Price, 20 cents.

6070　6070

Infants' Sack, with
Cape and Hood.
One size: Price, 20 cents.

7612　7612

(Issued June, 1881.)
Infants' Cloak.
One size: Price, 20 cents.

7469　7469

(Issued April, 1881.)
Infants' Cloak, with Cape.
One size: Price, 20 cents.

6069　6069

Infants' Circular.
with Hood. One size:
Price, 20 cents.

4148

Babies' Shawl Hood.
One size:
Price, 20 cents.

4819　4819

Infants' Skirt.
One size: Price, 20 cents.

6985　6985

(Issued April, 1880.)
Infants' Flannel
Petticoat. One size:
Price, 15 cents.

4127　4127

Infants' Pinning Blanket.
One size; Price, 20 cents.

7476

(Issued April, 1881.)
Child's Hood: 8 sizes.
Ages, 2 to 9 years.
Any size, 10 cents.

7762

(Issued October, 1881.)
Child's Cap: 4 sizes.
Ages, 2 to 8 years.
Any size, 5 cents.

7189

(Issued Sept., 1880.)
Child's Cap: 4 sizes.
Ages, 2 to 8 years.
Any size, 5 cents.

7188

(Issued Sept., 1880.)
Child's Cap: 4 sizes.
Ages, 2 to 8 years.
Any size, 5 cents.

7896

(Issued Jan., 1882.)
Child's Cap: 4 sizes.
Ages, 2 to 8 years.
Any size, 10 cents.

7613

(Issued June, 1881.)
Child's Hat: 4 sizes.
Ages, 2 to 8 years.
Any size, 10 cents.

7305

(Issued Nov., 1880.)
Child's Cap: 4 sizes.
Ages, 2 to 8 years.
Any size, 5 cents.

7 2 8

Child's Hood, in one
Piece: 3 sizes.
Ages, 2 to 6 years.
Any size,10 cents.

7376

7376

(Issued Jan., 1881.)
Child's Hood.
One size:
Price, 5 cents.

6516　6516

(Issued April, 1879.)
Infants' Bib.
One size:
Price, 10 cents.

7135　7135

(Issued August, 1880.)
Infants' Bib.
One size:
Price, 5 cents.

8029

(Issued April, 1882.)
Infants' Bib.
One size:
Price, 10 cents.

7073　7073

(Issued June, 1880.)
Infants' Bib.
One size:
Price, 5 cents.

7786　7786

(Issued October, 1881.)
Child's Sailor Collar:
5 sizes. Ages, 2 to 6 yrs.
Any size, 5 cents.

6015

Childs' Stocking:
10 sizes. Length of
foot, 4 to 8½ inches.
Any size, 10 cents.

3393

Infants' Boot.
One size:
Price, 10 cents.

3909

Infants' Boot.
One size:
Price, 10 cents.

7382

(Issued February, 1881.)
Child's Drawers: 5 sizes.
Ages, 2 to 6 years.
Any size, 10 cents.

2417

Babies' Drawers.
One size:
Price, 15 cents.

7744

(Issued October, 1881.)
Child's Drawers: 3 sizes.
Ages, 1 to 3 years.
Any size, 10 cents.

7904   **7904**
(Issued Jan., 1882.)
Infants' Apron.
One size: Price, 10 cents.

6545   **6545**
(Issued April, 1879.)
Babies' House Sack.
One size: Price, 15 cents.

3382   **3382**
Infants' Shirt.
One size:
Price, 10 cents.

6455   **6455**
(Issued February, 1879.)
Infants' Shirt. One
size: Price, 10 cents.

431
Infants' Under-
Shirt. One size:
Price, 10 cents.

4817
Infants' Flannel
Band. One size:
Price, 10 cents.

BOYS' AND GENTLEMEN'S PATTERNS.

7198   **7198**
(Issued Sept., 1880.)
Boys' Single-Breasted
Sack Overcoat: 8 sizes.
Ages, 3 to 10 years.
Any size, 20 cents.

7429   **7429**
(Issued March, 1881.)
Boys' Overcoat, with
Shawl Collar: 8 sizes.
Ages, 3 to 10 years.
Any size, 20 cents.

7727   **7727**
(Issued September, 1881.)
Boys' Ulster Overcoat:
4 sizes. Ages,
3 to 6 years.
Any size, 25 cents.

4862   **4862**
Boys' Single-Breasted
Duster: 9 sizes.
Ages, 7 to 15 years.
Any size, 25 cents.

7738   **7738**
(Issued September, 1881.)
Boys' Sack Overcoat:
9 sizes. Ages,
7 to 15 years.
Any size, 25 cents.

7430   **7430**
(Issued March, 1881.)
Boys' Overcoat:
9 sizes. Ages,
7 to 15 years.
Any size, 25 cents.

7848   **7848**
(Issued Nov., 1881.)
Boys' Double-Breasted
Sack Overcoat: 9 sizes.
Ages, 7 to 15 years.
Any size, 25 cents.

7737   **7737**
(Issued Sept., 1881.)
Boys' Double-Breasted
Overcoat: 8 sizes.
Ages, 3 to 10 years.
Any size, 20 cents.

7986   **7986**
(Issued March, 1882.)
Boys' Jacket, with
Kilted Skirt: 5 sizes.
Ages, 3 to 7 years.
Any size, 25 cents.

7993   **7993**
(Issued March, 1882.)
Boys' Jacket, with Sailor
Collar: 8 sizes.
Ages, 3 to 10 years.
Any size, 20 cents.

7736   **7736**
(Issued September, 1881.)
Boys' Double-Breasted
Blouse Jacket: 8 sizes.
Ages, 3 to 10 years.
Any size, 15 cents.

7733   **7733**
(Issued Sept., 1881.)
Boys' Jacket: 8 sizes.
Ages, 3 to 10 years.
Any size, 15 cents.

7440   **7440**
(Issued March, 1881.)
Boys' Coat, to be worn
with a kilt: 5 sizes.
Ages, 2 to 6 years.
Any size, 15 cents.

6325   **6325**
Boys' School Jacket:
8 sizes. Ages,
3 to 10 years.
Any size, 15 cents.

7732   **7732**
(Issued September, 1881.)
Boys' Double-Breasted
Jacket: 8 sizes.
Ages, 3 to 10 years.
Any size, 15 cents.

7432   **7432**
(Issued March, 1881.)
Boys' Jacket: 8 sizes.
Ages, 3 to 10 years.
Any size, 15 cents.

7730   **7730**
(Issued September, 1881.)
Boys' Cutaway Sack:
8 sizes. Ages,
3 to 10 years.
Any size, 15 cents.

7984   **7984**
(Issued March, 1882.)
Boys' Single-Breasted
Sack Coat: 9 sizes.
Ages, 7 to 15 years.
Any size, 25 cents.

7990   **7990**
(Issued March, 1882.)
Boys' Coat: 9 sizes.
Ages, 7 to 15 years.
Any size, 25 cents.

7205   **7205**
(Issued September, 1880.)
Boys' Single-Breasted
Sack Coat: 9 sizes.
Ages, 7 to 15 years.
Any size, 20 cents.

7442   **7442**
(Issued March, 1881.)
Boys' Single-Breasted,
Four-Buttoned Cutaway
Coat: 9 sizes. Ages, 7 to
15 years. Any size, 20 cents.

7191   **7191**
(Issued September, 1880.)
Boys' Single-Breasted
Sack Coat: 8 sizes.
Ages, 3 to 10 years.
Any size, 15 cents.

7193   **7193**
(Issued September, 1880.)
Boys' Coat: 8 sizes.
Ages, 3 to 10 years.
Any size, 15 cents.

7991   **7991**
(Issued March, 1882.)
Boys' Sack Coat:
8 sizes. Ages,
3 to 10 years.
Any size, 20 cents.

7445   **7445**
(Issued March, 1881.)
Boys' Single-Breasted
Sack Coat: 9 sizes.
Ages, 7 to 15 years.
Any size, 20 cents.

7741   **7741**
(Issued September, 1881.)
Boys' Sack Coat: 9 sizes.
Ages, 7 to 15 years.
Any size, 20 cents.

7438   **7438**
(Issued March, 1881.)
Boys' Sack Coat:
8 sizes. Ages,
3 to 10 years.
Any size, 15 cents.

7436   **7436**
(Issued March, 1881.)
Boys' Cutaway Coat:
8 sizes. Ages,
3 to 10 years.
Any size, 15 cents.

7997   **7997**
(Issued March, 1882.)
Boys' Plaited Blouse:
8 sizes. Ages,
3 to 10 years.
Any size, 25 cents.

7433   **7433**
(Issued March, 1881.)
Boys' Sailor Blouse:
8 sizes. Ages,
3 to 10 years.
Any size, 15 cents.

7994   7994

(Issued March, 1882.)
Boys' Box-Plaited Blouse:
8 sizes. Ages, 3 to
10 years. Any size, 25 cents.

7995   7995

(Issued March, 1882.)
Boys' Box-Plaited Blouse,
with Sailor Collar: 8 sizes.
Ages, 3 to 10 years.
Any size, 25 cents.

7731   7731

(Issued September, 1881.)
Boys' Blouse: 8 sizes.
Ages, 3 to 10 years.
Any size, 15 cents.

7148   7148

(Issued August, 1880.)
Boys' Camisole: 8 sizes,
Ages, 3 to 10 years.
Any size, 15 cents.

7251   7251

(Issued October, 1880.)
Boys' Camisole: 8 sizes.
Ages, 3 to 10 years.
Any size, 15 cents.

4277

Boys' Blouse Shirt
Waist: 8 sizes.
Ages, 3 to 10 years.
Any size, 20 cents.

6009   6009

Boys' Sailor Blouse-
Waist: 8 sizes.
Ages, 3 to 10 years.
Any size, 20 cents.

6470   6470

(Issued March, 1879.)
Boys' Sailor Blouse:
10 sizes. Ages, 6 to
15 yrs. Any size, 20 cents.

6243   6243

Boys' Shirt-Waist:
9 sizes. Ages, 2 to
10 years.
Any size, 20 cents.

7740   7740

(Issued September, 1881.)
Boys' Single-Breasted
Vest, with Notched Collar:
9 sizes. Ages, 7 to 15 years.
Any size, 10 cents.

7728

Boys' Long Vest:
8 sizes. Ages, 3 to
10 years.
Any size, 10 cents.

7743   7743

(Issued Sept., 1881.)
Boys' Single-Breasted
Vest, without a Collar:
8 sizes. Ages, 3 to 10 yrs.
Any size, 10 cents.

7989

(Issued March, 1882.)
Boys' Single-Breasted
Vest: 9 sizes.
Ages, 7 to 15 years.
Any size, 15 cents.

7987

(Issued March, 1882.)
Boys' Single-Breasted
Vest: 8 sizes.
Ages, 3 to 10 years.
Any size, 15 cents.

7431

(Issued March, 1881.)
Boys' Single-Breasted Vest,
Buttoned to the Neck: 8 sizes.
Ages, 3 to 10 years.
Any size, 10 cents.

7204

(Issued Sept., 1880.)
Boys' Single-Breasted
Vest, without a Collar:
9 sizes. Ages, 7 to 15
yrs. Any size, 10 cents.

7437

(Issued March, 1881.)
Boys' Vest: 8 sizes.
Ages, 3 to 10 years.
Any size, 10 cents.

7444

(Issued March, 1881.)
Boys' Single-Breasted
Vest: 9 sizes.
Ages, 7 to 15 years.
Any size, 10 cents.

7983   7983

(Issued March, 1882.)
Boys' Costume: 5 sizes.
Ages, 3 to 7 years.
Any size, 25 cents.

7735   7735

(Issued September, 1881.)
Boys' Costume: 5 sizes.
Ages, 2 to 6 years.
Any size, 20 cents.

7197   7197

(Issued September, 1880.)
Boys' Costume: 5 sizes.
Ages, 2 to 6 years.
Any size, 20 cents.

6924   6924

(Issued March, 1880.)
Boys' Costume: 5 sizes.
Ages, 2 to 6 years.
Any size, 25 cents.

7729   7729

(Issued Sept., 1881.)
Boys' Knickerbocker
Pants: 8 sizes.
Ages, 3 to 10 years.
Any size, 10 cents.

7998   7998

(Issued March, 1882.
Boys' Knee Pants:
8 sizes.
Ages, 3 to 10 years.
Any size, 15 cents.

7196   7196

(Issued Sept., 1880.)
Boys' Sailor Costume:
8 sizes. Ages, 3 to 10
yrs. Any size, 25 cents.

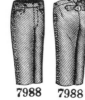
6382   6382

Boys' Sailor Costume:
8 sizes.
Ages, 3 to 10 years.
Any size, 25 cents.

7988   7988

(Issued March, 1882.)
Boys' Suspender
Pants: 9 sizes.
Ages, 7 to 15 years.
Any size, 20 cents.

6469   6469

(Issued March, 1879.)
Boys' Sailor Pants:
10 sizes.
Ages, 6 to 15 years.
Any size, 15 cents.

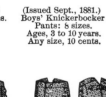
7739   7739

(Issued Sept., 1881.)
Boys' Suspender
Pants: 9 sizes.
Ages, 7 to 15 years.
Any size, 15 cents.

7443   7443

(Issued March, 1881.)
Boys' Suspender
Pants: 9 sizes.
Ages, 7 to 15 years.
Any size, 15 cents,

7734   7734

(Issued Sept., 1881,)
Boys' Short Pants:
8 sizes.
Ages, 3 to 10 years.
Any size, 10 cents.

7985   7985

(Issued March, 1882.)
Boys' Pants, Buttoned to
below the Knee: 8 sizes.
Ages, 3 to 10 years.
Any size, 15 cents.

7992   7992

(Issued March, 1882.)
Boys' Pants, Extending
below the Knee: 8 sizes.
Ages, 3 to 10 years.
Any size, 15 cents.

7996   7996

(Issued March, 1882.)
Boys' Knee Pants,
with Fly: 8 sizes.
Ages, 3 to 10 years.
Any size, 15 cents.

7434

(Issued March, 1881.)
Boys' Short Pants:
8 sizes.
Ages, 3 to 10 years.
Any size, 10 cents.

7742   7742

(Issued Sept., 1881.)
Boys' Short Pants:
8 sizes.
Ages, 3 to 10 years.
Any size, 10 cents.

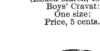
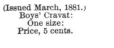
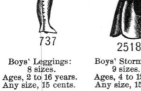

7435

7439

4753   **4753**

7441   **7441**

737

2518

(Issued March, 1881.)
Boys' Pants: 8 sizes.
Ages, 3 to 10 years.
Any size, 10 cents.

(Issued March, 1881.)
Boys' Kilt Skirt: 5 sizes.
Ages, 2 to 6 years.
Any size, 15 cents.

Chest Protector:
5 sizes. Chest measures,
8x9 to 12x13 inches.
Any size, 15 cents.

(Issued March, 1881.)
Boys' Cravat:
One size:
Price, 5 cents.

Boys' Leggings:
8 sizes.
Ages, 2 to 16 years.
Any size, 15 cents.

Boys' Storm Cap:
9 sizes.
Ages, 4 to 12 years.
Any size, 15 cents.

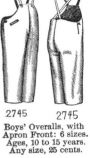

2746   **2746**

2745   **2745**

3613   **3613**

909

905

7617   **7617**

Men's Overalls, with Apron
Front: 23 sizes. Waist meas-
ures, 28 to 50 inches.
Any size, 25 cents.

Boys' Overalls, with
Apron Front: 6 sizes.
Ages, 10 to 15 years.
Any size, 25 cents.

Boys' Drawers and
Under-Shirt: 6 sizes.
Ages, 3 to 8 years.
Any size, 15 cents.

Gentlemen's Drawers:
16 sizes. Waist measures,
29 to 44 inches.
Any size, 25 cents.

Boys' Drawers:
8 sizes.
Ages, 7 to 14 years.
Any size, 25 cents.

(Issued June, 1881.)
Men's Working Pants:
19 sizes. Waist meas-
ures, 28 to 46 inches.
Any size, 25 cents.

4453

4887

3978

3033

4747

6672   **6672**

Men's Working Blouse:
8 sizes. Breast meas-
ures, 32 to 46 inches.
Any size, 30 cents.

Waiters' Jacket:
15 sizes. Breast meas-
ures, 30 to 44 inches.
Any size, 30 cents.

Men's Blouse Waist:
10 sizes. Breast meas-
ures, 28 to 46 inches.
Any size, 25 cents.

Boys' Double-Breasted
Dressing-Gown: 9 sizes.
Ages, 7 to 15 years.
Any size, 30 cents.

Gentlemen's House Jacket:
15 sizes. Breast meas-
ures, 30 to 44 inches.
Any size, 50 cents.

(Issued August, 1879.)
Gentlemen's Smoking Jacket:
13 sizes. Breast meas-
ures, 32 to 44 inches.
Any size, 50 cents.

6674   **6674**

6673   **6673**

7616

6671   **6671**

(Issued August, 1879.)
Gentlemen's Single-Breasted Dressing
Gown: 13 sizes. Breast measures,
32 to 44 inches. Any size, 50 cents.

(Issued August, 1879.)
Gentlemen's Double-Breasted Dressing
Gown: 13 sizes. Breast measures,
32 to 44 inches. Any size, 50 cents.

(Issued June, 1881.)
Gentlemen's *Pajamas*: 7 sizes.
Breast measures, 32 to 44 inches.
Any size, 30 cents.

(Issued August, 1879.)
Gentlemen's Duster: 15 sizes.
Breast measures, 32 to 46 inches.
Any size, 30 cents.

4863   **4863**

6258

7618

6359

1952

7087

Gentlemen's Duster:
15 sizes. Breast measures,
32 to 46 inches.
Any size, 30 cents.

Gentlemen's Bathing
Suit: 11 sizes.
Breast measures, 32
to 52 inches.
Any size, 50 cents.

(Issued June, 1881,)
Gentlemen's Sack Night-
Shirt: 10 sizes. Breast
meas., 28 to 46 inches.
Any size, 25 cents.

Gentlemen's Night-
Shirt: 10 sizes.
Breast measures,
28 to 46 inches.
Any size, 25 cents.

Gentlemen's Night-Shirt:
10 sizes. Breast measures,
28 to 46 inches.
Any size, 25 cents.

(Issued June, 1880.)
Gentlemen's Sack Shirt,
Open in the Front: 16 sizes.
Breast meas., 32 to 50 ins.
Any size, 25 cents.

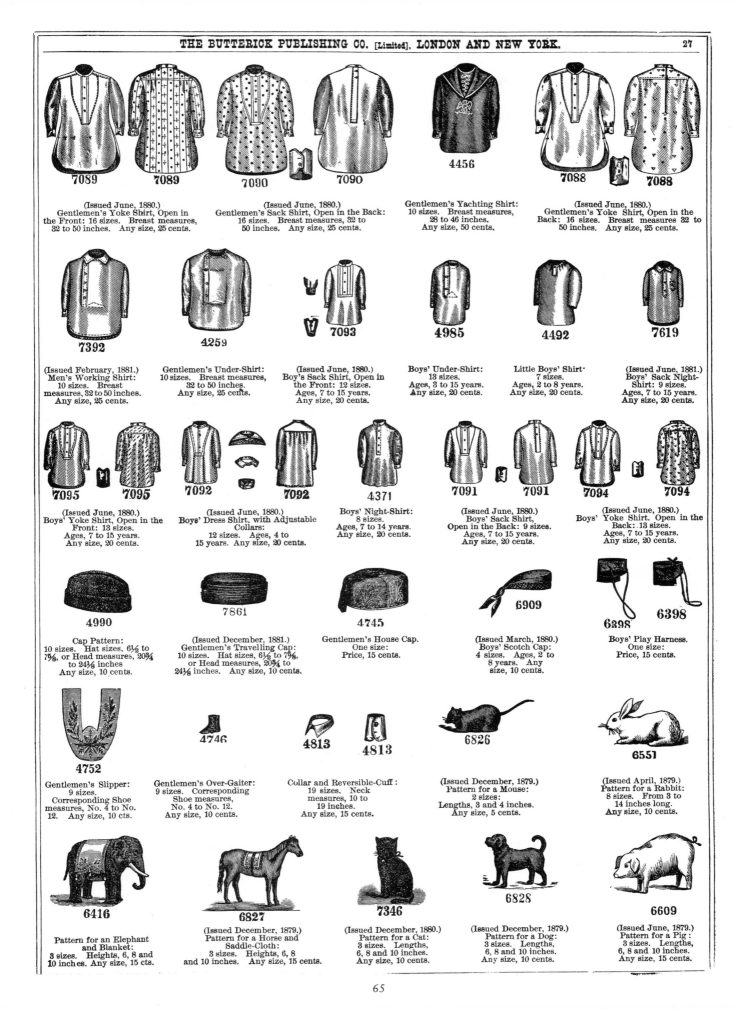

7089   **7089**   **7090**   **7090**   **4456**   **7088**   **7088**

(Issued June, 1880.)
Gentlemen's Yoke Shirt, Open in
the Front: 16 sizes. Breast measures,
32 to 50 inches. Any size, 25 cents.

(Issued June, 1880.)
Gentlemen's Sack Shirt, Open in the Back:
16 sizes. Breast measures, 32 to
50 inches. Any size, 25 cents.

Gentlemen's Yachting Shirt:
10 sizes. Breast measures,
28 to 46 inches.
Any size, 50 cents.

(Issued June, 1880.)
Gentlemen's Yoke Shirt, Open in the
Back: 16 sizes. Breast measures 32 to
50 inches. Any size, 25 cents.

7392   **4259**   **7093**   **4985**   **4492**   **7619**

(Issued February, 1881.)
Men's Working Shirt:
10 sizes. Breast
measures, 32 to 50 inches.
Any size, 25 cents.

Gentlemen's Under-Shirt:
10 sizes. Breast measures,
32 to 50 inches.
Any size, 25 cents.

(Issued June, 1880.)
Boy's Sack Shirt, Open in
the Front: 12 sizes.
Ages, 7 to 15 years.
Any size, 20 cents.

Boys' Under-Shirt:
13 sizes.
Ages, 3 to 15 years.
Any size, 20 cents.

Little Boys' Shirt·
7 sizes.
Ages, 2 to 8 years.
Any size, 20 cents.

(Issued June, 1881.)
Boys' Sack Night-
Shirt: 9 sizes.
Ages, 7 to 15 years.
Any size, 20 cents.

7095   **7095**   **7092**   **7092**   **4371**   **7091**   **7091**   **7094**   **7094**

(Issued June, 1880.)
Boys' Yoke Shirt, Open in the
Front: 13 sizes.
Ages, 7 to 15 years.
Any size, 20 cents.

(Issued June, 1880.)
Boys' Dress Shirt, with Adjustable
Collars:
12 sizes. Ages, 4 to
15 years. Any size, 20 cents.

Boys' Night-Shirt:
8 sizes.
Ages, 7 to 14 years.
Any size, 20 cents.

(Issued June, 1880.)
Boys' Sack Shirt,
Open in the Back: 9 sizes.
Ages, 7 to 15 years.
Any size, 20 cents.

(Issued June, 1880.)
Boys' Yoke Shirt. Open in the
Back: 13 sizes.
Ages, 7 to 15 years.
Any size, 20 cents.

4990   **7861**   **4745**   **6909**   **6398**   **6398**

Cap Pattern:
10 sizes. Hat sizes, 6½ to
7⅝, or Head measures, 20¾
to 24⅛ inches
Any size, 10 cents.

(Issued December, 1881.)
Gentlemen's Travelling Cap:
10 sizes. Hat sizes, 6½ to 7⅝,
or Head measures, 20¾ to
24⅛ inches. Any size, 10 cents.

Gentlemen's House Cap.
One size:
Price, 15 cents.

(Issued March, 1880.)
Boys' Scotch Cap:
4 sizes. Ages, 2 to
8 years. Any
size, 10 cents.

Boys' Play Harness.
One size:
Price, 15 cents.

4752   **4746**   **4813**   **4813**   **6826**   **6551**

Gentlemen's Slipper:
9 sizes.
Corresponding Shoe
measures, No. 4 to No.
12. Any size, 10 cts.

Gentlemen's Over-Gaiter:
9 sizes. Corresponding
Shoe measures,
No. 4 to No. 12.
Any size, 10 cents.

Collar and Reversible-Cuff:
19 sizes. Neck
measures, 10 to
19 inches.
Any size, 15 cents.

(Issued December, 1879.)
Pattern for a Mouse:
2 sizes.
Lengths, 3 and 4 inches.
Any size, 5 cents.

(Issued April, 1879.)
Pattern for a Rabbit:
8 sizes. From 3 to
14 inches long.
Any size, 10 cents.

6416   **6827**   **7346**   **6828**   **6609**

Pattern for an Elephant
and Blanket:
3 sizes. Heights, 6, 8 and
10 inches. Any size, 15 cts.

(Issued December, 1879.)
Pattern for a Horse and
Saddle-Cloth:
3 sizes. Heights, 6, 8
and 10 inches. Any size, 15 cents.

(Issued December, 1880.)
Pattern for a Cat:
3 sizes. Lengths,
6, 8 and 10 inches.
Any size, 10 cents.

(Issued December, 1879.)
Pattern for a Dog:
3 sizes. Lengths,
6, 8 and 10 inches.
Any size, 10 cents.

(Issued June, 1879.)
Pattern for a Pig:
3 sizes. Lengths,
6, 8 and 10 inches.
Any size, 15 cents.

DOLLS' PATTERNS.

(Issued December, 1880.)
Lady Dolls' Set No. 59.—Consisting
of a Princess Walking Dress and Wrap:
7 sizes. Lengths, 12 to 24 inches.
Any size, 20 cents.

(Issued January, 1881.)
Lady Dolls' Set No. 65.—Consisting
of a Walking Skirt and Polonaise:
7 sizes. Lengths, 12 to 24 inches.
Any size, 20 cents.

(Issued January, 1882.)
Lady Dolls' Set No. 72.—Consisting
of a Polonaise and Walking Skirt:
7 sizes. Lengths, 12 to 24 inches.
Any size, 20 cents.

(Issued December, 1879.)
Lady Dolls' Set No. 41.—Consisting
of a Wrap and Ulster:
7 sizes. Lengths, 12 to 24 inches.
Any size, 15 cents.

(Issued December, 1879.)
Girl Dolls' Set No. 42.—Consisting
of a Wrap and Ulster:
7 sizes. Lengths, 12 to 24 inches.
Any size, 15 cents.

(Issued January, 1882.)
Girl Dolls' Set No. 75.—Consisting
of a Dress and Cloak:
7 sizes. Lengths, 12 to 24 inches.
Any size, 20 cents.

(Issued January, 1881.)
Girl Dolls' Set No. 66.—Consisting
of a Yoke Slip and Jacket:
7 sizes. Lengths, 12 to 24 inches.
Any size, 15 cents.

(Issued January, 1882.)
Girl Dolls' Set No. 76.—Consisting of a Basque and Walking
Skirt: 7 sizes. Lengths, 12 to 24
inches. Any size, 20 cents.

Baby Dolls' Set No. 11.—Consisting
of a Dress, Cloak and Hood:
7 sizes. Lengths, 12 to 24 inches.
Any size, 20 cents.

Baby Dolls' Set No. 9.—Consisting of a
Chemise, Pinning-Blanket and Petticoat:
7 sizes. Lengths, 12 to 24 inches.
Any size, 20 cents.

(Issued January, 1880.)
Girl Dolls' Set No. 50.—Consisting
of a Night-Dress and Night-Cap:
7 sizes. Lengths, 12 to 24 inches.
Any size, 15 cents.

Baby Dolls' Set No. 10.—Consisting
of a Night-Dress, Wrapper and Bib:
7 sizes. Lengths, 12 to 24 inches.
Any size, 20 cents.

Baby Dolls' Set No. 17.—Consisting of a
Christening Robe, Gored Dress and Bonnet:
7 sizes. Lengths, 12 to 24 inches.
Any size, 25 cents.

Lady Dolls' Set No. 1.—Consisting
of a Chemise, Drawers and Yoke
Night-Dress: 7 sizes. Lengths,
12 to 24 inches. Any size, 10 cents.

Girl Dolls' Set No. 20.—Consisting
of a Chemise, Drawers and Petticoat:
7 sizes. Lengths, 12 to 24 inches.
Any size, 15 cents.

(Issued December, 1879.)
Girl Dolls' Set No. 48.—Sailor Costume:
Consisting of a Kilt and Blouse:
7 sizes. Lengths, 12 to 24 inches.
Any size, 15 cents.

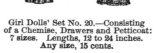

(Issued December, 1881.)
Nurse Dolls' Set No. 71.—Consisting
of a Dress, Cap and Apron:
7 sizes. Lengths, 12 to 24 inches.
Any size, 20 cents.

(Issued January, 1881.)
Lady Dolls' Set No. 63.—Consisting
of a Coat Basque and Demi-Train Skirt:
7 sizes. Lengths, 12 to 24 inches.
Any size, 20 cents.

(Issued December, 1880.)
Girl Dolls' Set No. 57.—Consisting
of a Walking Skirt and Polonaise:
7 sizes. Lengths, 12 to 24 inches.
Any size, 15 cents.

(Issued January, 1882.)
Lady Dolls' Set No. 73.—Consisting of a Wrap, Hat and Muff:
7 sizes. Length, 12 to 24 inches.
Any size, 20 cents.

(Issued December, 1879.)
Gentlemen Dolls' Set No. 40.—
Consisting of a Pants, Smoking
Jacket and Cap: 7 sizes.
Lengths, 12 to 24 inches.
Any size, 15 cents.

(Issued December, 1879.)
Gentlemen Dolls' Set No. 39.—Dress Suit:
Consisting of a Pants, Swallow-Tail Coat
and Low-Cut Vest, with Rolling Collar:
7 sizes. Lengths, 12 to 24 inches.
Any size, 20 cents.

(Issued December, 1880.)
Gentlemen Dolls' Set No. 62.—
Consisting of a Prince Albert Coat,
Pants and Vest: 7 sizes.
Lengths, 12 to 24 inches.
Any size, 20 cents.

(Issued December, 1881.)
Gentlemen Dolls' Set No. 70.—
Consisting of a Cutaway Coat,
Pants and Vest: 7 sizes.
Lengths, 12 to 24 inches.
Any size, 20 cents.

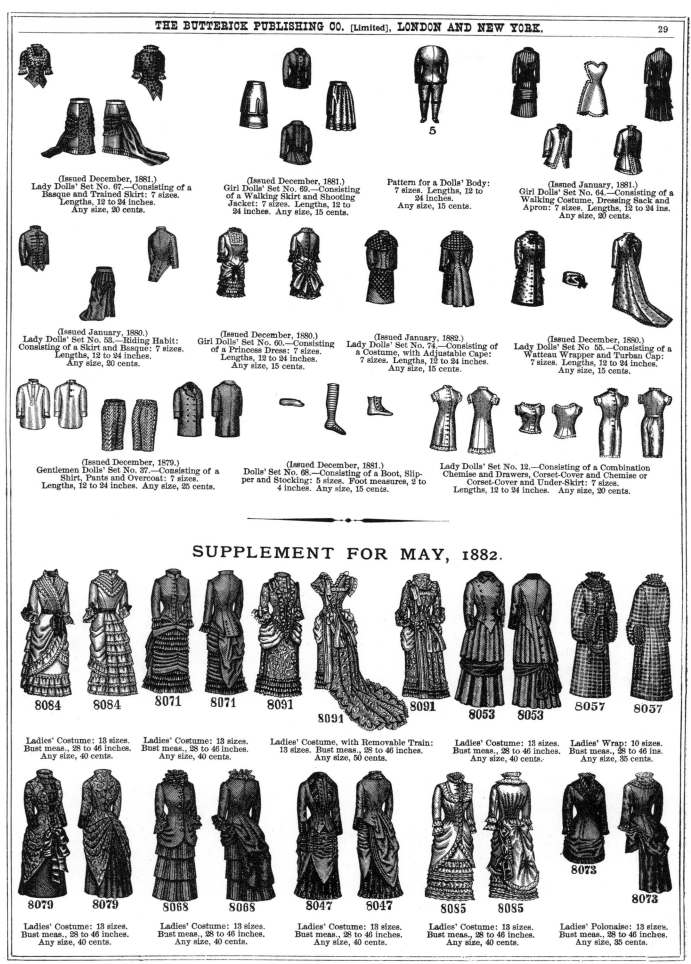

(Issued December, 1881.)
Lady Dolls' Set No. 67.—Consisting of a
Basque and Trained Skirt: 7 sizes.
Lengths, 12 to 24 inches.
Any size, 20 cents.

(Issued December, 1881.)
Girl Dolls' Set No. 69.—Consisting
of a Walking Skirt and Shooting
Jacket: 7 sizes. Lengths, 12 to
24 inches. Any size, 15 cents.

Pattern for a Dolls' Body:
7 sizes. Lengths, 12 to
24 inches.
Any size, 15 cents.

(Issued January, 1881.)
Girl Dolls' Set No. 64.—Consisting of a
Walking Costume, Dressing Sack and
Apron: 7 sizes. Lengths, 12 to 24 ins.
Any size, 20 cents.

(Issued January, 1880.)
Lady Dolls' Set No. 53.—Riding Habit:
Consisting of a Skirt and Basque: 7 sizes.
Lengths, 12 to 24 inches.
Any size, 20 cents.

(Issued December, 1880.)
Girl Dolls' Set No. 60.—Consisting
of a Princess Dress: 7 sizes.
Lengths, 12 to 24 inches.
Any size, 15 cents.

(Issued January, 1882.)
Lady Dolls' Set No. 74.—Consisting of
a Costume, with Adjustable Cape:
7 sizes. Lengths, 12 to 24 inches.
Any size, 15 cents.

(Issued December, 1880.)
Lady Dolls' Set No 55.—Consisting of a
Watteau Wrapper and Turban Cap:
7 sizes. Lengths, 12 to 24 inches.
Any size, 15 cents.

(Issued December, 1879.)
Gentlemen Dolls' Set No. 37.—Consisting of a
Shirt, Pants and Overcoat: 7 sizes.
Lengths, 12 to 24 inches. Any size, 25 cents.

(Issued December, 1881.)
Dolls' Set No. 68.—Consisting of a Boot, Slipper and Stocking: 5 sizes. Foot measures, 2 to
4 inches. Any size, 15 cents.

Lady Dolls' Set No. 12.—Consisting of a Combination
Chemise and Drawers, Corset-Cover and Chemise or
Corset-Cover and Under-Skirt: 7 sizes.
Lengths, 12 to 24 inches.   Any size, 20 cents.

SUPPLEMENT FOR MAY, 1882.

8084   8084   8071   8071   8091   8091   8091   8053   8053   8057   8057

Ladies' Costume: 13 sizes.
Bust meas., 28 to 46 inches.
Any size, 40 cents.

Ladies' Costume: 13 sizes.
Bust meas., 28 to 46 inches.
Any size, 40 cents.

Ladies' Costume, with Removable Train:
13 sizes. Bust meas., 28 to 46 inches.
Any size, 50 cents.

Ladies' Costume: 13 sizes.
Bust meas., 28 to 46 inches.
Any size, 40 cents.

Ladies' Wrap: 10 sizes.
Bust meas., 28 to 46 ins.
Any size, 35 cents.

8079   8079   8068   8068   8047   8047   8085   8085   8073   8073

Ladies' Costume: 13 sizes.
Bust meas., 28 to 46 inches.
Any size, 40 cents.

Ladies' Costume: 13 sizes.
Bust meas., 28 to 46 inches.
Any size, 40 cents.

Ladies' Costume: 13 sizes.
Bust meas., 28 to 46 inches.
Any size, 40 cents.

Ladies' Costume: 13 sizes.
Bust meas., 28 to 46 inches.
Any size, 40 cents.

Ladies' Polonaise: 13 sizes.
Bust meas., 28 to 46 inches.
Any size, 35 cents.

SUPPLEMENT FOR MAY, 1882,—Continued.

8063   8063

Ladies' Walking Skirt:
9 sizes. Waist meas., 20 to
36 ins. Any size, 35 cents.

8051   8051

Ladies' Walking Skirt:
9 sizes. Waist meas., 20 to
36 ins. Any size, 35 cents.

8077   8077

Ladies' Walking Skirt:
9 sizes. Waist meas., 20 to
36 ins. Any size, 35 cents.

8090   8090

Ladies' Walking Skirt:
9 sizes. Waist meas., 20 to
36 ins. Any size, 35 cents.

8055   8055

Ladies' Walking Skirt:
9 sizes. Waist meas., 20 to
36 ins. Any size, 35 cents.

8072   8072

Ladies' Basque: 13 sizes.
Bust measures, 28 to
46 inches.
Any size, 30 cents.

8095   8095

Misses' Basque: 8 sizes.
Ages, 8 to 15 years.
Any size, 25 cents.

8094   8094

Ladies' Basque: 13 sizes.
Bust measures, 28 to
46 inches.
Any size, 30 cents.

8052   8052

Ladies' Basque: 13 sizes.
Bust measures, 28 to
46 inches.
Any size, 30 cents.

8054   8054

Ladies' Basque: 13 sizes.
Bust measures, 28 to
46 inches.
Any size, 30 cents.

8096   8096

Ladies' Coat: 13 sizes.
Bust measures, 28 to
46 inches.
Any size, 30 cents.

8074   8074

Ladies' Wrap: 10 sizes.
Bust measures, 28 to
46 inches.
Any size, 30 cents.

8088   8088

Ladies' Wrap: 10 sizes.
Bust measures, 28 to
46 inches.
Any size, 25 cents.

8064   8064

Ladies' Basque: 13 sizes.
Bust measures, 28 to
46 inches.
Any size, 30 cents.

8076   8076

Ladies' Basque: 13 sizes.
Bust measures, 28 to
46 inches.
Any size, 30 cents.

8056   8056

Ladies' Basque: 13 sizes.
Bust measures, 28 to
46 inches.
Any size, 30 cents.

8087

Ladies' Shopping
Bag.
One size:
Price, 10 cents.

8048   8048

Ladies' Walking Skirt:
9 sizes.
Waist meas., 20 to 36 ins.
Any size, 35 cents.

8058

Ladies' Walking Skirt,
with Yoke: 9 sizes.
Waist meas., 20 to
36 ins. Any size, 30 cts.

8082

Misses' Walking
Skirt: 8 sizes.
Ages, 8 to 15 years.
Any size, 25 cents.

8081   8081

Misses' Walking Skirt:
8 sizes.
Ages, 8 to 15 years.
Any size, 30 cents.

8089   8089

Ladies' Over-Skirt:
9 sizes.
Waist measures, 20 to 36 inches.
Any size, 30 cents.

8092   8092

Ladies' Coat:
13 sizes.
Bust meas., 28 to 46 ins.
Any size, 30 cents.

8075   8075   8049   8049

Misses' Costume, with De-
tachable Cape: 8 sizes.
Ages, 8 to 15 years.
Any size, 35 cents.

Misses' Costume:
8 sizes.
Ages, 8 to 15 years.
Any size, 35 cents.

8093   8093

Misses' Polonaise:
8 sizes.
Ages, 8 to 15 years.
Any size, 30 cents.

8065   8065

Ladies' Wrap:
10 sizes.
Bust measures, 28 to 46 ins.
Any size, 30 cents.

8062   8062

Ladies' Polonaise, with Ad-
justable Cape: 13 sizes.
Bust measures, 28 to 46 ins.
Any size, 35 cents.

8059   8059

Misses' Wrap:
8 sizes.
Ages, 8 to 15 years.
Any size, 35 cents.

SUPPLEMENT FOR MAY, 1882—Concluded.

8083   8083   8070   8070   8061   8061   8066   8066   8067   8067   8078   8078

Child's Costume: 5 sizes. Ages, 2 to 6 years. Any size, 25 cents.

Child's Dress, with Removable Collar: 5 sizes. Ages, 2 to 6 years. Any size, 20 cents.

Girls' Cloak: 7 sizes. Ages, 3 to 9 years. Any size, 25 cents.

Girls' Costume: 7 sizes. Ages, 3 to 9 years. Any size, 25 cents.

Girls' Costume: 7 sizes. Ages, 3 to 9 years. Any size, 25 cents.

Girls' Blouse Costume: 7 sizes. Ages, 3 to 9 years. Any size, 25 cents.

8050   8086   8086   8080   8080   8097   8097   8069   8069

Girls' Zouave Basque: 7 sizes. Ages, 3 to 9 years. Any size, 20 cents.

Misses' Jacket: 8 sizes. Ages, 8 to 15 years. Any size, 25 cents.

Child's Dress: 8 sizes. Ages, 2 to 9 years. Any size, 25 cents.

Child's Costume: 5 sizes. Ages, 2 to 6 years. Any size, 25 cents.

SUPPLEMENT FOR JUNE, 1882.

8130   8130   8142   8142   8116   8116   8100   8100   8124   8124

Ladies' Costume: 13 sizes. Bust measures, 28 to 46 inches. Any size, 40 cents.

Ladies' Costume: 13 sizes. Bust measures, 28 to 46 inches. Any size, 40 cents.

Ladies' Costume: 13 sizes. Bust measures, 28 to 46 inches. Any size, 40 cents.

Ladies' Polonaise: 13 sizes. Bust measures, 28 to 46 inches. Any size, 35 cents.

Ladies' Riding-Habit, with Princess Skirt: 13 sizes. Bust meas., 28 to 46 inches Any size, 50 cents.

8098   8098   8122   8122   8114   8114   8126   8126   8147   8147

Ladies' Nursing Wrapper: 13 sizes. Bust measures, 28 to 46 inches. Any size, 35 cents.

Misses' Long Coat: 8 sizes. Ages, 8 to 15 years. Any size, 30 cents.

Ladies' Polonaise: 13 sizes. Bust measures, 28 to 46 inches. Any size, 35 cents.

Misses' Costume: 8 sizes. Ages, 8 to 15 years. Any size, 30 cents.

Gentlemen's Duster: 15 sizes. Breast measures, 32 to 46 inches. Any size, 30 cents.

8109   8109   8112   8112   8131   8131   8106   8106   8148   8148

Ladies' Walking Skirt: 9 sizes. Waist measures, 20 to 36 inches. Any size, 35 cents.

Ladies' Walking Skirt: 9 sizes. Waist measures, 20 to 36 inches. Any size, 35 cents.

Ladies' Walking Skirt; 9 sizes. Waist measures, 20 to 36 inches. Any size, 35 cents.

Ladies' Petticoat: 9 sizes. Waist measures, 20 to 36 inches. Any size, 30 cents.

Boys' Single-Breasted Duster: 9 sizes. Ages, 7 to 15 years. Any size, 25 cents.

SUPPLEMENT FOR JUNE, 1882—Continued.

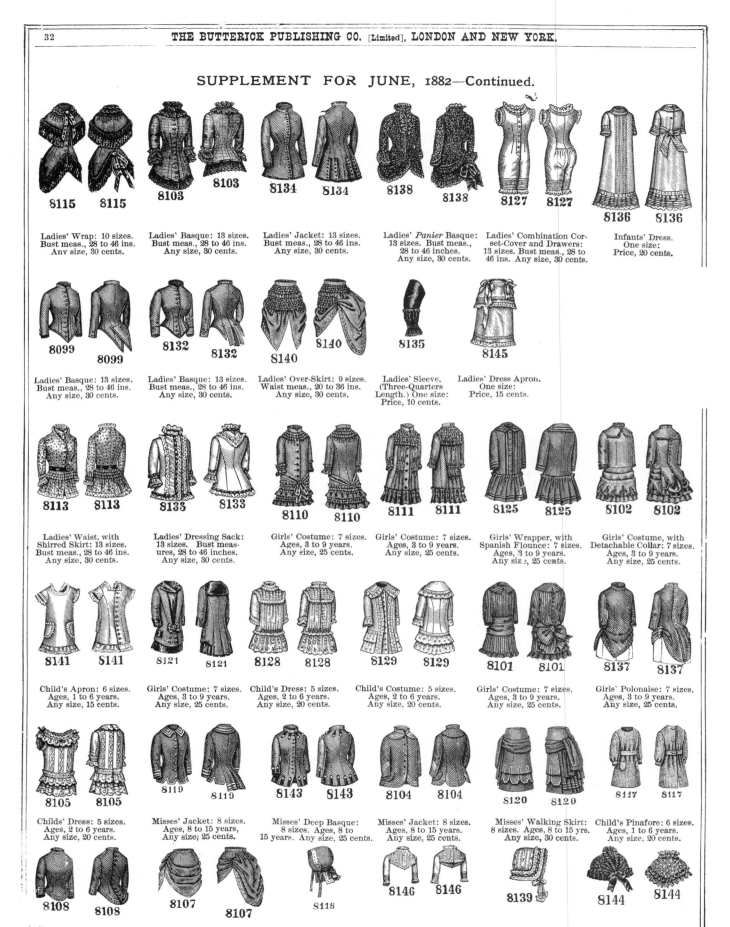

8115   8115

Ladies' Wrap: 10 sizes.
Bust meas., 28 to 46 ins.
Any size, 30 cents.

8103   8103

Ladies' Basque: 13 sizes.
Bust meas., 28 to 46 ins.
Any size, 30 cents.

8134   8134

Ladies' Jacket: 13 sizes.
Bust meas., 28 to 46 ins.
Any size, 30 cents.

8138   8138

Ladies' *Panier* Basque:
13 sizes. Bust meas.,
28 to 46 inches.
Any size, 30 cents.

8127   8127

Ladies' Combination Cor-
set-Cover and Drawers:
13 sizes. Bust meas., 28 to
46 ins. Any size, 30 cents.

8136   8136

Infants' Dress.
One size:
Price, 20 cents.

8099   8099

Ladies' Basque: 13 sizes.
Bust meas., 28 to 46 ins.
Any size, 30 cents.

8132   8132

Ladies' Basque: 13 sizes.
Bust meas., 28 to 46 ins.
Any size, 30 cents.

8140   8140

Ladies' Over-Skirt: 9 sizes.
Waist meas., 20 to 36 ins.
Any size, 30 cents.

8135

Ladies' Sleeve,
(Three-Quarters
Length.) One size:
Price, 10 cents.

8145

Ladies' Dress Apron.
One size:
Price, 15 cents.

8113   8113

Ladies' Waist, with
Shirred Skirt: 13 sizes.
Bust meas., 28 to 46 ins.
Any size, 30 cents.

8133   8133

Ladies' Dressing Sack:
13 sizes. Bust meas-
ures, 28 to 46 inches.
Any size, 30 cents.

8110   8110

Girls' Costume: 7 sizes.
Ages, 3 to 9 years.
Any size, 25 cents.

8111   8111

Girls' Costume: 7 sizes.
Ages, 3 to 9 years.
Any size, 25 cents.

8125   8125

Girls' Wrapper, with
Spanish Flounce: 7 sizes.
Ages, 3 to 9 years.
Any size, 25 cents.

8102   8102

Girls' Costume, with
Detachable Collar: 7 sizes.
Ages, 3 to 9 years.
Any size, 25 cents.

8141   8141

Child's Apron: 6 sizes.
Ages, 1 to 6 years.
Any size, 15 cents.

8121   8121

Girls' Costume: 7 sizes.
Ages, 3 to 9 years.
Any size, 25 cents.

8128   8128

Child's Dress: 5 sizes.
Ages, 2 to 6 years.
Any size, 20 cents.

8129   8129

Child's Costume: 5 sizes.
Ages, 2 to 6 years.
Any size, 20 cents.

8101   8101

Girls' Costume: 7 sizes.
Ages, 3 to 9 years.
Any size, 25 cents.

8137   8137

Girls' Polonaise: 7 sizes.
Ages, 3 to 9 years.
Any size, 25 cents.

8105   8105

Childs' Dress: 5 sizes.
Ages, 2 to 6 years.
Any size, 20 cents.

8119   8119

Misses' Jacket: 8 sizes.
Ages, 8 to 15 years.
Any size, 25 cents.

8143   8143

Misses' Deep Basque:
8 sizes. Ages, 8 to
15 years. Any size, 25 cents.

8104   8104

Misses' Jacket: 8 sizes.
Ages, 8 to 15 years.
Any size, 25 cents.

8120   8120

Misses' Walking Skirt:
8 sizes. Ages, 8 to 15 yrs.
Any size, 30 cents.

8117   8117

Child's Pinafore: 6 sizes.
Ages, 1 to 6 years.
Any size, 20 cents.

8108   8108

Misses' Basque: 8 sizes.
Ages, 8 to 15 years.
Any size, 25 cents.

8107   8107

Misses' Over-Skirt: 8 sizes.
Ages, 8 to 15 years.
Any size, 25 cents.

8118

Child's Sun-Bonnet:
3 sizes. Ages, 2 to
6 years. Any size, 15 cts.

8146   8146

Infants' Dress-Yoke
and Sleeves. One size:
Price, 10 cents.

8139

Girls' Cap   8 sizes.
Ages, 2 to 9 years.
Any size, 10 cents.

8144   8144

Ladies' Shoulder-Cape:
10 sizes. Bust meas., 28 to
46 inches. Any size, 15 cts.

Figure No. 1.—LADIES' MULL TOILETTE.   Figure No. 2.—LADIES' PROMENADE TOILETTE.

FIGURE No. 1.—Ladies' Mull Toilette.—This illustrates a Basque and Skirt, the labels of which represent them in different materials, with different trimmings. The Pattern to the Basque is No. 8099; 13 sizes: Bust measures, 28 to 46 inches; Any size, 30 cents.   The Pattern to the Skirt is No. 8109; 9 sizes: Waist measures, 20 to 36 inches; Any size, 35 cents.

FIGURE No. 2.—Ladies' Promenade Toilette.—This illustrates a Polonaise and Skirt, the labels of which show other views of their patterns.   The Pattern to the Polonaise is No. 8100; 13 sizes; Bust measures, 28 to 46 inches; Any size, 35 cents.   The Pattern to the Skirt is No. 726. . 9 sizes; Waist measures, 20 to 36 inches; Any size, 25 cents.

THE LADIES STANDARD Magazine.

Devoted to Fashions and the HOME.

APRIL, 1894.

50 CTS. A YEAR. 5 CTS. A COPY.

STANDARD FASHION COMPANY · STANDARD · NEW YORK

PUBLISHED MONTHLY BY THE STANDARD FASHION CO.
342 WEST 14TH STREET, NEW YORK.

Entered as Second Class Matter at the New York, N. Y., Post Office, February 28, 1891.

Standard Measurements for Ladies, Misses & Girls.

Take bust measure under the arms, around the fullest part of figure, holding tape well up across the back, drawing it moderately tight.

Ladies' garments requiring bust measure are cut in 8 sizes, from 30 to 44 inches.

Ladies' garments requiring waist measure only are cut in 8 sizes, from 20 to 34 inches.

In sending for Misses', Girls', Children's, or Boys' patterns, be sure to order for the *age corresponding* with the *actual measure*.

Misses' garments requiring bust measure are cut in 4 sizes, viz. :

Age,	10	12	14	16	years.
Bust measure,	29	30	31	33	inches.

Substitute for hip measure : pass tape over fullest part of bust and over arms.

Misses' garments requiring waist measure are cut in 4 sizes, viz. :

Age,	10	12	14	16	years.
Hip measure,	31	34	37	40	inches.
Waist measure,	25	24¼	24	23½	"

Girls' garments requiring bust measure are cut in 4 sizes, viz. :

Age,	6	7	8	9	years.
Bust measure,	24	25	26	27	inches.

Girls' garments requiring waist measure are cut in 4 sizes, viz.:

Age,	6	7	8	9	years.
Hip measure,	27	28	29	30	inches.
Waist measure,	23	23¼	23½	24	"

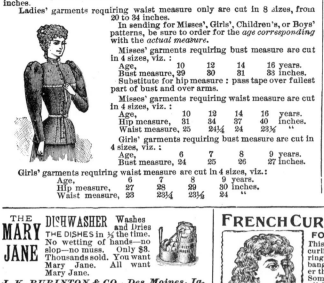

Standard Measurements for Children, Boys and Men.

Children's garments are cut in 4 sizes (½ to 3, or 2 to 5 years), viz. :

Age,	½	1	2	3	4	5	years.
Breast measure,	18	19	20	21	22	23	inches.

Boys' coat or vest measurements : Pass tape around the body under arms, drawing it moderately tight.

Boys' overcoat measurements : Measure over coat or jacket the garment is to be worn over.

Boys' trousers measurements : Pass tape around the waist over the trousers, drawing it moderately tight.

For men's and boys' shirts, take the exact neck measurement and add one inch.

For coats, take breast measure, close under arms, drawing tape moderately tight.

Men's Measurements for Shirts.

Neck	14	14½	14½	15	15	15½	15½	16	16	16½	16½	17	17	17½
Breast	34	34	36	36	38	38	40	40	42	42	44	44	46	46

Boys' Measurements.

Age,	2	3	4	5	6	7	years.
Breast,	21	21¾	22½	23¼	24	24¾	inches.
Waist,	21	22	22½	23	23½	24	"
Age,	8	9	10	12	14	16	years.
Breast,	25½	26¼	27	28½	30	31½	inches.
Waist,	24½	25	25½	26½	27½	28½	"
Neck,	10½	11	11½	12½	13½	14½	"

Notice.

The schedule shows how much greater variation there is in the size of the hips than the waists of girls from 6 to 9 years, and misses from 10 to 16 years, and proves that the *only correct* way of ordering skirts, etc., is by HIP MEASURE, instead of waist measure.

THE **MARY JANE** DISHWASHER Washes and Dries THE DISHES in ⅓ the time. No wetting of hands—no slop—no muss. Only $3. Thousands sold. You want Mary Jane. All want Mary Jane.

J. K. PURINTON & CO., Des Moines, Ia.

$10 TO $25 per week made working for us. Ladies are equally as successful as men. Parties preferred who can devote their entire time and attention to the business, but spare moments may be used to good advantage. A splendid opportunity. Address, for particulars, B. F. JOHNSON & CO., No. 5 S. 11th Street, Richmond, Va.

---

10 CENTS (silver) pays for our handsome PEOPLE'S JOURNAL one year, *on trial*, and your address in our "AGENTS' DIRECTORY," which goes whirling all over the United States to firms who wish to mail **FREE**, sample papers, magazines, **books**, pictures, cards, etc., with terms, and our patrons receive bushels of mail. Greatest bargain in America. ***Try it*; you will be Pleased.**

T. D. CAMPBELL, X 201, Boyleston, Ind.

High Arm **FREE TRIAL** in your own home for 30 days without paying one cent in advance; machine to be returned at our expense if unsatisfactory. We take all risks, **pay freight,** ship anywhere, to anyone, in any quantity at wholesale prices. $65 **Kenwood** machine, **$24.50; $55 Arlington, $20.50; $45** Arlington, **$17.50;** $35 High Arm Gem, **$12.** We sell all makes and styles, from cheapest $7.95 to best "Kenwood," $24.50, **All attachments free.** THREE HIGHEST WORLD'S FAIR MEDALS AWARDED. Over 100,000 now in use. Buy direct from factory Save agents large profits. Catalogue and testimonials **free. Write at once.** Address (in full) **CASH BUYERS' UNION, 158-164 W. VanBuren St., Dept. A 106, Chicago, Ill.**

Warranted Ten Years.

There is no position more suitable for a lady desirous of earning her living than that of Secretary for a business house. This necessitates a knowledge of the Typewriter. In selecting an instrument choose one that does the finest and greatest variety of work and **is the easiest to learn.** This machine is

THE HAMMOND TYPEWRITER.

FRENCH CURLING CREAM

FOR MEN AND WOMEN.

This preparation is used for curling stiffest hair into wavy ringlets, without injury. Keeps bangs and frizzes in curl longer than any other preparation. Something that would accomplish this without injuring the texture of the hair has been a long-felt want. To this end various remedies have been introduced, all of which have proved to be wanting in some one or more particulars. They have either produced a dryness or a gumminess of the hair. We believe we are offering the public THE BEST Hair Curler yet produced.

The Curling Cream does not injure the hair or skin, but is calculated to impart everything necesary to its beauty, causing the hair of any person to curl after the first application. Every package is securely sealed with plain printed directions for use, and sent by mail, under extra cover, for **25 cents.** One dozen, **$1.75.** Agents wanted everywhere. Address FRANCIS WEHOSKIEE, 35 Eddy St., Providence, R. I.

GRAY HAIR MADE DARK by a harmless Home Wash. Will also make the hair grow. Full directions for 25 cents. **MRS. HUNTER, 2660 Lucas Ave, St. Louis, Mo.**

LADIES Mail 2c. stamp for sealed instructions how to enlarge your bust 5 inches, by using **"Emma" Bust Developer.** Guaranteed. 24 page illustrated catalogue for 6 cents. Address EMMA TOILET BAZAR, 224 Tremont Street, BOSTON, MASS. Mention this paper.

LADIES! GOOD PAYING WORK AT HOME, NO CANVASSING. Send stamp to MISS J. B. MILLER, Battle Creek. Mich.

HOW TO WIN, control and influence others, also the real secret of Mesmerizing. New Illustrated Book $1. Satisfaction guaranteed. 100 page Circular 10 cents. **PROF. ANDERSON. L. S. Q., 182 State Street, Chicago.**

·BRIGHTEST·AND·BEST·

Ladies' STANDARD Magazine.

Issued Monthly. Illustrates in splendidly executed Large Fashion Engravings the very latest and newest designs in Ladies', Misses' and Children's Garments, and the latest information on Fabrics, What to Wear, Millinery, Trimmings, Household Decoration and Furnishing; Cooking and Domestic Receipts. Subscription price, only 50 cents per year. Sample copies, 10 cents. Send Money Order or Bank Draft to **Standard Fashion Co., 342 W. 14th St., New York.**

TO YOUNG MEN AND WOMEN. Light, honorable employment at home. Will pay $20 to $40 per week. Write us. Address MATTOON & CO., Oswego, N. Y.

REAL ARSENIC.

FREE.—The truth is that so-called "Arsenic Wafers," which contain no arsenic, have been sold for years on the reputation of what **REAL** arsenic will do in giving health, rounded form, fine complexion, brilliant eyes, strength, happiness. Real chemically pure refined arsenic (not such as is sold by druggists to kill rats) will do this, and is perfectly safe when used under instructions from a competent doctor. ☞ We will prove this by sending you one month's treatment free, and our Chief Physician will instruct you. Send postage. Address, **Chemists' Assoc'n, San Francisco, Cal.**

MARRIAGE PAPER FREE. 500 ladies and gents want correspondents **GUNNELS' MONTHLY, TOLEDO, OHIO.**

A WOMAN'S SUCCESS For two years I have made **$25 a week at Home.** Instructions FREE to lady readers. Send stamp. (No humbug.) **MRS. J. A. MANNING, Box 85, ANNA, OHIO.**

I WILL PAY A FEW LADIES A SALARY of $10 per week to work for me in their locality and at home. Light work, good pay for part of time. Write with stamp. Mrs. E. E. Bassett, Suite 904, Marshall Field Bldg, Chicago.

Gray Hair or Whiskers restored to perfectly natural color by using **Van's Mexican Hair Restorative.** It removes all dandruff, stops hair from falling out and cures all disease of the scalp. **It is no Dye,** and is warranted absolutely harmless. Money refunded if it does not do everything claimed for it. Sent to any address on receipt of price, $1 per bottle. Full information free. Agents wanted. **Allen & Co.,** 312 Inter Ocean B'd'g, Chicago, Ill.

LADIES you can obtain a safe, reliable, never-failing French Remedy for Female Troubles by enclosing **10c.** for sealed particulars. **One Box FREE. Dr. Murat Co.,** Sole Amer. Agts., **Cincinnati, O.**

ONE MONTH AGO A lamp chimney was mended with **Apple's Adhesive Pencil.** The lamp burns every night. The chimney still holds firm.—nuf ced. **Agents Wanted.** 400 per cent. profit. Sample and terms for 2 cent stamp. APPLE CHEMICAL CO., Lock Box 29, Indiana, Pa.

You Dye in 30 minutes Turkey red on cotton that won't freeze, boil or wash out. No other will do it. Package to color 2 lbs., by mail, 10 cts.; 6, any color—for wool or cotton, 40c. Big pay Agents. Write quick. *Mention this paper.* **FRENCH DYE CO. Vassar, Mich**

RUBBER GOODS BY MAIL Ladies or Gents send for Free catalogue. **Big Profits To Agents. A. U. BETTS & CO., 54 Water St. Toledo, O.**

MY WIFE CANNOT SEE HOW YOU DO IT AND PAY FREIGHT.

$14 Buys our 2 drawer walnut or oak **Improved High Arm Singer** sewing machine finely finished, nickel plated, adapted to light and heavy work; guaranteed for **10 Years;** with **Automatic Bobbin Winder, Self-Threading Cylinder Shuttle, Self-Setting Needle** and a complete set of **Steel Attachments;** shipped any where on **30 Day's Trial.** No money required in advance. 75,000 now in use. World's Fair Medal awarded machine and attachments. Buy from factory and save dealer's and agent's profits. **FREE** Cut This Out and send to-day for machine or large free catalogue, testimonials and Glimpses of the World's Fair. **OXFORD MFG. CO. 342 Wabash Ave. CHICAGO, ILL.**

AGENTS WANTED

to sell **Lace Curtains** to consumers direct from the factory. Write for illustrated catalogue mailed free. **Big Commission,** large sales. NORTH BRITISH LACE MILLS, 115 Worth Street, New York.

PILLOW SHAMS AND BED SETS.

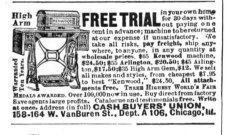

THE LADIES' Standard Magazine

SHOULD BE IN EVERY HOUSEWIFE'S HANDS.

IT WILL TEACH HER HOW TO . . . .

DRESS HERSELF AND DRESS HER CHILDREN
WISELY AND WELL . . . .

IT COSTS NO MORE TO DRESS WELL THAN OTHERWISE. IT ACTUALLY COSTS LESS IF THE STANDARD PATTERNS ARE USED . . . .

For 10 cents EXTRA
WE WILL SEND A COPY OF OUR LARGE CATALOGUE, CURRENT ISSUE. REGULAR PRICE, 20 CENTS.

THEY ARE PREFERRED BY THE LEADING DRESS-MAKERS — THEY REQUIRE VERY LITTLE REFITTING .

The Ladies' Standard Magazine . . . . costs but Fifty Cents a year. A book Every Month. Postage Paid by the Publishers to any part of the United States, Canada, Newfoundland or Mexico. 50 cents extra (for postage) must be added to each subscription for any other foreign country.

. . . ADDRESS . . .

STANDARD FASHION COMPANY,
342 West Fourteenth Street, New York.

The attractive figures above show two styles of costumes for bicycling.   The first, in cloth, braid-trimmed, is worn with a silk blouse, the second, requiring only a chemisette of linen or silk to fill in the neck, as the jacket is double-breasted.   The first figure illustrates Bicycling Costume, No. 2124 ; the second consists of the double-breasted Eton Jacket, No. 2046, and Divided Skirt Bloomers, No. 2148.   Both costumes are described on page 103.

The first figure here shown illustrates the back view of Bicycling Costume, No. 2124, showing the adjustment of the circular hip-piece which is designed to conceal the outlines of the figure, as the skirt beneath is scant. The second illustration shows the Divided Skirt Bloomers, No. 2148, and Eton Jacket, No. 1934, worn with a silk blouse. Each of the riders wears a jaunty cap, cut by Pattern, No. 1353. Both costumes are described on page 104.

Two charming street toilettes are here shown, the first combining Ladies' Wrap, No. 2142, and Serpentine Skirt, No. 2037. Brown satin and novelty cloth were used in making, with a rich garniture of lace. Back and front views of wrap again shown on page 79.

The second illustration is a Ladies' Ulster, No. 2120, suitable for traveling or as a mackintosh, as it is made without sleeves. Slate gray waterproof, lined with plain gray taffeta silk, were the materials selected. For a full description of the garments shown on both figures see page 71.

THE LADIES STANDARD MAGAZINE

VOL. XI. No. 2.   APRIL, 1894.   NEW YORK CHICAGO

Fashions and Fabrics.

THE PROMISE of Easter-tide brings its usual suggestions of downy little chicks gazing in unfathomable yet stupid wonder at the fragments of their late habitation, and an influx of dainty hats, bonnets and smart, jaunty wraps for early Spring wear. The bonnets somehow remind one of the chicks, inasmuch as they greet us at the shops in a guise so new, so tasteful and at such a variance with the heavy and sombre head coverings which we have worn during the Winter. About wraps, too, there is an airiness which seems gleeful in its freedom from the weight of heavy fabrics, and they are "brave in ribbons," jets, lace and intricate flutes and frills.

MOIRE is growing more and more popular, and continues to be used for all manner of garments. It enters into various combinations or is used alone, and of such a range are its colorings and designs that one is bewildered in a selection. Taffetas, glace and a rich *gros grain* are still favorites, and while the changeable effects of last season are subdued and modified they will still have no peers for this. Foulards are no more, and the long wail of the oppressed is at last silenced in a surety that one may this Summer be fashionably gowned, and *not* in foulard.

THE Eton jacket has not as yet passed away, and a good make opens over a distinctive waistcoat, braided to resemble a Swiss belt, and also in lines from the neck, ending on the bust in curves. Many women find ties and waistcoats mannish and objectionable, and for them have been introduced a double-breasted bodice, opening with one large revers on the right and a smaller one on the left, which close in to the neck band. The skirt with this is quite plain, having trouser pockets at the side. The rounded basque of a double-breasted bodice is new. This style can be left open, or fastens at the waist with three buttons, and has a velvet collar and flap pockets. There are introduced some broad box pleats into the front of the skirt ; the jacket had a turn-down collar and opened over a waistcoat.

THERE are some new and uncommon materials, among them a dull red, splashed with white, the splashes oval ; and it made a pretty country house gown, which many women call now one of the three-day-visit gowns. Checks are ordered freely, some with double lines, but all of a fancy character. The outer jackets are made with check linings, beaver collars and facings, and some, besides double revers, are made with hoods. As to the cut of skirts and bodices, three and a half yards is considered a comfortable width ; double box pleats are frequently introduced at the back, a great object being to render the skirt as narrow as possible toward the top. Small cross cut gores at the hem frequently widen the lower portion. Bodices, in contradistinction to jackets, are often worn, cut in tabs at the waist ; and black silk, cloth and jet seem to find their way onto many plain cloths by way of trimming. Brown is still peculiarly the fashion, especially when trimmed with black.

TO put it in the poetic—the ball gown is the rose of all gowns. Like the rose, it has an ever-pleasing charm and an evanescent glory, a splendor and beauty distinctive and complete. To carry the parallel further—just as violets, orchids and mignonette engage the popular fancy for a time, yet never really displace the American Beauty rose, so tailor-made costumes, the paddock and reception dresses, although they absorb special attention from time to time, never interfere with the continuous creation of enchanting costumes for the ball.

ONE of all colors was pink ; most cheerful of shades. It was moire just the appetizing pink of a luscious, ripe watermelon. The decollete bodice was adorned with a wide black satin scarflike belt which was drawn across the front in a pleasingly intricate fold, one end going diagonally up, losing itself under the armhole, and the other end was artistically fastened underneath the upper band of the black satin. The effect was a bit like a surplice. The basque in the back was finished with three wide points nearly six inches long. The striking feature of this waist was the pretty collarette of white satin that encircled the corsage. It was edged with a narrow band of sable above which was inwrought in jet a threadlike embroidered tracery, lacelike in its delicacy Above this jet embroidery was another narrow band of sable. The skirt was simple, its distinctive feature being the three bias breadths that were inserted in the back. It was edged with a little flounce of white satin bordered with narrow bands of sable and embroidered with the dainty jet design similar to the collarette on the corsage. If the one who wears it adorns the corsage with a bunch of mignonette, the combination of coloring is simply soul-satisfying.

BERTHAS are being relegated to the past, the severely characteristic revers taking their place. These revers are deeply peaked and cross one another over the chest. Notwithstanding their severe aspect they are undoubtedly pleasing and becoming to most figures. Oddly shaped, as well as slashed ornamental pieces are much used in the decoration of the modish waists and basques. Hip garnitures continue to find favor and panniers are being introduced gradually and will be in high favor with slender beauties ; plump maidens will look askance at them, fearing ponderous effects, but if worn judiciously they will add a pleasing softness to the full figure. No prevailing style is ever wholly unbecoming unless misused.

PARURE is a potent rival to velours-du-Nord, having a cotton back and being thinner and more easily manipulated. It is used for mantles and for trimming gowns, and is to be had in all the colorings of velvet. It will stand rain and is unrivaled in combination with other materials. One of the new woolens resembles shot Astrakhan in curious combinations of color, such as magenta, green and blue, and this also was draped with velvet. The French watered velvets are particularly noticeable from the exquisite softness of the watering.

A NEW and pretty notion for bridal gowns is a trail of orange blossoms carried down each seam and forming a tasseled end. This looks charming if allowed to drop at the hem over a full lace flounce. Chiffon is employed for the vest of the bodice. A trail of orange blossoms bordering each side starts from a large bow at the neck. Talking of bridal gowns reminds me how often bridesmaids now wear white, relieved by a color, such as light maize on white figured satin.

———

THERE is no doubt that with the present style of bodices, the cape is the best wrap, and it will be seen in various guises for Spring wear. They will be made chiefly of velvet and are very full, quite short and richly decorated. Many of them are made with long stoles or tabs reaching below the knees. Fur will be worn late into the season, for we are yearly growing more like our English and Canadian cousins in this respect.

———

A GOWN gracefully worn by a well-known tragic actress was of the new satin-faced velvet, sapphire blue on the surface, with the reverse of Nile green ; stripes of green, gold and pale blue, looking like baby ribbon run on with one edge unconfined, were woven upon the surface with unique effect ; bunches of baby ribbon of the same colors were placed down one side in the guise of a cascade, the other consisting of a panel of black lace over gold color ; the bodice was of gold satin entirely covered with black lace, and confined by a girdle of Egyptian gold.

———

WALKING suits are almost invariably made with the medium flaring skirt and full three-quarter coat ; the tight-fitting ones are the most stylish. Green, a rich garnet, plum inclining to purple are the leading shades in vogue just now. Blue has lost some of its prestige on account of its universal adoption for seaside suits the past Summer. The lower edges of skirts are to be once more finished with heavy cord, a pretty and protective arrangement.

———

ACCORDION-PLEATED tea-gowns are among the newest things ; one of particular beauty was of gold-colored India silk. It had a tunic reaching to the knees, and laid in fine accordion pleating over an under bodice of gathered silk ; black Chantilly and black satin ribbon relieved the intensity of the color.

———

AN evening gown which was quite a picture, had a cerise velvet petticoat ; over this a black grounded brocade with red flowers, and some light pink-and-gold foliage. The overskirt of this was cut in four large points, reaching above the red velvet petticoat almost to the hem. The low bodice had a waistband of the same velvet with three folds, and the puffed sleeves, formed with two puffs and lace ruffles, were of velvet, reaching to the elbows, the bodice being of brocade, cut somewhat square on the shoulders, and trimmed with a Medicis cape of lace over soft folds of velvet. This was quite effective and suitable for a woman of regal appearance.

———

A MORNING gown made of black moiré, bordered with sable, headed by jet, had a most important bodice. This was also made of moiré, the basque, cut on the round, was attached at the waist line, the rest of the bodice as far as the bust being entirely worked in jet, the trimming forming a pointed corslet, headed by narrow sable ; the sleeves had gigantic pufflings, intermixed with fur and jet, and over the shoulders was a pointed lace bertha, tucked in beneath the fur so that the corners appeared below. It was a most beautiful dress and one suitable for wear late into the season, when a twist of velvet can replace the fur edging. A gray cloth was made in much the same style, but with steel embroidery and gray velvet instead of fur.

———

THE long basques are decidedly coming in. An emerald green velvet has been made in this way, with white satin revers in front, trimmed in gold galon intermixed with emeralds. This was to be worn with a white satin skirt and large green velvet puffed sleeves. A new mode of cutting the skirt was demonstrated in a black velvet gown arranged en princesse as far as the train was concerned. It had apparently no fullness at the back, this being hidden underneath, but in such a way that a great width and spring were given to the flow of it. The bodice was trimmed with a fichu of white lace, and white lace was ruffled at the neck.

———

AN evening toilette for a lady of stout proportion was admirably designed. It had a bodice of black merveilleux, with one revers of this and one of velvet. The vest, made of terra-cotta silk, was gathered horizontally down the centre, a heart-shaped transparent piece of lace at the back. There was a great amount of handsome lace upon it, and elbow sleeves with large lace ruffles. The skirt was made of black lace embroidered in jet for the front, having a broad breadth of black satin introduced in the centre of the back.

———

THE skirts for large figures are frequently draped, being drawn up slightly on the hips apparently to show an under petticoat. Most of us suffer from the inconvenience of pockets placed in an inaccessible portion of the dress, but there is now a way of getting over this, and enabling them to be placed at the side, a slight box pleat hiding them, and apparently forming a portion of the skirt drapery.

———

A BLACK satin for evening had been trimmed with ombré yellow velvet, the sleeves formed of black chiffon and the ombré velvet, while a cream grounded chiné moire, with floral bouquets scattered all over it, opened over a front breadth of pink satin, a flounce of fine old Venetian point being drawn into three festoons at the hem, a point between each caught up with pink velvet. The bodice had a pointed stomacher of pink satin veiled with the lace, and the large double-puffed satin sleeves were caught up with diamond buckles.

———

AN extremely dainty basque, suitable for the house, evening or street wear, is high neck, but sleeveless ; the sleeves are inserted for out-of-door occasions. The lining is fitted by the usual front bust darts and is closed down the middle of the front Over this is arranged a perfectly plain vest facing which is attached on one side and arranged to fold over the closing, and be invisibly fastened on the other. The outer portion is in three pieces, a seamless back, fitted to the waist by two fine pleats, one on either side of the centre, and two fronts. These front pieces are laid in double surplice folds which slope from the shoulder and meet in a point at the lower edge. One odd feature is the shoulder decoration, which is a large diamond-shaped piece with the points coming down below the bust line in front, like little sharp jacket pieces, and similarly adjusted in the back. The points are trimmed off at the armhole and collar seam. The other points are a quaintly folded collarette with full frills at either edge, and square bretelles, finished with lace, the lower edge, coming down in a shallow point back and front, is finished by a narrow, upturned, bias fold.

———

ANOTHER jaunty waist has the outer sections adjusted to a fitted lining by tiny folds at the neck and drawn into the waist. A pretty decoration simulating a short square jacket is laid in two forward-turning pleats from the shoulder seams. This is a particularly good design for this Spring when such a quantity of deep lace will be used. A novelty in this basque is the little epaulette straps which come from the collar seam to overlap the sleeve line. A circular bib-piece lies under the collar back and front and forms a pretty finish. The waist ends at the belt line and has a bias folded girdle terminating in a buckle fold.

LADIES' STREET TOILETTE.

(For illustration see page 68.)

Nos. 2142 and 2037.—The two garments here tastefully combined are Ladies' Wrap, No. 2142, and Ladies' Skirt (with Serpentine Drapery), No. 2037. The patterns are in eight sizes, thirty to forty-four inches bust and twenty to thirty-four inches waist measure, respectively, and will require for the medium size three and three-quarters yards of material twenty-two, three yards combined with figured novelty cloth buttonholed at the edges; while Venetian lace forms an effective decoration for the skirt and wrap. Price of wrap, 25 cents; skirt, 35 cents.

LADIES' ULSTER.

(WITHOUT SLEEVES, SUITABLE FOR WATERPROOF.)

(For illustration see page 68.)

No. 2120.—One of the most serviceable garments of the season

No. 2127.—LADIES' BALL COSTUME. (See page 72.)

twenty-seven, one and five-eighths yard forty-four, or one and one-half yard fifty-four inches wide for the wrap, and nine and one-quarter yards of material twenty-two, six and five-eighths yards thirty-two, five and three-eighths yards forty-four, or four yards fifty-four inches wide, for the skirt. Brown satin was here is here pictured. The material chosen in this instance was slate gray waterproof cloaking, with lining of plain gray taffeta silk. The fronts are shaped loosely without darts and closed to knee depth with buttons and buttonholes. Cape portions are inserted in the side-back and shoulder seams covering the opening for the arm underneath; it is neatly finished at the neck with close-fitting straight and rolling revers collars.

The pattern is cut in eight sizes for ladies measuring from thirty to forty-four inches bust measure, and cost 35 cents. In making for the medium size it will require seven yards of material twenty-seven inches, four and three-quarters yards forty-four inches, or three and one-half yards fifty-four inches in width.

LADIES' BALL COSTUME.
(For illustration see page 71.)

No. 2127.—The exquisitely charming costume here portrayed will be one of the season's favorites, combining, as it does, many of the fashionable attributes of the present modes. A richly shaded, checkered and brocaded satin was used in making, with garniture of lace, chiffon, ribbon and ostrich pompons. Delicate

Nos. 2133 AND 2112.—LADIES' TOILETTE.   (See page 73.)

No. 2145.—LADIES' COSTUME.   (See page 74.)

Serge, heptonette, cravenette, rubber lined silk, homespun, pongee, etc., are suitable fabrics, and it may be made without lining if desired, a medium wide facing being sufficient finish.

This is an excellent wrap for Summer travel as it will protect its wearer from smoke and dust, and is still sufficiently loose to promote comfort and ease to the highest degree.

heliotrope, maize, apple green, blue and blanc d'Argent are the colors blended in the satin, the chiffon matching the green in color, the lace blanc d'Argent and the ribbon and pompons combining all the shades. Stylish panniers, a handsome front gore, graceful bretelles and short puffed sleeves are the noticeable attributes of this delightful gown. By referring to page 77, back and front views may be seen showing different development, and also as made with high neck and long sleeves.

The pattern is cut in eight sizes for ladies from thirty to forty-four inches bust measure, and costs 40 cents. To make for a lady of medium size it will require fifteen yards twenty-two, ten and one-half yards thirty-two, seven and three-quarters yards

LADIES' TOILETTE.

(For illustration see page 72.)

Nos. 2133 and 2112.—Quite pleasing is the combination of the new Spencer Waist, No. 2133, and Yoke Front Skirt (with Drapery omitted), No. 2112, shown in this illustration.

A very beautiful novelty silk of turquoise blue was used in

Nos. 2125 and 2135.—Ladies' Toilette. (See page 74.)   Nos. 2134 and 2094.—Ladies' Toilette. (See page 75.)

forty-four, or six and one-eighth yards of material fifty-four inches in width. This costume is admirably adapted to make in moiré antique; satin, faille, rich brocades and velvet will be greatly favored amongst the more elaborate materials, while equally suitable are the dainty China and India silks, glace, taffetas, Henrietta, delaine, India mulls, Swiss muslin, crêpons, etc.

making with dainty ribbon garniture. The Spencer Waist, No. 2133, is shaped to the figure by shoulder and under-arm seams, fitting smoothly across the shoulders and bust; the fullness being drawn into position by tiny gathers in the front and back at the waist line. Three bands of ribbon slightly overlapping and closed at the throat with a tiny bow and jabot of lace form the dainty neck finish. Leg-o'-mutton sleeves trimmed with ribbon spaced perpendicularly around the wrist complete the waist. Back and front views may be seen by referring to page 82.

The pattern is cut in eight sizes for ladies from thirty to forty-four inches bust measure, and costs 20 cents. To make for a lady of medium size requires three and one-eighth yards twenty-two, three yards twenty-seven, two and one-half yards thirty-six, or two and one-eighth yards of material forty-four inches in width.

The Skirt, No. 2112, is shaped smoothly about the hips by a front yoke prettily decorated with ribbon, the back breadth falling straight and full; around the lower edge three rows of ribbon are applied with very stylish effect. A jaunty piece of ribbon encircles the waist and is tied in a careless bow at the front.

The pattern is cut in eight sizes for ladies from twenty to thirty-four inches waist measure, and costs 30 cents. To make in the medium size will require eleven yards twenty-two, seven and seven eighths yards thirty-two, five and one-half yards forty-four, or four and three-quarters yards of material fifty-four inches in width.

This pretty toilette is adaptable to a variety of charming materials, amongst which are the dainty ginghams, lawns, muslins, etc. Serge, cashmere, Henrietta, veiling, albatross and all the novelty weaves are equally suitable. Lace, velvet, appliqué, braid, gimp and various other trimmings may be used according to material chosen and individual taste.

Silk-weft ginghams are well adapted to this style of toilette and may serve for any occasion from afternoon wear to more pretentious affairs. They are so lovely in appearance, so easily adjusted to the figure and comparatively inexpensive as to promise great popularity.

LADIES' COSTUME.
(For illustration, see page 72.)

No. 2145.—This figure illustrates a very *chic* costume suitable for street and house wear. As represented it was handsomely developed in aubergine novelty goods and trimmed with silk and braiding. Other views showing different combinations may be seen on page 78.

The pattern is cut in eight sizes for ladies from thirty to forty-four inches bust measure, and costs 35 cents. To make for a lady of medium size it will require thirteen yards twenty-two, eight and one-eighth yards thirty-two, six yards forty-four, or five and one-quarter yards of material fifty-four inches in width. Any desired material or combination may be used as suggested by individual taste.

LADIES' TOILETTE.
(For illustration, p. 73.)

Nos. 2125 and 2135. —Two of our newest models, Ladies' Waist (with fitted lining), No. 2125, and Ladies' Skirt, No. 2135, are here charmingly associated, showing in their development the most fashionable material and very latest garniture. A beautiful brown moiré was the fabric chosen with trimmings of creamy white point Venise lace and moiré ribbon. The waist, other views of which are given on page 78, is shaped by shoulder and under-arm gores, and arranged upon a tight-fitting lining. Stylish epaulettes of lace ripple upon the leg-o'-mutton sleeves, a collar and

Y. A. K.
S. F. Co.

No. 2151.—LADIES' WATTEAU DRESS. (See page 76.)

jabot of lace forming an effective finish at the neck. The ribbon is twisted and applied in yoke shape above the bust, ending in a rosette bow upon the left shoulder. Perpendicular rows of ribbon coming from under the twist of ribbon, are looped gracefully at the waist line, the ends of which are of graduated lengths. The pattern is cut in eight sizes for ladies from thirty to forty-four inches bust measure, and costs 30 cents. To make for a lady of medium size it will require five and three-eighths yards twenty-two, three and three-quarters yards thirty-two, two and seven-eighths yards forty-four, or two and one-eighth yards of material fifty-four inches in width. Ladies' Skirt, No. 2135, is gracefully shaped by a wide front gore and back breadth ; five graduated slashes, through which the lace peeps forth flutteringly,

Nos. 2132 and 2135.—Ladies' Evening Toilette. (See page 76.)

are made in the front gore, dainty rosette bows emphasizing the effect.

The pattern is cut in eight sizes for ladies from twenty to thirty-four inches waist measure, and costs 25 cents. In making for a lady of medium size it will require seven and one-half yards twenty-two, five yards thirty-two, three and three-quarters yards forty-four or three and one-quarter yards of material fifty-four

inches in width. Henrietta, serge, delaine, novelty silk and wool mixture, brocade, satin, and also many of the thinner fabrics, such as gingham, lawn, batiste, etc., will all adapt themselves to the mode with exquisite results.

LADIES' TOILETTE.
(For illustration see page 73.)

Nos. 2134 and 2094, are here admirably associated in a street toilette which is equally suitable for home, visiting or carriage wear. Plain magenta, serge and black moiré were the materials used in this instance—a very effective and ultra fashionable combination. Ladies' Basque, No. 2134, is close fitting and formed to the figure by the regulation seams and darts. The peplum or skirt piece corresponds with the cape collar in shape and is

No. 2132.—Ladies' Evening Basque. (See page 77.)
(Showing Back View.)

extremely graceful in design. A high rolling collar completes the neck finish and the sleeves are of the new leg-o'-mutton shape. Other views showing the basque made entirely of one material are given on page 80.

The pattern is cut in eight sizes for ladies from thirty to forty-four inches bust measure, and costs 30 cents. To make for a lady of medium size it will require five and one-eighth yards twenty-four, four and one-half yards thirty-two, three and one-eighth yards forty-four, or two and five-eighths yards of material fifty-four inches in width.

No. 2094, Ladies' Two-seamed Skirt, is here used without the circular ripple flounce, a blocked flounce substituting it, matching in character the stylish decoration of the basque. A broad front gore and plain back breadth flares the skirt gracefully towards its lower edge, the upper part fitting smoothly around the hips.

The pattern is cut in eight sizes for ladies from twenty to thirty-four inches waist measure, and costs 30 cents. To make for a lady of medium size it will require eight yards twenty-two, five and five-eighths yards thirty-two, three and seven-eighths yards forty-four, or three and one-quarter yards of material fifty-four inches in width.

Cashmere, Henrietta, camel's-hair, cheviot, French novelties, satin or rich brocades will make up well by this mode. The garniture may be of lace, novelty gauze, velvet, or of the same material used in making; a contrasting material, however, will give a more stylish effect.

LADIES' WATTEAU DRESS.
(For illustration see page 74.)

No. 2151.—This illustration portrays a charming dress as made of dainty beurre Pompadour brocade with garniture of point

No. 2142.—LADIES' WRAP. (See page 77.)

d'Venise and aubergine velvet. The waist is cut open in V-shape back and front exposing the neck prettily, and the sleeves are very bouffant and banded just above the elbow. A graceful Watteau pleat is formed at the back between the shoulders, falling free to the edge of the skirt.

The pattern is cut in eight sizes for ladies from thirty to forty-four inches bust measure, and costs 30 cents. To make for a lady of medium size it will require twelve and three-eighths yards twenty-two, seven and three-quarters yards thirty-two, or six and one-eighth yards of material forty-four inches in width.

All evening materials will make up charmingly by this exquisite mode ; also delicate challis, batiste, silk warp gingham, etc.

Although this is very suitable for dressy occasions it is a remarkably sweet design for house or garden parties, when it is effectively developed in silk-weft gingham, dotted Swiss, grena-

dine, silk mull, flowered or plain silk with lace or ribbon garniture. Lace is especially pretty.

LADIES' EVENING TOILETTE.
(For illustration see page 75.)

Nos. 2132 and 2135.—In this illustration Ladies' Evening Basque, No. 2132, is very attractively associated with Ladies' Skirt, No. 2135. The materials chosen in the development were green and rose shaded moiré showing pinhead watered dots and sprays of neutral tinted flowers, with garniture of lace, chiffon and ribbon. The Basque, No 2132 back and front views of which may be seen by referring to page 77, is shaped over a fitted lining, the right front overlapping the left and vice versa in the back. It is gracefully short over the hips, tapering to slight points back and front. The neck is cut quite low and the opening partially filled with a triple box pleating of chiffon ; charmingly full sleeves, ending in deep elbow frills and strapped from shoulder to elbow with ribbon, complete this artistic basque.

The pattern is cut in eight sizes for ladies from thirty to forty-four inches bust measure, and costs 25 cents. To make for a lady of medium size requires three and three-quarters yards twenty-two, two and one-half yards thirty-two, two yards forty-

No. 2141.—LADIES' CIRCULAR CAPE WRAP. (See page 78.)

four, or one and five-eighths yard of material fifty-four inches in width.

Ladies' Skirt, No. 2135, is a two-seamed skirt having a broad front gore and plain back breadth. The front gore is cut in five graduated slashes and fluffy gores of lace inserted, each one headed by a butterfly bow of ribbon. Other views are given on page 81.

The pattern is cut in eight sizes for ladies from twenty to thirty-four inches waist measure, and costs 25 cents. To make for a lady of medium size it will require seven and one-half yards twenty-two, five yards thirty-two, three and three-quarters yards forty-four, or three and one-quarter yards of material fifty-four inches in width.

Many handsome materials may be chosen in making by this mode, amongst which velvet, satin and brocade will be favored.

LADIES' EVENING BASQUE.

(For illustration see p. 75.)

No. 2132.—A very tasteful and extremely stylish model for an evening basque is portrayed on this figure, other views of which are here given. In this instance novelty figured moiré with dainty ribbon and lace garniture was used in the construction.

The pattern is cut in eight sizes for ladies from thirty to forty-four inches bust measure, and costs 25 cents. To make for a lady of medium size it will require three and three-quarters yards

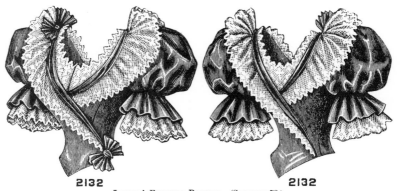

2132   2132
Ladies' Evening Basque. (See page 78.)

for ball toilettes and will be much used in making up evening toilettes for seaside and country wear.

LADIES' WRAP.

(For illustration see page 76.)

No. 2142.—This dainty figure portrays a very graceful wrap suitable for early Spring wear; other views may be seen by referring to page 79. The materials used in combination as illustrated were aubergine ladies' cloth, fancy velvet and jet edging.

The pattern is cut in eight sizes for ladies from thirty to forty-four inches bust measure, and costs 25 cents. To make for a lady of medium size it will require three and three-quarters yards twenty-two, three yards twenty-seven, one and five-eighths yards forty-four, or one and one-half yards of material fifty-four inches in width. Any desired fabric and combination may be used as suggested by individual taste.

Velvet promises to be very popular for Spring wraps and either plainly completed or trimmed with moiré ribbon or jet is suitable

2127   2127
Ladies' Costume. (See page 78.)

twenty-two, two and one-half yards thirty-two, two yards forty-four, or one and five-eighths yard fifty-four inches in width.

This attractive basque may be developed in all materials suitable

for this mode. Cloth the material of the costume with which it is to be worn, or moiré silk may also be effectively combined with lace or ribbon.

LADIES' CIRCULAR CAPE WRAP.
(For illustration see page 76.)

No. 2141.—This stylish figure illustrates an extremely pretty cape wrap, very suitable for opera or carriage wear. As represented, it was made of tabac moiré and lined throughout with taffeta glacé of the same shade. It is shaped in circular style with one seam at the centre of the back. The upper cape and ripple collar are similarly shaped. For other views see page 79.

The pattern is cut in eight sizes for ladies from thirty to forty-four inches bust measure, and costs 20 cents. To make for a lady of medium size three and one-half yards twenty-two, three and one-eighth yards twenty-seven, one and three-quarters yards forty-four, or one and five-eighths yard of material fifty-four inches wide will be necessary. Other materials may be used in making, such as cloth, cheviot, serge, velvet, brocade, satin, etc.

2125 **2125**
LADIES' WAIST (WITH FITTED LINING) (See page 79.)

forty-four, or one and five-eighths fifty-four with six and one-quarter yards of lace for garniture. Price of pattern, 25 cents.

LADIES' COSTUME.
(For illustration see page 77.)

No. 2127.—A very handsome and remarkably stylish costume is portrayed in this illustration, the small outline view showing it with short sleeves and the neck cut decollete, for evening and reception wear. As pictured, the materials used in making were plain and brocaded silk of a rich petunia shade, velvet a shade darker and point guipure lace. The basque is formed with the regulation seams and darts, it is curved over the hips and slightly pointed in the front and back. Very stylish circular bretelles ripple in graceful billows upon the shoulders continuing smoothly to points at the centre of the back and front. Charmingly bouffant is the dainty puff arranged at the top of the sleeves. ending in a frill at the bend of the elbow ; from elbow to wrist the sleeves are in coat shape style overlaid with velvet ; lace tastefully applied in the form of a cuff adds a pretty finish at the wrist. Overlaid velvet in yoke form, below which the silk is shirred tapering to a point in V-shape, are the noticeable features of the front arrangement. The skirt has a front gore of velvet handsomely trimmed with lace, tiny panniers surmount the side gores which are made of the brocade and the train of plain silk is straight and gracefully full.

The pattern is cut in eight sizes for ladies from thirty to forty-four inches bust measure, and costs 40 cents. To make for a lady of medium size it will require fifteen yards twenty-two, ten and one-half yards thirty-two, seven and three-quarters yards forty-four, or six and one-eighth yards of material fifty-four inches in width. If made of a combination as portrayed five yards of brocade twenty-two, six and seven-eighths yards plain silk and three yards of velvet will be necessary, with one and three-quarters yard wide and one-half yard narrow lace for

LADIES' EVENING BASQUE.
(For illustration see page 77.)

No. 2132.—Silk and lace was used in making the charming evening basque here portrayed ; other fabrics may be used as desired. Velvet, brocades and satins will be greatly favored, while the more simple veiling, albatross, etc., will be equally suitable ; chiffon, tulle, and embroidered net are pretty substitutes for lace garniture. The basque is shaped snugly to the figure, the right side overlapping the left in the front and finished with a tiny butterfly bow at the left side, and in the back the left side overlaps the right. Full puff sleeves of the Empire style, finished with a deep frill under which a fall of lace is gathered, complete this artistic mode with exquisite grace.

The pattern is cut in eight sizes for ladies from thirty to forty-four inches bust measure. To make for a lady of medium size it will require three and three quarters yards twenty-two, two and one-half yards thirty-two, two

2145 **2145**
LADIES' COSTUME. (See page 79.)

garniture. Other materials may be chosen in making this costume, such as novelty silk and wool, or all wool mixtures, silk, satin, cashmere or Henrietta; passementerie, rich braiding, appliqué, ribbon, etc., will be pretty decorations.

LADIES' WAIST, WITH FITTED LINING.
(For illustration see page 78.)

No. 2125.—Corail satin, figured in white, with trimming of white lace was used in making this neat and serviceable waist, as

2141   2141
LADIES' CIRCULAR CAPE WRAP.

shown in the illustration. It is arranged over a fitted lining, and although perfectly smooth and plain across the shoulders and bust it is gracefully loose below and will look remarkably well on slender figures. The lace is applied in pointed yoke shape and gathered in a flaring epaulette over the leg-o'-mutton sleeves. A medium broad belt completes the adjustment.

The pattern is cut in eight sizes for ladies from thirty to forty-four inches bust measure, and costs 30 cents. To make for a lady of medium size it will require five and three-eighths yards twenty-two, three and three-quarters yards thirty-two, two and seven-eighths yards forty-four, or two and one-eighth yards of material fifty-four inches in width. If made as represented five and one-eighth yards twenty-two, with three and one-eighth yards of lace, one quarter of a yard in width, will be necessary. China or India silk, taffeta, glacé, pongee, cambric, gingham, mull, lawn, or any light-weight novelty mixture are suitable fabrics for making. This waist may be worn with all the modish skirts and will be much favored for outing as well as home wear.

LADIES' COSTUME.
(For illustration see page 78.)

No. 2145.—This illustration portrays a stylish and very useful costume which is well adapted for the promenade, shopping, calling or for house wear It admits of many handsome combinations both of color and material; in this instance it was made of an extremely happy combination; nut brown wale serge and chamois cloth were the materials used. The basque fits the figure snugly in the back to just below the waist line, where it is shaped into graceful flutes. The fronts are prettily rounded and open to expose the tight-fitting vest underneath; at the throat stylish cascade revers are arranged and the neck is finished with a high rolling collar. Slashed sleeve-caps add a dignified appearance to the leg-o'-mutton sleeves. The skirt is gored to flare stylishly, having for its simple decoration an inserted panel of the chamois

cloth, on each side of which handsomely wrought tortoise-shell buttons are placed in tailor-made style. The pattern is cut in eight sizes for ladies from thirty to forty-four inches bust measure, and costs 35 cents. To make for a lady of medium size it will require thirteen yards twenty-two, eight and one-eighth yards thirty-two, six yards forty-four, or five and one-quarter yards of material fifty-four inches in width, or, if made as represented, five and one-half yards forty, with two yards twenty-four inches wide will be necessary. Camel's-hair, ladies' cloth, cheviot, crêpon, Henrietta, cashmere, Thibet, gingham, lawn, percale, batiste, etc., may all be used in making by this mode.

LADIES' CIRCULAR CAPE WRAP.

No. 2141.—This is a very useful and attractive wrap; it will be found quite an addition to the season's wardrobe and handy for all incidental occasions, especially for wear on cool Summer evenings. As portrayed, silver-gray ladies' cloth was used in making. It is shaped by a centre back seam and is in circular style flaring prettily about the figure. The upper cape is cut in similar fashion, a standing ripple collar completing the stylish effect.

The pattern is cut in eight sizes for ladies from thirty to forty-four inches bust measure, and costs 20 cents. To make for a lady of medium size it will require three and one-half yards twenty-two, three and one-eighth yards twenty-seven, one and three-quarters yard forty-four, or one and five-eighths yard of material fifty-four inches in width.

The upper cape and collar may be of a contrasting color and fabric if desired; velvet, brocade, moiré, rep silk, serge, cheviot, diagonal or any cloaking material may be used by this mode. The upper and lower capes are usually lined with silk or satin of

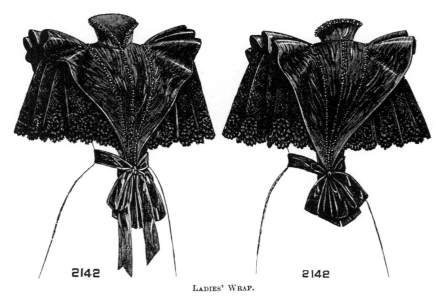

2142   2142
LADIES' WRAP.

the same or an effectively contrasting shade. Bright linings are not seen in the best models.

LADIES' WRAP.

No. 2142.—A very delightful wrap is here pictured which admits of a variety of charming combinations and effects; as portrayed it was effectively developed in moiré antique of a rich tabac color, black lace and moiré ribbon.

The pattern is cut in eight sizes for ladies from thirty to forty four inches bust measure, and costs 25 cents. To make for a lady of medium size it will require three and three-quarters yards twenty-two, three yards twenty-seven, one and five-eighths yard forty-four, or one and one-half yard of material fifty-four inches in width. If made as represented, two and three-quarters yards of moiré, two yards lace flouncing and three and one-quarter yards of ribbon will be necessary.

Serge, camel's-hair, ladies' cloth, brocade, satin or velvet, are all admirably suited to this mode.

LADIES' BASQUE.

No. 2134. — Polka dotted novelty silk was used in making this stylish basque portrayed in this illustration. It is shaped to the figure by the regulation number of seams and bias darts; the closing is effected down the centre of the front with buttons and buttonholes. The sleeves are in the newest leg-o'-mutton shape, having the under-arm seam gathered from the elbow bend to the arm's eye which adds a more gracious fullness to the upper part. Shapely peplums or hip-pieces cut *en forme* and matching the cape collar in design are attached to the basque with charming effect. A

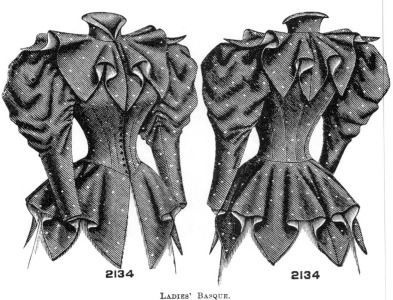

2134   **2134**

LADIES' BASQUE.

high collar rolling softly at its free edges completes the neck finish. The pattern is cut in eight sizes for ladies from thirty to forty-four inches bust measure, and costs 30 cents. To make for a lady of medium size it will require five and one-eighth yards twenty-four, four and one-half yards thirty-two, three and one-eighth yards forty-four, or two and five-eighths yards of material fifty-four inches in width, with two and three-eighths yards of silk twenty-four inches wide to line peplum and cape collar.

Serge, camel's-hair, Henrietta, llama, delaine, pongee, moiré, gingham, batiste, brilliante, lawns, etc., are excellent materials for making.

LADIES' WATTEAU DRESS.

No. 2151. — A Watteau dress made of satin-striped material, geranium red in color, and decorated with black lace and moiré ribbon is here pictured. This charming dress is especially adapted for an afternoon tea, but will be favored for evening wear as well. It is made with a slight train, the Watteau is gathered and attached to the waist just below the V-shaped opening at the back of the neck. The back of the body is shaped by the usual seams and a Spencer arrangement is used in the front where it is closed invisibly. Full puff elbow sleeves complete this delightful gown. Moiré ribbon belts the waist and is tied in a jaunty bow at the side, the long ends falling nearly to lower edge.

The pattern is cut in eight sizes for ladies from thirty to forty-four inches bust measure, and costs 30 cents. To make for a lady of medium size it will require twelve and three-eighths yards twenty-two, nine and five-eighths yards twenty-seven, seven and three-quarters yards thirty-two, or six and one-eighth yards of material forty-four inches in width; if made as represented three and one-half yards wide lace for zouave and sleeves and one yard narrow for the neck will be necessary.

Pongee, China and India silk, silk novelties, satin, moiré Française, brocades or challis, llama, nun's-veiling, albatross, crêpon, etc., are all admirable materials for making. Dotted Swiss is a very suitable material to develop this mode, and may be finished by Swiss frills or lace. Swiss frills will be used to finish a number of Summer materials.

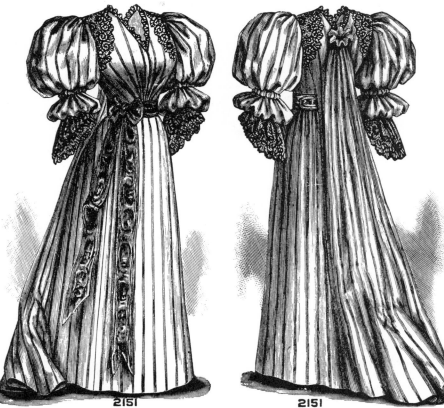

2151   **2151**

LADIES' WATTEAU DRESS.

LADIES' OUTING JACKET.

No. 2146.—Portrayed in this illustration is a charmingly comfortable jacket suitable for many occasions and especially well adapted for bicycling, tennis, etc. It may be made of any light-weight woolen material sufficiently warm to afford necessary protection after becoming over-heated from the exercise; homespun, serge or flannel will be most generally used. As shown here it was made of gray serge neatly finished with machine stitching. The outline view shows a plain coat sleeve substituting the leg-o'-mutton sleeve, as many bicyclists prefer this style. The back is seamless

LADIES' OUTING JACKET.

and drawn into the waist by gathers held into position by a strap; loose double-breasted fronts and an under-arm gore complete the shaping. A turn-over notched revers collar finishes the neck.

The pattern is cut in eight sizes for ladies from thirty to forty-four inches bust measure, and costs 25 cents. To make for a lady of medium size it will require three and three-quarter yards twenty-seven, two and one-quarter yards forty-four, or one and five-eighths yard of material fifty-four inches in width.

LADIES' SKIRT.

No. 2135.—A very modish skirt is here given with which any of the new basques or waists may be worn satisfactorily The materials used in making, as shown in the illustration, were prune novelty silk and mirror velvet. A wide front gore and plain back breadth are the principal features of this skirt, the garniture consisting of five inserted gores of the velvet, which, if preferred, may be made more ample.

The pattern is cut in eight sizes for ladies from twenty to thirty-four inches waist measure, and costs 25 cents. To make for a lady of medium size it will require seven and one-half yards twenty-two, five yards thirty-two, three and three-quarter yards forty-four, or three and one quarter yards of material fifty-four inches in width, or if made as represented three and three-quarters

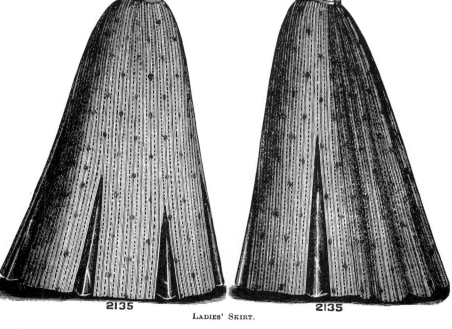

LADIES' SKIRT.

yards forty with one and three-eighths yard of velvet. This skirt may be made throughout of one material or in any combination suggested by individual taste, but two materials will show the mode to its best advantage, especially of silk and wool, or wool and velvet.

LADIES' SPENCER WAIST.

(For illustration p. 82.)

No. 2133.—An effective waist and one combining ease and grace is here shown as made up in pale blue and white striped wash silk, but any soft material such as crêpe, crêpon, albatross, nuns' veiling, challis, gingham, crêpon zephyr, batiste, Chambery, lawn or any preferred material may be used with equally good effect. This is a charming waist for Spring and Summer wear, being comfortable and at the same time shapely of design; it fits smoothly over the bust and is joined to a belt at the waist, giving symmetry and outline to the figure. A plain standing collar forms a neat and simple finish to the neck; the sleeve is of the popular leg-o'-mutton style which falls in its own graceful folds to the elbow.

The pattern is cut in eight sizes, from thirty to forty-four inches bust measure, and will require for a lady of medium size three and one-eighth yards of material twenty-two, three yards twenty-seven, two and one-half yards thirty-six, or two and one-eighth yards forty-four inches wide, and costs 20 cents. This dainty waist is again shown in a figure view on page 72.

LADIES' NORFOLK JACKET.

(For illustration p. 82.)

No. 2150.—Figured novelty goods was used in making the jacket here portrayed, the shaping of which is accomplished over a tightly fitted lining; three box pleats arranged at the back and front, and an under-arm gore are the principal features of this charming mode. Leg-o'-mutton sleeves, a turn-down collar and natty little belt complete this comfortable jacket, which will be found a very convenient adjunct in the season's wardrobe; it is also exceedingly suitable for outdoor recreations, such as bicycling, tennis, etc.

The pattern is cut in eight sizes for ladies from thirty to forty-four inches bust measure, and costs 25 cents. To make for a lady of medium size it will require four yards twenty-seven, three and seven-eighths yards thirty-two, two and three-quarters yards forty-four, or two and three-eighths yards of material fifty-four inches in width. Other materials may be used in making, among which dainty check cheviots and all wool novelties will be much favored; later in the season ginghams and launderable fabrics will obtain popularity.

LADIES' YOKE PETTICOAT without Darts.

No. 2130.—An exceedingly comfortable petticoat is here shown as made of silver-gray striped mohair. Front, side gores and a plain back breadth shape the skirt part freely about the limbs; a medium deep yoke fitting it snugly at the top. Other materials may be chosen in making, and it may have a foot trimming of lace or tiny ruffles of silk if preferred. Pongee, taffeta, glacé, gingham, lawn, etc., will be much favored. The pattern is cut in eight sizes for ladies measuring from twenty to thirty-four inches waist, and thirty-six to fifty inches hip measure. To make for a lady of medium size it will require five and seven-eighths yards twenty-

2150   2150
Ladies' Norfolk Jacket.   (See page 81.)

two, four and three-quarters yards twenty-seven, three and three-quarters yards thirty-six, or three and one-eighth yards of material fifty-four inches in width. Price of pattern, 25 cents. This mode is also suitable for cambric or muslin, with trimmings of lace, needlework or embroidery.

LADIES' BICYCLING TROUSERS.
(BLOOMER OR ZOUAVE STYLE.)
(For illustration see page 83.)

No. 2123.—Dark-blue cravenette was selected in making this serviceable and sensible garment, which is one of the most successful of all our bicycling models. The bloomer, or zouave style is recommended in glowing terms by ladies who ride, and this style is pronounced safe, elegant and comfortable beyond compare. For touring trips it is indispensable, and is then accompanied by any skirt, which is rolled up and carried so as to be in readiness when required for wear in the hotels or whenever the riders stop for rest. The fullness is disposed in small pleats around the belt, which is buttoned each side a little beyond the hip line. The lower hems are run through with strong elastic and are then kept in position below the knee. Long leggings or English stockings are worn with these trousers.

The pattern is cut in six sizes for ladies

measuring from twenty to thirty inches waist measure, and requires to make for a lady of medium size four and three-eighths yards of material twenty-seven, three and one-quarter yards forty-four,

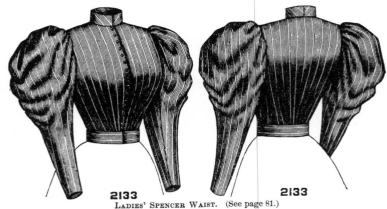

2133   2133
Ladies' Spencer Waist.   (See page 81.)

or two and one-eighth yards fifty-four inches in width, with five-eighths yard of elastic braid, and eight buttons. Price, 20 cents. Serge, cravenette, flannel, cloth, Jersey cloth, waterproof, English weaves and similar materials suitable for outdoor wear may be used in making.

LADIES' BICYCLING COSTUME.
(For illustration see page 83.)

No. 2124.—As shown in this illustration this suitable and attractive costume was made of hunters' green wale serge and polka dotted China silk, with trimming of wide and narrow braid. A shirt blouse of the silk is jauntily emphasized by a prettily formed Eton jacket, finished with broad revers collar. The peplum or hip-piece, is arranged on the belt and extends around the waist from each side of the box pleat in the centre of the skirt front, one seam only shaping the skirt at the back. The sleeves are of the leg-o'mutton order, quite full at the upper part, snugly fitting below the elbow, and finished with a neatly pointed cuff. The pattern is cut in eight sizes for ladies from thirty to forty-four inches bust measure, and costs 35 cents.

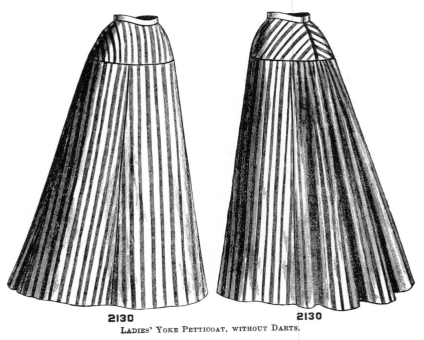

2130   2130
Ladies' Yoke Petticoat, without Darts.

To make for a lady of medium size it will require ten and five-eighths yards twenty-two, seven and three-quarters yards thirty-two, five and seven-eighths yards forty-four, or five and one-quarter

falls free. The upper and smaller view shows the elastic attached by a button on the outside and drawn around the ankle, the free end having a loop which is caught over the button, thus making

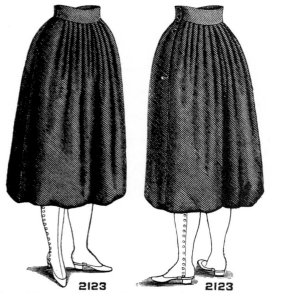

2123
LADIES' BICYCLING TROUSERS BLOOMER, OR ZOUAVE STYLE. (See p. 82.)

2148 **2148**
LADIES' DIVIDED SKIRT BLOOMERS.

yards of material fifty-four inches in width. In making of two materials, as represented in the illustration, five and three-quarters yards forty, with two yards of twenty-two and nine yards of wide and narrow braid respectively will be necessary.

Camel's - hair cheviot, cloth and homespun are excellent fabrics for making, and the most pleasing colors are blue, brown, steel gray or black; any neutral shade may be chosen. Glaring effects are to be avoided, as they are neither durable nor suitable.

LADIES' DIVIDED SKIRT BLOOMERS.
(USED FOR BICYCLING, MOUNTAIN CLIMBING AND CROSS SADDLE RIDING.)

No. 2148.—We here portray a comfortable and almost indispensable adjunct of the outing wardrobe. These bloomers will be worn with any of the blouse waists and also with the reefer and sack coats usually worn when bicycling. Gray flannel was used in the making as shown in this illustration, but navy blue, brown or black will be much used and cheviot, serge, camel's-hair and similar fabrics are suitable for making, also checked woolen materials. The left view shows the skirt gathered above the ankle with an elastic which is run through a casing on the inside and is invisible when the skirt

the frill finish preferred by many. The pattern is cut in six sizes for ladies from twenty to thirty inches waist measure, and costs 20 cents. To make for a lady of medium size it will require six yards of twenty-seven, or three and five-eighths yards of material forty four or fifty-four inches in width.

LADIES' CORKSCREW SLEEVE.
(WITH CLOSE LINING.)
(For Illustration see page 84.)

No. 2147. — This is a charmingly graceful sleeve and will be much favored in making both house and street toilettes. It is gathered full over the shoulder and at the elbow, giving a balloon effect to the upper part, the lower part having two seams in coat shape style. It may be made of the same material as the garment, or of a contrasting color and fabric if preferred.

The pattern is cut in four sizes for ladies measuring from eleven to seventeen inches around the largest part of arm, and costs 10 cents. To make in the thirteen-inch size it will require four and one half yards twenty-two, three and one-quarter yards twenty-seven, two and three-eighths yards thirty-six to forty-four, or two yards of material fifty-four inches in width, with one and one-half yard of twenty-seven-inch wide lining.

2124 **2124**
LADIES' BICYCLING COSTUME. (See page 82.)

LADIES' BICYCLING SKIRT.

No. 2155.—An exceedingly attractive bicycling skirt is here given which will obtain great popularity, as it affords protection against any objectionable exposure of the figure in wearing the bloomer suit which is fast gaining favor with tourists. The skirt, as portrayed here is made of nut-brown flannel. It is shaped in five-gore style, rather scant, but sufficiently ample for comfort; on the inner side of each seam are attached four rings through which ribbon is run these ribbons are brought through eyelets made at the waist, and are drawn together in a bunch and tied gracefully causing the skirt to fold in tunic fashion, and freeing the limbs from all restriction while riding or climbing. When walking or in the house these ribbons are untied and the skirt falls free, covering the bloomers completely.

The pattern is cut in six sizes for ladies from twenty to thirty inches waist measure, and costs 20 cents. To make for a lady of medium size it will require five and seven-eighths yards twenty-two, four and seven-eighths yards twenty-seven, three and three-eighths yards forty-four, or two and five-eighths yards of material fifty-four inches in width, with six and one-quarter yards of ribbon, and twenty rings. Silk or cambric blouses will be much worn with the skirt and an Eton jacket of the skirt material will add sufficient warmth on chilly days, and

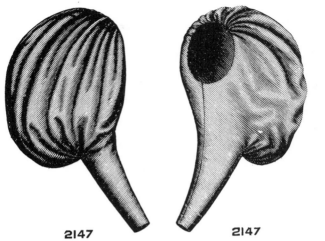

2147   2147
LADIES' CORKSCREW SLEEVE, WITH CLOSE LINING. (See page 83.)

LAST YEAR the picturesque crept into our raiment, this year it dominates it ! Hats, cloaks, dresses are all picturesque ; and if, in our desire for the picturesque, we sometimes overstep the narrow line which divides the sublime from the ridiculous, we are, after all, quite unconscious of the fact, and unconsciousness has its advantages. Do we not wear our sleeves hugely puffed outwards, until we look as broad as we are long ; our hats waved in outline until every natural curve is lost, and our necks and hips frilled with capes ; altogether over-burdening the upper part of our bodies with grandeur, weight and width, until our poor little extremities, which are all unhonored and unsung—I mean untrimmed and uncared for—look too absurdly insignificant to be allowed the honor of bearing our shoulders ?

But never mind, we are very happy. Fashion smiles upon our idiosyncrasies, and we flatter ourselves that in no period of history was ever costume so beautiful, and withal more reasonable than it is now. And maybe we are right, for, after all, our ancestresses were not patterns of wisdom.

———

THE tendency of Spring fashions is towards the broadening of the figure ; the wide revers, the flaring collars, the big ruffs, the drooping sleeves, and the lengthened shoulder seams counter-

2155

2155   2155   2155
LADIES' BICYCLING SKIRT.

when resting, thus making a very stylish suit. Serge, camel's-hair, tweed, homespun, cheviot and various all-wool novelties will make up very suitably by this mode. Sensible women will gladly adopt this style of skirt for shopping and tramps in muddy and stormy weather as it can be elevated with more ease and grace than the ordinary style.

balancing the full flaring skirts, and the new overdresses which, while graceful, add bulk to the figure.

———

AMONG the novelties for evening wear are collarettes of black "footing," edged with white inserting. They are about ten inches deep with double ruffles around the neck.

MISSES' COSTUME.

No. 2149.—A very delightful costume is here pictured made of violet challis prettily figured with garniture of lace and ribbon. It is gracefully shaped over a close fitting lining ; lace is overlaid at the neck in yoke fashion, the lower part of the sleeves are also overlaid with lace, large puffs form the upper part ending in elbow frills. The skirt is shaped to flare fashionably, and is decorated around its lower edge with ribbon tastefully bowed. For other views of this dainty costume see page 88.

The pattern is cut in four sizes for misses from ten to sixteen

MISSES' COSTUME.

No. 2137.—This illustration portrays a very graceful costume appropriate both for street and house wear. The materials chosen in this instance were delicate heliotrope novelty silk, moiré antique and point d'Venise of a rich beurre shade. Deep slashes are made at regular intervals across the lower part of front gore in which are inserted gores of moiré ; these gores may be made more ample if preferred. A sharply pointed bertha bretelle gives an artistic grace to the costume, and falls over the full puff at the top of the sleeves with charming effect. The lace is tastefully

No. 2149.—MISSES' COSTUME.

No. 2137.—MISSES' COSTUME.

years of age, and costs 30 cents. To make for a miss of fourteen it will require seven and one-half yards twenty-two, seven yards thirty-two, three and seven-eighths yards forty-four or three and one eighth yards of material fifty-four inches in width, with one and one-half yard of twenty-seven-inch waist lining.

Veiling, gingham, soft silks and all the dainty Spring and Summer fabrics will make up admirably by this mode.

Lace is a suitable decoration and may be used in profusion and with good effect. Point d'Venise, Irish point, or any delicate colored style may be selected. Ribbon or velvet are also used.

arranged about the neck, elbows and waist line. Garment views may be seen by referring to page 87.

The pattern is cut in four sizes for misses from ten to sixteen years of age, and costs 25 cents. To make in the fourteen year size it will require eight and one-quarter yards twenty-two, five and five-eighths yards thirty-two, four and three-eighths yards forty-four or three and three-eighths yards of material fifty-four inches in width.

Any of the seasonable combinations and materials will make up admirably by this mode.

MISSES' TOILETTE.

Nos. 2153 and 2139.—The charming figure here portrayed illustrates Misses' Toilette, consisting of Misses' Waist, No. 2153, again shown on page 88, and Misses' Skirt, No. 2139, again pictured on page 87.

The pattern of the waist is in four sizes for misses from ten to sixteen years of age, and will require for a miss of fourteen three and three-quarters yards of material twenty-two, three and three-eighths yards twenty-seven, two and seven-eighths yards thirty-

materials, such as crêpon, zephyr, silk, Chambery, percale, lawn, challis, delaine, albatross, nun's-veiling, etc., may be used with pleasing effect. This comfortable waist is fitted to the form by shoulder and under-arm seams and drawn to the waist by forward-turning pleats, giving symmetry and grace to the form. The closing is invisibly effected by means of hooks and loops in front.

No. 2154.—Misses' Cutaway Jacket.

Nos. 2153 and 2139.—Misses' Toilette.

This waist has large drooping puff sleeves, and is finished at the neck by a high collar, which is slightly rolled, giving freedom and grace to the appearance.

The skirt has small inserted gores which makes it a very desirable model, especially for out-door sports.

The pattern of this skirt is in five pieces—front, back and three small gores ; these are most effective when made up in a material contrasted with the rest of the skirt. They may be interlined with soft crinoline if desired. Silk, satin, moiré or velvet are often seen. These gores are sometimes widened with good effect. A handsome decoration is a rosette bow at the top point of each with the streamers tacked down each side seam to the lower edge.

MISSES' CUTAWAY JACKET.

No. 2154.—Portrayed on this figure is a very modish jacket suitable for Spring wear and all outing occasions during the season. It is shown here as made of fawn lady's cloth. The shaping is accomplished by the regulation seams in the back, fitting the figure snugly ; it is closed with a button and buttonhole just over the bust, the fronts flaring gracefully in blazer effect. A stylish lapel collar finishes the neck, and leg-o'-mutton sleeves complete the fashioning of this neat and comfortable jacket, other views of which may be seen on page 88.

The pattern is cut in four sizes for misses from ten to sixteen years of age, and costs 20 cents. To make in the fourteen year size it will require three and one-half yards twenty-seven, two and one-half yards forty-four or one and five-eighths yard of material fifty-four inches in width.

Cheviot, serge, homespun, novelty coating, diagonal, French twill or any material generally used for street wear will make up well in this style.

two, or two and three-eighths yards forty-four inches wide, with seven-eighths yard of lining twenty-seven inches wide for lining pieces, and costs 20 cents.

The pattern of the skirt is in four sizes for misses from ten to sixteen years of age, and will require for a miss of fourteen, four and five-eighths yards of material twenty-two, three and one-eighth yards thirty-two, two and three-eighths yards forty-four, or two yards fifty-four inches wide, and costs 20 cents.

Plain and fancy gingham were here tastefully associated in making the stylish garment illustrated above, but many other

MISSES' DRESS.

No. 2137.—The attractive features of this charming dress are the gracefully fluted bretelle, and the fluted gores in the skirt. Rich *tabac* brown diagonal cloth had in this instance figured brown and gold silk in combination, this appearing in the bretelle, lower sleeve, skirt gore and piping for seams.

The pattern is cut in four sizes for misses from ten to sixteen years of age, and requires to make in the fourteen-year size eight and one-quarter yards of material twenty-two, five and five-eighths yards thirty-two, four and three-eighths yards forty-four, or three and three-eighths yards fifty-four inches in width. As represented, three and three-quarters yards of material forty, with two and one-half yards of fancy silk were sufficient. Price of pattern, 25 cents.

Serge, drap d'ete, camel's-hair cloth, novelty goods, gingham or any fashionable fabric may be selected in making.

MISSES' SKIRT.

No. 2139.—This new and fashionable model is shown in the costume above, and again upon a figure on page 86. The slashed front section offers a means of introducing a pretty effect by combining different materials as in this instance.

The pattern is cut in four sizes for young girls from ten to sixteen years, and made in the fourteen-year size requires two and three-eighths yards of material forty, with one yard of twenty-two-inch silk for inserted gores. Two yards of fifty-four-inch material will make the entire garment. Price of pattern, 20 cents.

Gray serge was here combined with polka-dotted silk, but cloth, silk, cheviot or novelty suiting may be as suitably employed.

MISSES' BLOOMERS.

No. 2152.—The bloomers here illustrated are remarkably comfortable, and well adapted for bicycling, mountain climbing and cross-saddle riding. They are pictured made of navy-blue flannel, and may be worn with a loose waist of the same, or any fancy silk blouse, as preferred. The construction is very simple and easily accomplished by the home needlewoman.

The pattern is cut in four sizes for misses from ten to sixteen years of age, and costs 15 cents. To make for a miss of fourteen it will require three and one-half yards twenty-seven, two and one-eighth yards forty-four, or one and three-quarters yard of material fifty-four inches in width. Any soft woolen material will be suitable in making. Gray, brown and all dark colors are to be preferred.

MISSES' COSTUME.

(For illustration see page 88.)

No. 2149.—The costume given in this illustration is simplicity itself, and at the same time attractively pretty. The shaping of the body is accomplished over a fitted lining, and the skirt is gored to flare fashionably, a ribbon belt encircles the waist, and is tied into a long loopy bow and ends at the back.

The pattern is cut in four sizes for misses from ten to sixteen years of age, and costs 30 cents. To make in the fourteen-year size it will require seven and one-half yards twenty-two, seven yards thirty-two, three and seven-eighths yards forty-four, or three and one-eighth yards of material fifty-four inches in width, with one and one-half yards of waist lining, or if made as represented four and one-half yards forty, with one and three-quarters yards of silk twenty-two inches wide for yoke facing, collar, belt, etc.

MISSES' WAIST, WITH FITTED LINING.

(For illustration see page 88.)

No. 2153.—This is a neat and simple model for Spring and Summer fabrics, especially for lawn or silk, and by the addition of ruffles or bretelles is dressy enough for the most delicate fabrics.

The pattern is cut in four sizes from ten to sixteen years, and costs 20 cents. A miss of fourteen will require three and three-

2137 **2137**

MISSES' DRESS.

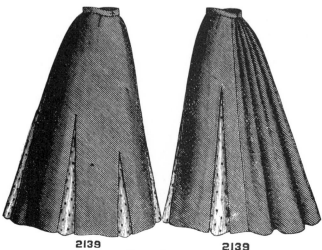

2139 **2139**

MISSES' SKIRT.

2152 **2152**

MISSES' BLOOMERS.

quarters yards of material twenty-two, three and three-eighths yards twenty-seven, two and seven-eighths yards thirty-two, or two and three-eighths yards forty-four inches wide, with seven-eighths yard of material twenty-seven inches wide for lining pieces.

MISSES' CUTAWAY JACKET.

No. 2154.—A stylish and neat jacket is here shown as made of nut-brown cloth plainly finished with machine stitching. It is shaped to fit the figure in the back with the usual seams, the side-back seams terminating in short underlaps, thus giving stylish ease to the skirt part. The fronts are buttoned at the bust and flare in blazer fashion. A turn-over lapel collar deeply overfaced with dark brown velvet finishes the neck effectively.

The pattern is cut in four sizes for misses from ten to sixteen years of age, and costs 20 cents. To make in the fourteen-year size it will require three and one-half yards twenty-seven, two and one-half yards forty-four, or one and five-eighths yard of material fifty-four inches in width, with three-eighths yard of velvet for collar facing. Any of the fashionable coatings will make up well by this mode, especially serge, homespun, cheviot or rough and ready effects.

This jacket is exceedingly well adapted for all outing expeditions and ordinary street and promenade wear; it may be trimmed with braid or gimp if desired.

GIRLS' DRESS.
(For illustration see page 89.)

No. 2126.—A quaint and novel design for a girl's dress is here shown, which will be found extremely suitable for all occasions. Its plain simplicity recommends it very forcibly for a school dress. As pictured it was made of dull blue figured cashmere with trimmings of cream-colored appliqué lace, blue mirror velvet and bebé ribbon. It is shaped to the figure by shoulder and underarm seams, the skirt being slightly gathered and attached to the waist, from which it falls with graceful ease. A V of velvet

2149

2149

MISSES' COSTUME.   (See page 87.)

The pattern is cut in four sizes for girls from six to nine years of age, and costs 25 cents. To make for a girl of eight requires five and five-eighths yards twenty-two, four yards thirty-two, two and seven-eighths yards forty-four, or two and three-eighths yards of material fifty-four inches in width.

This mode is adapted to all the Spring and Summer fabrics. Challis, veiling, silk, albatross, gingham and cambric, will take the place of the heavier goods, such as serge, homespun, cheviot, wool novelties, etc., which are all suitable for making.

GIRLS' DRESS, WITH BODY LINING.
(For illustration see page 89.)

No. 2136.—On this charming little figure is portrayed a stylish and most effective dress of, fancy figured India silk trimmed with velvet and bebé ribbon. It hangs in free graceful fashion around the little figure, and is very simple of construction. For other views see page 90.

The pattern is cut in four sizes for girls from six to nine years of age, and costs 20 cents. To make for a girl of eight it will require six and five-eighths yards twenty-two, four and three-eighths yards thirty-two, three and three-eighths yards forty-four or two and a half yards of material fifty-four inches in width.

This mode is adaptable to gingham, cambric, lawn, dimity, brilliante or any of the launderable fabrics, and may be trimmed with lace or embroidery, as preferred.

GIRLS' JACKET.
(For illustration see page 89.)

No. 2138.—A very neat, serviceable and comfortable jacket is portrayed in this illustration. It is made of fawn-colored cloth and finished with rows of machine stitching. The back is

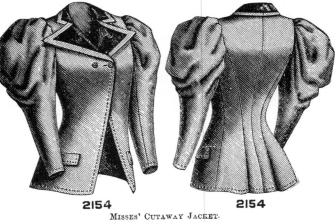

2154

2154

MISSES' CUTAWAY JACKET.

2153

2153

MISSES' WAIST, WITH FITTED LINING.   (See page 87.)

overlaid with lace is inserted in the front of the body and pointed seamless pieces are flatly applied over the shoulders, making a novel garniture. Velvet epaulettes ripple full and free upon the fashionable leg-o'-mutton sleeves.

shaped to the figure, and the double-breasted front hangs perfectly plain and loose. A rolling lapel collar finishes the neck prettily, from under which falls a pointed cape collar with charming effect. Leg-o'-mutton sleeves complete the arrangement. Convenient little pockets are inserted in each side of the front just below the waist line.

The pattern is cut in four sizes for girls from six to twelve years of age, and costs 20 cents. To make for a girl of eight

GIRLS' GUIMPE.

No. 2144.—This illustration shows a very neat and serviceable guimpe, the shaping of which is accomplished by shirrings at the neck and waist, shoulder and under-arm seams. Full bishop

No. 2126.—GIRLS' DRESS. (See page 88.)

No. 2136.—GIRLS' DRESS, WITH BODY LINING. (See page 88.)

requires four and one-quarter yards of material twenty-two, three and five-eighths yards twenty-seven, two and one-eighth yards forty-four, or one and seven-eighths yard fifty-four inches in width.

sleeves gathered into frills at the wrists complete the garment, the neck having a turn-down collar or plain finish, as shown in the outline view, as preferred. Nainsook was the fabric used in making, French cambric, delicate silks, sheer muslin, lawn or any similar materials are equally suitable.

The pattern is cut in four sizes for girls from six to twelve years of age. In making for a girl of eight it will require three yards twenty-two, two and one-half yards twenty-seven, one and

2138   2138

GIRLS' JACKET. (See page 88.)

2144   2144

GIRLS' GUIMPE.

Serge, homespun, cheviot, novelty cloaking, diagonal, hopsacking, matelasse, tweed, and a variety of other materials will all give satisfaction in making by this mode.

seven-eighths yard thirty-six, one and one-half yards forty-four or one and one-quarter yard of material fifty-four inches in width. Price of pattern, 15 cents.

GIRLS' JACKET.

No. 2138.—The jacket so charmingly illustrated on this figure is well adapted for all occasions, and is an extremely stylish mode. It is shown as made of tan-colored diagonal with trimming of

GIRLS' JACKET.

No. 2138.—Illustrated on this girlish figure is a jacket made of beurre lady's cloth with cape collar of dark brown moiré. Other views may be seen by referring to page 89.

NO. 2138.—GIRLS' JACKET.

very narrow gimp. The chief feature of this jacket is the handsome cape collar which falls in a peculiarly graceful fashion ; back and front views may be seen by turning to page 89.

The pattern is cut in four sizes for girls from six to twelve years of age, and costs 20 cents. To make for a girl of eight it will require four and one-quarter yards twenty-two, three and five-eighths yards twenty-seven, two and one-eighth yards forty-

NO. 2138.—GIRLS' JACKET.

The pattern is cut in four sizes for girls from six to twelve years of age, and costs 20 cents. To make for a wee maiden of eight it will require four and one quarter yards twenty-two inches

2136   2136

GIRLS' DRESS, WITH FITTED LINING. (See page 91.)

2126   2126

GIRLS' DRESS. (See page 91.)

four or one and seven-eighths yard of material fifty-four inches in width.

This jacket may be satisfactorily developed in all material used for coatings ; such as serge, cheviot, cloth, etc.

in width. Other materials may be chosen in making ; a delicate shade of gray serge with deep green velvet collar would be a pretty combination.

GIRLS' DRESS, WITH FITTED LINING.
(For illustration see page 90.)

No. 2136.—This dainty dress, here pictured, was made of turquoise blue figured llama prettily trimmed with lace. The skirt part is quite ample, gathered at the top and attached to the full neck portions above which a scalloped garniture overlaid with lace is applied in yoke effect. The sleeves are **charmingly**

woolen fabrics are admirable for making. Embroideries, ribbons and other decorations may be substituted.

GIRLS' DRESS.
(For illustration see page 90.)

No. 2126.—A neat and simple dress is here given that is exceedingly well adapted for all ordinary wear, and will be found excel-

No. 2140.—CHILD'S CLOAK. (See page 92.)

No. 2131.—CHILD'S DRESS, WITH BODY LINING. (See page 92.)

puffed above the elbow, the lower part is in coat-shape style over-laid with lace.

The pattern is cut in four sizes for girls from six to nine years of age, and costs 20 cents. To make for a girl **of** eight it will **require** six and five-eighths yards twenty-two, four and three-eighths yards thirty-two, three and three-eighths yards forty-four, **or** two and one-half yards of material fifty-four inches in width,

lent for the school-room. In this instance it was made of fine French novelty flannel in a rich geranium shade, with trimmings of leaf-green velvet and gold braid. The body is shaped by shoulder and under-arm seams, and the garniture is applied flatly, as portrayed in the illustration ; rippling epaulettes float gracefully above the leg-o'-mutton sleeves with charming effect, the skirt being gathered and attached to the body with a fine piping ; a bias

2128　　　　**2128**
CHILD'S DRESS. (See page 92.)

2140　　　　**2140**
CHILD'S CLOAK. (See page 92.)

with seven-eighths yard of lace to trim, and one and three-eighths **yard** of lining twenty-seven inches wide.

Gingham, lawn, cambric, batiste, brilliante, also silken and

fold of the velvet sewn on with gold braid just above the **hem** adds a very pretty finish.

The pattern is cut in four sizes for girls from six to nine **years** of age, and costs 25 cents. To make for a girl of eight it will require five and five-eighths yards twenty-two, four yards thirty-two, two and seven-eighths yards forty-four, or two and three-eighths yards of material fifty-four inches in width; or if made as represented, two and three-quarters yards forty, with

No. 2128.—Child's Dress.

two yards twenty-two, and seven and three-quarters yards of braid.

Gingham, lawn, mull, veiling, cashmere, Henrietta, albatross and all the light-weight silks will make up favorably by this mode.

CHILD'S CLOAK.

(For illustration see page 91.)

No. 2140.—This little girlie wears a very modish cloak, other views of which may be seen by referring to page 91. As

2131   2131

Child's Dress, with Body Lining.

portrayed here, the materials used in making were nut-brown serge and moiré antique of same color. This garment fits the little figure snugly in the back, the front falling full and free. A stylish cape collar adds grace and beauty to this serviceable cloak.

The pattern is cut in four sizes for children from two to five years of age, and costs 20 cents. In making for a child of four it will require four and one-half yards twenty-two, four and one-quarter yards twenty-seven, two and one-quarter yards forty-four or two yards of material fifty-four inches in width.

This garment is suitable for general every-day wear, and can be made of cheviot, homespun, wale serge, novelty cloaking, diagonal or any desired material

CHILD'S DRESS, WITH BODY LINING.

No. 2131.—This cunning little darling wears one of the daintiest dresses of the month made up in this instance of dainty rose-pink figured and dotted China silk simply trimmed with bebé ribbon. It is shirred to fit prettily around the neck and shoulders, the shirrings being outlined with the ribbon. A full puff ending in a graceful frill surmounts the coat-shape sleeve.

2129

Infant's Slip, in One Piece. (See p. 93.)

The pattern is cut in five sizes for children from one to five years of age, and costs 20 cents. To make for a child of four it will require four yards of material twenty-two, three yards thirty-two, or two and one-quarter yards forty-four or fifty-four inches in width.

Challis, batiste, brilliante, linen lawn, dimities and silk-weft ginghams will be favored in making.

CHILD'S DRESS.

(For illustration see page 91.)

No. 2128.—A very delightful little dress of the Mother Hubbard style is here pictured as made of ruby-red silk combined with polka-dotted silk of the same shade. The yoke is shaped by shoulder and under-arm seams, the front prettily shirred, while the back is perfectly plain with closing down its centre of buttons

2143   2143

Child's Guimpe. (See page 93.)

and buttonholes. A narrow frill of the dotted silk conceals the joining of the skirt to the yoke, full puffs of the same are attached to the sleeves ending in a graceful frill at the elbow.

The pattern is cut in five sizes for children from one to five years of age, and costs 20 cents. To make for a child of four it will require four and three-quarters yards twenty-two, three and one-half yards thirty-two, two and three-eighths yards forty-four or two yards of material fifty-four inches in width. If made as represented three and one-eighth yards twenty-two, and one yard dotted forty inches in width will be necessary.

Cashmere, Henrietta, serge, veiling, albatross, China silk, cambric, gingham or lawn will make up prettily by this mode.

CHILD'S CLOAK.

(For illustration see page 91.)

No. 2140—A comfortable cloak for the little maiden is here given as made of novelty homespun with trimming of narrow hercules braid. It is shaped to the little form in the back. Two narrow pleats each side of the closing, which is made invisibly at the centre of the front, give a pretty fullness to the garment. The sleeves are in the leg-o'-mutton style, full and shapely. From below the tiny upright collar falls a primitive-looking cape, very plain across the back and arranged in cascades at the front.

The pattern is cut in four sizes for children from two to five years of age, and costs 20 cents. To make for a little one of four requires four and one-half yards twenty-two, four and one-quarter yards twenty-seven, two and one-quarter yards forty-four, or two yards of material fifty-four inches in width, with nine yards of braid for garniture.

Serge, cheviot, diagonal, corduroy, hop-sacking, bengaline, rep silk, or any cloaking material may be used by this model.

CHILD'S DRESS.

(For illustration see page 99.)

No. 2128.—This winsome little tot wears a dainty dress of dotted Swiss very prettily fashioned in Mother Hubbard style, and trimmed with embroidered edging. The yoke is shirred in front and perfectly plain in the back, and the sleeves are stylishly puffed above the elbow. For other views of this charming dress see page 91.

The pattern is cut in five sizes for children from one to five years of age, and costs 20 cents. To make for a wee one of four it will require four and three-quarters yards twenty-two, three and one-half yards thirty-two, two and three-eighths yards forty-four, or two yards of material fifty-four inches in width.

Challis, veiling, cashmere, China or India silk, crêpon, lawn, gingham and various other fabrics will all give satisfaction in making by this mode.

CHILD'S DRESS, with Body Lining.

(For illustration see page 91.)

No. 2131.—The pattern of this simple and comfortable little dress is cut in five sizes for children from one to five years of age, and will require for a child of four, four yards of material twenty-two, three yards thirty-two, two and one-quarter yards forty-four or fifty-four inches wide, and costs 20 cents.

Polka-dotted challis, combining the two popular colors, brown and tan, was here used in making this stylish little garment, but many other materials, such as Chambery, crêpon, gingham, crêpon zephyr, nun's veiling, albatross, percale, batiste, mull, challis, delaine, lawn, silk or any material that may be selected will make up satisfactorily after this model.

This charming little garment, which is both neat and easy of construction, is shirred to a fitted lining in a manner simulating a round yoke, from where it falls in its own folds and is finished by a hem at the bottom. It also has a ruffle standing up well around the neck, doing away with the necessity of the collar band, which is at all times uncomfortable to the little one in the merry games so common among them. Another pleasing feature of this little gown is the sleeve, which has a fitted foundation overlapped by a full puff extending to the elbow, where it is joined in the form of a frill. The closing is invisibly effected in the back by means of hooks and eyes.

INFANTS' SLIP, in One Piece.

(For illustration see page 92.)

No. 2129.—A very dainty little slip is here given, suitable for making in nainsook, lawn, cambric or silk. As represented it was made of fine nainsook trimmed with feather stitching and Valenciennes lace.

The pattern is cut in one size, and costs 15 cents. In making it will require two and one-eighth of material from twenty-seven to thirty-six inches in width, with one and one-quarter yard of lace to trim the neck and sleeves. For comfort and extreme simplicity this garment thoroughly recommends itself.

CHILD'S GUIMPE.

(For illustration see page 92.)

No. 2143.—Simple, comfortable and altogether suitable is this neat little guimpe ; devoid of trimming and made entirely of the sheerest of lawn, it is just the thing for the wee one. The shaping is accomplished by shoulder and under-arm seams, and gathers at the neck and around the waist. A turn-over collar finishes the neck, and the sleeves, in bishop style, are gathered into a frill at the wrist.

The pattern is cut in four sizes for children from two to five years of age, and costs 10 cents. To make for a child of four it will require two and three-eighths yards twenty-two, two yards twenty-seven, one and five-eighths yard thirty-six, or one and one-quarter yard of material forty-four inches in width.

Flashes of Humor.

Doctor—What you want now, my man, is fresh air. You want to be taken out.

Patient—Shall I engage a cabman, doctor ?

" You misunderstand me, sir. I did not say you wanted to be ' taken in,' but taken out."—*Yonkers Statesman.*

Physician—What is your profession, sir ?

Patient (pompously)—I'm a gentleman.

Physician—Well, you'll have to try something else ; it doesn't agree with you.—*Tit-Bits.*

Friend (calling on dentist)—My head aches terribly.

Dentist (absent-mindedly)—Why don't you have it out.—*Exchange.*

Caller—Is your sister in, Bobby ?

Bobby—She's both in and out.

Caller—Both in and out ? How can that be ?

Bobby—It depends on who calls.—*Tit Bits.*

Young Mother (displaying the baby)—Do you think he looks like his father, Mr. Oldboy ?

Mr. Oldboy—Well, ye—es, there is a family resemblance, but it isn't striking enough to worry about.—*London Exchange.*

" What must precede baptism ? " asked the rector, when catechising the Sunday-School.

" A baby," exclaimed a bright boy, with the air of one stating self-evident truth.— *Tit-Bits.*

Astronomy is a lovely study—especially when you have a real bright, pretty girl to go out with you gazing at the stars.—*Somerville Journal.*

If poverty is a crime, wealth must be a capital offense.—*New Orleans Picayune.*

Mrs. Peterby—What a poor spirited creature you are. I wish you would be either a man or a mouse.

Mr. Peterby—I wish I was a mouse. I'd make you climb up the wall in a minute.—*Exchange.*

Jones—I read the other day that good liquor strengthens the voice.

Smith—I guess there is something in that. I know it makes my breath stronger.—*Texas Siftings.*

A young man in Evanston, Ill., went to sleep in church, Sunday, and remained in that state four days. This is rather longer than the average church nap.—*Lowell Courier.*

April Millinery.

AT this season "maiden's fancies lightly turn to thoughts of bonnets." It is now high time to lay aside the heavy felt, velvet and fur of the Winter and seek the dainty lace, ribbon and flower confections which are, if possible, more beautiful than ever.

It is now settled beyond all questioning that the coming season will be a ribbon and lace reign. Ribbons and ribbons and ribbons are shown in all hues, textures and widths. Moiré may be said to predominate, although it has a fearless rival in the satin-faced brocades, while plain satin and gros-grain hold their own.

The "something new for Easter," generally applies to the Easter bonnet. Very few indeed are they who have the courage to appear in the Winter head-gear, or even last season's bonnet on this day. An entirely new outfit is deemed necessary by many although the more sensible delay deciding upon a Spring toilette until the weather becomes more settled and they can crown themselves "Queen of the May" without fearing threatening smiles and tears from the fickle weather God, who, fickle as he generally is, is always at his worst pranks in April. Dame Fashion may also be said to be a trifle fickle at this stage of transition; she has to put out little feelers like a strawberry plant, and, like

No. 1.

No. 2.

the same little plant, frequently gets frost-bitten. However, a new bonnet can always be worn with impunity, provided the English fashion of carrying an umbrella be adopted.

The following suggestions for Spring millinery comes from the pen of our Parisian correspondent:

"The latest novelty is called pearl chip. It is in two shades of green bronze, with a red iridescence or reflex. At night it changes to the purple shade called aubergine. This pearl chip is most beautifully woven and will make up into a wondrously stylish hat to go with a changeable silk warp crépon in green bronze and aubergine shades. Another real novelty is chip covered with Cuba bast, giving the effect of *changeable* chip. It is made up in ruby, emerald, orange, canary chip and covered with cream or bronze bast; also in combinations, black over red, navy blue over scarlet, black over purple, buff over green, and white over olive.

"The latest use for sea weed is to make it up into hats. It is dyed in solid or mixed colors and wrought into flat round shapes like a plate. These are supple and as tough as felt, and can be turned inside out or outside in, both sides being alike. They are rather heavy looking, but will find great favor with all young people who adopt Tam-O'Shanter headgear, for they are infinitely lighter than felt or wool and exceedingly original. Decorated with a silk pompon and held in place with a Japanese hat pin they will very likely adorn the heads of thousands of tennis players and bicyclists during the Summer.

"I have also seen two novel pleats in straw, one is called watch chain, the other cockle-shell. The latter is made up in a combination of chip and straw, the watch chain in pure straw; gold, buff, cream and brown will be mixed with fancy chip when made up into hat shapes."

An exceedingly attractive Easter bonnet is shown in illustration No. 1. It is made of aubergine colored straw gracefully shaped to shade the piquant face beneath, and tastefully trimmed with cream chiffon, leaf-green ribbon, deep purple roses and ostrich plumes, having iridescent aigrettes and matching the straw in color.

No. 2 is a charming confection in black, of chenille, jet and ostrich plumes; the only touch of color is a crush Marechal Niel rose placed coquettishly on the brim.

A tamborine turban is given in Illustration No. 3. This shape is admirably adapted for traveling wear, and will often be made of the costume cloth. As portrayed, gray velvet and moiré with steel wings and white aigrette were the materials used.

No. 4 portrays the crescent shape, so much in vogue, as made of steel wire with trimming of soft ribbon in a delicate moss green shade and steel thistles.

No. 5 is a beurre colored fancy chip, somewhat in turban shape,

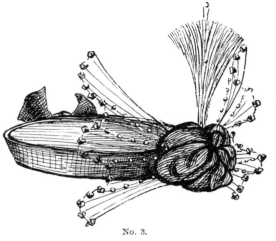

No. 3.

prettily trimmed with chiffon, roses and plumes. This is a typical Easter hat and extremely becoming to the majority of faces.

No. 6 illustrates a mourning hat for a young lady, made entirely of crape with ornaments of dull jet. The crape bows are wired invisibly into position.

No. 7 is a charming group of three ; the upper one is of novel design and suggestive of the briny deep. The crown is made of cockle-shell straw in cockle shape and color, and the brim of sea weed with decoration of ostrich feathers and poppies. The second of this pretty group is an artistically shaped leghorn hat, rather Frenchy in design, and charmingly trimmed with moiré-faced black velvet ribbon, silver buckle set with brilliants and an exquisite bunch of lilacs and roses. The ribbon is drawn through

Of all the garnitures ever designed for headgear lace is the *crême de la crême*, and on straw nothing is more *comme il faut* than flowers. To be sure, over decoration of flowers is suggestive of a "flower garden," but taste controls all elaborations of millinery, and it might as well be said of an over-trimmed hat in fur, that it resembles a menagerie of wild beasts. An over-abundance of any decoration is extremely bad taste. It is far better to have too little than too much trimming, although meagreness must be

No. 5.

avoided. A skimpy-looking hat or bonnet is always suggestive of "I-would-if-I-could" effect.

If you would be well bonneted consider these rules : Wear that

No. 6.

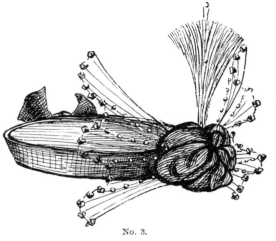

No. 4.

the brim in front and around the crown and tied in a long loopy bow at the back. The last of the group is an exquisite bandeau trimmed with white viking wings, pompon, aigrettes and crush roses ; this is a gem of millinery art and just the thing for ceremonious occasions and opera wear.

which is becoming ; choose a shape suited to the features ; next, a color that *adds* tone to the complexion ; never choose loud or gaudy trimmings ; avoid odd shapes, unless especially becoming, and not to be worn at all times ; do not get the latest fad, lest it be worn to death before you can say " Jack Robinson " ; startling effects may be beautiful for the moment, but the average woman wearies of them ; buy nothing but reliable materials ; cheap millinery is perishable.

Oblong buckles, curved more or less, are a most approved decoration for hats. When intended for this purpose they have rather formidable pointed tongues, which pierce the ribbon or drapery drawn through the buckle. Frequently they measure six or eight inches in length and will go nearly half round the crown of a sailor hat. But their use is not confined to this shape of hat ; they deck broad brims and toques equally well. Similar buckles are made in cut jet, but that in imitation diamonds is the favorite.

As a rule, there is always some old wire frame that can be bent and twisted into a new shape for an opera or fête bonnet. If the amateur milliner is absolutely fresh at the work, it is best to buy a frame that suits at once, although it is very rare that milliners use a wire frame as it comes from the maker.

Wire frames cost anywhere from nineteen cents up to fifty cents, but twenty-five cents is about the price of the frame. Be sure and consult the nasal appendage in

by modistes who, in connection with dress and cloak making, do some millinery work, but the largest class of patronage comes from millinery shops. The intruder is scorned by the women in the workroom, who not only make personal remarks, but depreciate everything he turns out. One milliner in Fifth avenue, near the Union League Club, hires a man trimmer every season to go over her trimmed goods and put on finishing touches, which he does to her entire satisfaction.

A feature in millinery for children is the extraordinary size of

selecting the frame. Not to buy by smell, but to be sure to find out whether your ears and nose harmonize with the wire shape.

Just a couple of wires forming a band to rest lightly on the hair and well down towards the face in front is a favorite shape and one easy to handle as well. Here is a very economical way to treat this for a young girl :

Wind the wires loosely but evenly with satin ribbon of some light color, pale pink being a great fad this season. Then make two little rosettes of the ribbon to place in front, with notched ends wired to stand up. That bonnet needn't cost a cent over $1. To make it more elaborate a tiny aigrette can be placed in each rosette, either to take the place of the standing ends of ribbon or with them.

It is not generally known, perhaps, that there are man milliners who hire out by the day or week as trimmers to New York modistes. It goes without saying that these trimmers are artists. Their greatest value lies in what they call original designing. The frames or shapes in stock are taken with whatever decorative material may be available, and unique bonnets and hats are evolved, which may serve as models or used for special orders. The men trimmers command a salary of fifty dollars a week or ten dollars a day of six hours. They are regularly employed

No 7.

the " granny " bonnet. The little faces of the children are hidden away and seem to be visible only at the end of a long tunnel. These bonnets are made in silk gauze, mull or silk drawn on to cane or cords, having large rosette bows at the sides and deep gathered curtains at the back.

An extremely pretty evening ornament for the hair of a brunette consists of a narrow band of silver, which almost encircles the head, ornamented with two little silver wings perched up erectly a little to either side of the parting in front.

The Princess of Wales has a remarkable collection of hats and bonnets, consisting of all those she has worn during the thirty years she has led London fashion. Each hat or bonnet, carefully put away, bears the date of the season of its use, and a history of the whims, vagaries and changes of feminine fashion. which are never so capricious as in matters of head gear. A volume which would be eagerly sought after by the curious might well be written upon this interesting collection.

Early Spring Fashions.

PARIS, December 30, 1893.

PARIS Fashion is a kaleidoscope whose gemlike atoms are the many bright fancies of a multitude of the cleverest and most cultured people, both men and women, whose training has fitted them for the task of selecting and adopting from the wealth of the past all the picturesque, graceful and elegant attire suitable for the present generation.

Doucet intends using the double puff sleeve for young people, and will revive the high puffed leg-of-mutton sleeve for early Spring dresses.

Probably gowns made in May and June will be of materials that hang softly draped, and the puffs will fall from the shoulders much as they have done this Winter.

The earliest Spring goods will be a woolen material with silk warp, called *crépon*. It resembles crape, but is made in all colors.

The fashionable tones will be all manners of bronze, brown, tan and tobacco.

Many of these very elegant crêpons will be changeable, and the highest novelties will have a small bud or tiny arabesque embroidered or woven in the stuff.

The tea gown or house dress should be made up in light pongee silk trimmed with lace. It can be made up in cashmere, and trimmed with guipure or embroidery, and although very elegant, it will be found a serviceable gown.

Children's dresses may be of cherry red, olive or hunters' green serge if for daily wear, or in light pongee silk, cream rose or blue, if intended for house or party dresses.

I have seen a dress for a girl of twelve which would be very pretty for a party gown. It is in one piece, buttoned at the back, V-shaped collar from the waist, with a chemisette of lace or crêpe de chine. Under the collar is a modified bertha of heavy lace in points, as well as at the elbow under the large puff which falls from the shoulder. There is a belt of moiré antique ribbon partly run through the pleats around the waist in a pretty style, reminding one of a boy's Norfolk jacket. The lace to be used is imitation Venice point or guipure, but I think Irish lace, or even crochet work could be used with pretty effect.

Another child's dress was for a church wedding, and extremely elegant. It had a vest and coat in Louis XVI. style, but with puffed sleeve and modified 1830 collar, under which was a deep trimming of heavy cream-colored lace. The chemisette, visible above the decollete vest, was of crêpe de chine. But this was for an India silk gown.

If made up in woolen goods the chemisette and lower part of sleeve, from elbow to wrist, should be of fine batiste edged with embroidery. It can likewise be made with a *piqué* vest buttoned high for a little boy still in skirts.

Embroidery will not be very largely used in Paris, though certain novelties will, no doubt, crop up later on in the season, and find some to favor this style of trimming.

But in laces there are two real novelties which, though extremely elegant, can be had at prices which place them within reach of moderate purses. Venice point is now being made in imitation so rich and careful that only an expert could distinguish it from the real.

The color is no longer light coffee or old lace tinge, which is really the effect of time and dirt, but all I have heard of and seen is to be in deep cream called "beurre," or butter. Then there is the same Venetian point made up in black silk.

It is just as heavy and far richer than real Venetian lace, the latter being always of linen thread and white or yellowish gray.

This black Venetian point is called black *guipure*, and will be worn on gowns where Spanish or Chantilly laces have been used.

I have seen some of this elegant black silk guipure at fifteen dollars a yard, but it is very wide, and if made in real Venetian point would be worth from eighty to two hundred dollars per yard.

Passementerie and jet trimming will not be largely used in the Spring time, though it may be found on very elegant costumes as a front piece or inserting. But lace will lead everything.

I have heard of a new lace of Spanish design and effect, and another that will go by the odd name of Arabian lace, and Doucet will use both of them, so, of course, they will be the fashion. These new "Spanish" laces will be very light in texture, not made of silk, like genuine Spanish, but of thread, and both black and white.

Large collars in points and square pendants will be worn, falling from the neck over the shoulders in Louis XVI. style. They will be suitable both for young girls and children wearing blouses.

For more elegant dresses these collars will be worn in real antique lace, either Florentine or Venetian point. They were largely in use in England during the reign of Charles I., and we in America would call them Van Dyke collars. Nothing could be more picturesque than such an adornment worn on a full puff-sleeved blouse of India or pongee silk.

Blouses will be just as much in vogue as ever, but, though richer in outline, that is, with more material in the sleeves, they will be simple in make, less inserting used and little gathering or smocking, as lace would hide all such details.

It is safe to predict an extensive use of moiré antique ribbon in plain colors, both for dresses and hats. Real novelties have not been made up in ribbons, and it is predicted that none will be in demand.

Moiré antique and watered silk was just becoming fashionable when fur took the place of it, and so it is expected that moiré antique will be very largely used at the opening of the Spring season, to the complete exclusion of all other ribbons.

Though moiré antique ribbon will be largely worn on hats, the latter are to be of such exquisite material that little trimming other than a few flowers and a bit of *mousseline de soie* need be used. The shapes will not be stamped with an authentic patent of good style until they have been submitted to and approved of by the leading modistes.

In the materials to be used for dresses there is always the same embarrassment of riches. Out of an ocean of new creations I am fain to accept what has been repeated over and over again to me, namely, that the most favored goods of all will be the *silk warped crapes*. The woof is of wool, the warp of silk, quite often of different colors. This makes a changeable material like changeable silk, only with a rich crepy effect in dark prune or purple; it is as rich as heaviest English crepe, and yet how soft, how light and supple. Made into gowns of 1830 shape, modified to suit the taste of 1894, these crêpons must be loosely fitted to a lining which fits the body neatly. In this way all difficulties of their giving quality are obviated. The puffed sleeves sometimes require a little haircloth lining, but even when they hang loosely from a richly gathered or smocked shoulder they have the same graceful effect as *crêpe de chine*, only with a little more body.

For Paris, crêpons will be all the rage, but here the novelty will be a little bud or tiny arabesque woven into the crêpon, like silk embroidery, to match the wool or body color. In silk materials the Summer goods will be moiré antique taffetas, glace silk, and light watered silks in which a tiny design is woven or printed. Pongee grenadines will be a high novelty, not only in color but in effect. They will be mostly in bronzes, navy blue and black being staples always in demand, and besides being printed in little figures, light blue mauve and whites on dark grounds, they will be woven in stripes of open-work that take the place of lace inserting.

The styles in which gowns will be made will continue to be largely those of 1830, and they are based on the old fashion plates dating from the reign of Charles X. and King Louis Philip.

MRS. B. F. PEIXOTTO.

Her Dress Considered.

"What shall we wear?" is a query rising from every channel of woman's life; for upon each occasion we must be suitably clad to enjoy its peculiar benefits. This is especially noticeable for such exercise as bicycling, for, in this case, it is not only a matter of appearing well, but the health, the comfort and safety demand a carefully selected costume and equipment.

endeavor to cater to all tastes, provided we can do so consistently with ease and safety, and from the suggestions which arrive from time to time we shall reinforce our list of garments suitable for wheelwomen.

In our designs we have always kept in view that simplicity is a first requisite and in no instance will even an amateur seam-

No. I. ILLUSTRATING LADIES' COSTUME, No 2122, WITH THE SKIRT LOOSENED FOR WALKING.

We have placed ourselves in correspondence with all the writers of note in America, and have received scores of suggestions for many details of dress, and from practical wheelwomen only do we look for ideas and points of experience. In this issue we are able to put forth a variety of garments ranging from the safe and jaunty bloomer to a complete costume of attractive design. We

stress experience any difficulty in making from our patterns. They are sensible, serviceable and handsome enough for the best weight and grade of material.

In the illustrations here given a variety will be seen, the figures showing the wearers in different position, thus illustrating their adaptability both when riding or walking beside the wheel.

Upon page 106 an additional assortment is offered in which connection a full description is given. Upon page 103 the figures are described, with detail as to costume, material and construction.

Fashion's decree has always required woman to clothe herself in draggling skirts whether on foot or horseback. Earnest endeavor has been, and efforts still continue to be made to secure emancipation from them, by the advocates of dress reform. Delsarte, Jenness-Miller, Dr. Walker and Mrs. Bloomer all have

of locomotion which offered to women this desideratum. As soon as the idea of the value of this position was appreciated, its novelty was forgotten. How well they have overcome this, at first a great objection, the history of women's wheels can testify. That women everywhere in the civilized world believe in the wheel and know its worth, is manifest on every highway in every town and city. There are to-day nearly 40,000 women cyclers in the United States alone. It behooves these women riders, and

No. II. ILLUSTRATING LADIES' COSTUME, No. 2132, WITH THE DIVIDED SKIRT CONFINED AS BLOOMERS. ALSO MISSES' BASQUE, No. 1466, AND SKIRT, No. 1854.

exerted themselves to secure converts to their teachings. These and hundreds of others have not aroused as much discussion, nor secured one iota of the interest which is aroused by the rational dress advocates in a sincere endeavor to secure a practical costume for women who ride bicycles. For years every teacher of physical education has insisted that sitting as women do on horse tends to produce a curved spine. It is well understood that the position of a man on horseback or upon a bicycle is the only one correct for perfect development. The bicycle was the first means

all others who are taking up cycling, to consider well the question of dress. At a reception, ball or party, the proper costume is worn, so for equestrian exercise; for bicycling the rule should be the same. Women should be especially particular about this point.

Mrs. L. C. Boardman says, in speaking of the costume she wears, that is a reefer coat, leggings and bloomer : " Simplicity should be the first object sought, and nothing is of more importance than the healthfulness of the costume. The whole body should be free from restraint of any kind, and be able to move in all directions with perfect ease. This and more "bloomers" give you, perfect freedom to mount and dismount, no skirts as a resistance to the wind, to get tangled in and around the pedals, and cause serious accidents For years the writer has been a practical wheelwoman trying all manner of dresses for the wheel. None have proven satisfactory ; until after reading the account of the French fashion, these were adopted and improved upon. Aside from the full Turkish trousers, the French use all manner of short skirts, which are still in the way of the wind, making pedaling hard for woman. This caused me to try the bloomers.

the fault of my skirt. Some friends and I were riding one day last summer against a very heavy wind, when it caught my skirt and wound it around my pedal, throwing me. The rapid gait I was going caused the force of the fall to break my arm It laid me up six weeks ; then it was I decided to wear almost any other costume, but never a skirt, and declared if ever I recovered the use of my arm, I should wear bloomers ; and truly glad I am that I did so decide, for never in the years of my experience as a bicycle rider have I derived such pleasure from cycling. I climb hills impossible before. It has increased my speed just double. I fear nothing from teams or roads, for if I slip I light on my feet.

No. III. ILLUSTRATING LADIES' BLOOMERS, No. 2123, AND REEFER, No. 2146.

I have found them to be perfect for cycling. I have been the first to brave public opinion and ride in them, and have received from men and women alike commendation. Encouraging letters have been sent from wheelwomen all over the country, saying to keep up the good work. Now there are hundreds who have taken to wearing bloomers. Many others in their attempts at a rational dress, have made Turkish trousers and bifurcated skirts in their endeavor to get a perfect cycling costume."

Mrs. George D. Johnston, who has adopted bloomers, says : " If I was compelled to go back to wearing a skirt on my wheel, I would give up cycling." Speaking further on the subject she said : " I shall never forget what I suffered with my arm, all from

With my bloomers and heavy undergarments, leggins to my knees, a corset waist, and in cool weather a double-breasted box coat, which amply protects me from chilling, I enjoy my riding."

Mrs. E. C. Hungerford, of New York City, is another who has discarded skirts. She is loud in praise of her suit, which is more on the Turkish style than the regular bloomer. It is very pretty and shows how easily a woman may dress becomingly for cycling, and at the same time be free from the trammels of skirts with their disadvantages. When asked if she would ever wear her skirt on her bicycle, she said, " never again. I do not care who rides in bloomer costume, I have too much pleasure and comfort. I never really knew what enjoyment there was in cycling until I got up this costume ; which I have made myself. Heretofore I always had trouble with my skirt, it would get caught in my pedal and throw me ; another thing, I could not keep it clean. Now I always present a neat appearance. With my bloomers I wear a pleated waist, and sash of cloth to match, leggins to my knee, and gloves and cap. With me I carry a skirt. All last summer I made weekly trips in the country or to Coney Island, then my skirt came in use. I could slip it on and none knew that I did not have petticoats under it. Numbers of my friends are wearing bloomers, and this year I know hundreds will follow."

Mrs. Boardman is very enthusiastic about her costume ; she further says : "Many objections are put forth by timid ones.

that beset the work of women who ride, were early presented for my consideration. The question was a severe one, but like a ray of sunlight came the solution of the problem in the advent of bloomers.

"My opinions have been corroborated by many wheelwomen. I give one from a prominent woman of Brooklyn, who has been a bicycle rider for years ; she says : 'As you know, I have adopted the bloomer costume for riding. My reasons for doing so are as follows : In riding the wheel the first requisite is safety. No lady can be as safe with skirts as with the bloomers. For three years I have ridden a wheel and have made a number of experiments with skirts ; I have tried skirts with and without weights, wide

No. IV. Illustrating Ladies' Costume, No. 2122, as it Appears in Riding.

With all that they say, they are lacking in strength of argument, because not one but admits the superiority of the style, and deplores the fact that it is a radical departure. To them the change from a tallow dip to the blazing glare of an electric arc light is too much, they must, therefore, to be consistent, follow the evolution by way of the candle, kerosene lamp and gas to the illumination of these *fin de siecle* days. When contemplating a riddance of skirts, it never for a moment entered my head that I would not wear bloomers unless, necessarily, others must follow the fashion. I was never strong-minded or inclined to follow teachings of Sorosis or dress reform, looking on such things with eyes askance. On taking to wheeling, the drawbacks and trials

skirts and narrow ones, all sorts, and found them cumbersome and at times positively dangerous on account of their tendency to catch in the wheel, chain and sprocket. With the bloomer costume one feels comfortable and safe, and, contrary to the general impression, they are as modest as any skirt, as we can rest secure in the consciousness that the wind cannot disarrange our costume. I do not wear it for its beauty, or to be odd or eccentric. I simply think it is the only proper suit for riding a wheel. My suit is made of the League gray ladies' cloth. The bloomers are pleated full on a wide band, gathered in with an elastic just under the knee, and fall over about three inches. Long buttoned leggings to match meet them at the knee, and with blouse waist and outside half fitting jacket, my costume is complete. The saving in the weight of the wheel is to be considered, for by wearing bloomers I am enabled to ride my wheel with the mud, dress and chain guards removed.'"

Mrs. Sidney B. Bowman, of New York, is also an enthusiastic convert to the bloomer costume. She wears a jaunty navy blue suit, reefer and bloomer, with tan Oxford ties and leggings. In cool weather she wears warm underwear and a white sweater, tied at the neck with a navy blue sailor knot. Over this her reefer is trimly buttoned, and her natty little officer's cap completes one of the prettiest and most attractive cycling costumes in the city. She is very sincere in her admiration of this style of dress, and says that although she has been riding several years

the bloomer and ordinary skirt comes the divided skirt. This dress is highly spoken of by those who have worn it. Each division of the skirt is side pleated or gathered, but plain on the inside, which is said to be a great aid in mounting and dismounting as compared with the ordinary skirt.

"Glancing back over years of experimenting with all sorts of costumes for the wheel, I have arrived at the conclusion that the rider's comfort depends on what she wears under the skirt, if the latter be properly lined (with silk or satin) and shaped, more than the skirt itself. The skirt should be cut so there is no unnecessary fullness about the hips, and yet unpleasant scantiness should be positively avoided. To begin with, a union undergarment should be worn next the skin varied in fabric and texture according to

No. V. Illustrating Misses' Costume, No. 1981.

she never fully realized the pleasure to be derived therefrom until she abandoned skirts.

On the other hand Mrs. S. E. Merry, who has resorted to riding for her health, still adheres to the skirt like our 2124, and seems perfectly satisfied with it.

The great favor with which bloomers are regarded by those who have adopted them is not universal, for many women will not adopt them this season or next, if at all; and for those who prefer skirts we have carefully investigated the field, and in this issue show designs which will cater to every taste.

Skirts have still some stanch advocates, and eminent riders maintain that for an ordinary spin in the park a skirt is no especial hinderance. They are very dangerous where there is much driving, car-tracks, cables, or where much speed is desired. Mary Sargent Hopkins, of Boston, writes : "As a compromise between

the weather. Over this suit should be worn woven equestrian tights in lieu of underskirts. Corsets should never be worn on the wheel. Well-fitting waists should be substituted. I have found the Equipoise to be most satisfactory, as it supports the figure without restricting it, and it can be worn without bones and still hold its shape.

"Equestrian" stockings should be black and under a smoothly lined skirt, allowing perfect freedom of motion with nothing to entangle in pedals or spokes. Shoes should be low and broad-toed.

For the head a light weight felt tourist's hat is almost universally becoming, but whatever style of hat is worn it should be entirely devoid of feathers or flowers.

Do not trust to pins where buttons or hooks belong
Jewelry should be left at home

Lisle thread gloves are better than kid or silk ; the former are too warm for Summer wear, the latter are apt to slip on the handles.

Every garment worn when riding should be kept exclusively for that purpose. After a long run, when one returns home heated and tired, a warm bath should be next in order, with an entire change of clothing. By following this rule many a cold would be avoided, and stiffened muscles would be unknown. After a run on a warm or windy day a little cold cream applied to the face and allowed to remain there a few minutes, to be removed with a soft cloth, will be found far more cooling and pleasant in its effect than a gallon of cold water dashed over your face, which only serves to intensify the glow. If you must use

Description of Figures Illustrating Garments for Bicycling.

The first figure on page 66 illustrates Ladies' Bicycling Costume, No. 2124, one of the most modest and comfortable garments ever designed for the wheel. It has an Eton jacket fitted by shoulder and under-arm seams finished with a wide notched lapel collar ; the sleeves are leg-o'-mutton in form, are full and drooping, and have gauntlet cuffs. The blouse, which is designed to conceal the contour of the figure, is loose and simply made. The closing is effected by means of buttons and buttonholes in front. The skirt, which is after all the important feature, is circular, quite scant and arranged so that the fullness is distributed over the knees in riding, giving freedom to the limbs. The circular hip-piece

No. VI. ILLUSTRATING MISSES' GYMNASIUM COSTUME, No. 1402, HERE USED FOR CYCLING.

water use it warm, not cold, and put in a few drops of ammonia. This will thoroughly cleanse and cool the skin.

I would lay down no cast-iron rules for the cycler ; each rider must be a law unto herself, but a few little hints may not come amiss to the new riders, and time and trouble be saved. As in olden days " all roads led to Rome," so now may all paths traveled by our wheels lead to joy and health.

The little miss on the next page is the daughter of the secretary of one of the largest cycle manufacturers in the United States. Her age is nine years. She is greatly in love with her machine and in the riding season, it is an almost inseparable companion. She has been perfectly well since she took to riding the bicycle, and I am positive that the use of the wheel has done her a great deal of good.

recommends itself to the wearer as being very modest, falling as it does from the line of the waist from the back and over the hips. It proceeds backward from either side of the front panel. The closing of the skirt is deftly concealed at the left of the panel, thus obviating the distaste for a back or side opening, which is likely to show as the wearer moves in the various positions on the wheel.

The pattern is cut in eight sizes for ladies from thirty to forty-four inches bust measure, and requires for a lady of medium size ten and five-eighths yards of material twenty-two, seven and three-quarters yards thirty-two, five and seven-eighths yards forty-four or five and one-quarter yards fifty-four inches wide, and costs 35 cents. It is here shown as made of Hunter's green cravenette with wide and narrow braid as decoration, and has the blouse of green and cream dotted silk.

Illustrated in the second figure view on page 67 is Ladies' Toilette, consisting of Ladies' Double-breasted Eton Jacket, No. 2046, and Ladies' Divided Skirt Bloomers, No. 2148. This jacket is fitted by shoulder, under-arm seams and darts, is closed double-breasted and has a notched revers collar, and may be suitably worn with a four-in-hand tie, a shirt waist or for extra warmth over any waist.

This jacket is cut in eight sizes from thirty to forty-four inches bust measure, and requires for the medium size four yards of material twenty to twenty-two, three and one-eighth yards twenty-seven, two yards forty-four or one and five-eighths yard fifty-four inches wide, and costs 20 cents.

These bloomers are easy of construction, very full and gathered to a band with the closing invisibly effected in the back; the lower edge is finished by a hem in which an elastic tape is run.

This pattern is cut in six sizes from twenty to thirty inches waist measure, and requires for the medium size six yards of material twenty-seven or three and five-eighths yards forty-four to fifty-four inches wide, and costs 20 cents. This handsome suit was effectively made of dark blue serge tastefully trimmed with braid.

In the first figure view on page 67, Ladies' Bicycling Costume, No. 2124, is again portrayed, here illustrating the garment as it would appear to an observer in the rear. In the second a Ladies' Toilette, consisting of Ladies' Eton Jacket, No. 1934, and Ladies' Divided Skirt Bloomers, No. 2148, are shown. The jacket is fitted by a front dart and under-arm gores, and has a wide notched lapel-collar; it has large drooping sleeves and is simply finished with machine stitching, and is well adapted to wear with any shirt waist.

This pattern is cut in eight sizes from thirty to

forty-four inches bust measure, and will require for the medium size three and one-quarter yards of material twenty-two, three yards twenty-seven, one and three-quarters yard forty-four or one and three-eighths yard fifty-four inches wide, and costs 20 cents.

In this figure view the divided skirt bloomers are shown as they appear when drawn up in a frill at the lower edge, preparatory to mounting the wheel; they are made full, and when loosened for walking have much the appearance of the ordinary skirt and may be made of serge, cheviot, cravenette, etc.

This charming little lady wears a suit of dark blue habit cloth, with a shirt waist of silk of the same shade, and an officer's cap of the same color made by Pattern No. 1353, cut in six sizes for heads measuring from nineteen and one-quarter to twenty-three inches, and will require to make for the medium size three-eighths

yard of material forty-four to fifty-four inches wide, with three-eighths yard of lining, and costs 10 cents.

In a figure view on page 98 Ladies' Bicycling Costume, No. 2122, is illustrated. It is made with a waist fitted by shoulder, under-arm seams and outward turning darts. It has a vest front, and is finished at the neck by a broad rolling collar. The sleeves, which are of the bishop style, are finished at the wrist by a frill. An attractive feature of this costume is the divided skirt trousers, so constructed as to have the appearance of an ordinary walking skirt when loosened after dismounting, preparatory to entering the house. A figure view on page 99 illustrates the same costume with the trousers drawn up as they appear after preparations have been made for mounting. The pattern is cut in six sizes from thirty to forty inches bust measure. The pattern allows for a loose, comfortable fit, to be worn without stays. It costs 30 cents. A lady of medium size will require nine and five-eighths yards of material twenty-seven, six yards forty-four or three and five-eighths yards of material fifty-four inches wide. Cravenette, serge, etc., may be used in making.

The first figure on page 99 shows Misses' Toilette, consisting of Misses' Basque (with pleats laid on), No. 1466, and Misses' Circular Skirt, No. 1854.

These patterns are in four sizes for misses from ten to sixteen years of age, and require for a miss of fourteen one and seven-eighths yard forty-four, and one and seven-eighths yard fifty-four inches wide for basque and skirt, respectively. Price of each, 25 cents. English tweed was the material here used in making, but serge, etc., may be selected.

The second figure on page 99 illustrates Ladies' Bicycling Costume, No. 2122, with the trousers drawn up as they would appear when the wearer was ready to mount the wheel. The figure on page 100 pictures Ladies' Bicycling Toilette, consisting of Ladies' Outing Jacket, No. 2146, and Ladies' Bicycling Zouave Trousers, No. 2123.

The pattern of the jacket is cut in eight sizes from thirty to forty-four inches bust measure, and requires for the medium size three and three-quarters yards of material twenty-seven, two and one-quarter yards forty-four, or one and five-eighths yard fifty-four inches wide, and costs 25 cents. The pattern of the trousers is cut in six sizes from twenty to thirty inches waist measure, and requires for the medium size four and three-eighths yards of material twenty-seven, three and one-quarter yards forty-four, or two and one-eighth yards fifty-four inches wide, with five-eighths yard of elastic, braid and buttons, and costs 20 cents.

The remaining illustrations show some serviceable garments.

Garments Suitable for Bicycling.

NOW that the balmy Springtide is once more here, bicycling enthusiasts eagerly turn their thoughts to dress. With roads in good condition, wheels in order, and a comfortably warm and suitable dress, the woman of '94 is supremely happy.

She mounts her wheel with glee, and spins through the still, frosty air, filling her lungs with oxygen, every breath full of life and health—a gloriously radiant being, the embodiment of health and healthy exercise, envied by all pedestrians, and the wonder

2124   2124

and admiration of even those who *try* to look horrified at the *seemingly* unladylike pastime.

To thoroughly enjoy riding thus early in the season, it is essential to be comfortably and warmly clad, and with this idea in view we give a number of illustrations of the most seasonable and suitable garments for this purpose.

All experienced riders wear a complete undersuit of flannel during all seasons. Corsets are done away with altogether by those who desire to obtain the height of comfort, and many discard the outer dress entirely in favor of the divided skirt or bloomer suit, which is certainly "the thing" on the wheel.

However, public opinion is divided on this as well as on all other subjects, and as no two people are ever supposed to think alike, we strive to furnish something to meet the requirements of each individual taste.

In illustration No. 2124, Ladies' Bicycling Costume is shown very charmingly; it may be made in a variety of pleasing combinations, serge, cravenette, flannel, and all woolen materials will be given

2155

2155

1353

2123

the preference, with linings of silk or satin. The pattern is cut in eight sizes from thirty to forty-four inches bust measure, and

2122

costs 35 cents. To make for a lady of medium size it will require ten and five-eighths yards twenty-two, seven and three-quarters

2146   2146

yards thirty-two, five and seven-eighths yards forty-four, or five and one-quarter yards of material fifty-four inches in width.

2123   2123   2148   2148

No. 2155.—LADIES' BICYCLING SKIRT.—The pattern is cut in six sizes for ladies from twenty to thirty inches waist measure, and costs 20 cents. To make in the medium size it will require five and seven-eighths yards twenty-two, four and seven-eighths yards twenty-seven, three and three-eighths yards forty-four, or two and five-eighths yards of material fifty-four inches in width, six and one-quarter yards of ribbon and twenty rings.

No. 1353.—OFFICERS' CAP.—Six sizes, nineteen and one-quarter to twenty-three inches head measure, and the medium size requires three-eighths yard forty-four inches wide, three-eighths yard of lining, three-quarters yard of cord, and four pearl buttons. Price, 10 cents.

2152   2152

No. 2122.—LADIES' BICYCLING COSTUME (having Divided Skirt Trousers).—This pattern is cut in six sizes for ladies from thirty to forty inches bust measure, and requires for the medium size nine and five-eighths yards of material twenty-seven inches wide, six yards forty-four inches wide, or three and five-eighths

medium size requiring one and one-eighth yard of thirty-six inch goods. Price, 25 cents.

No. 1981.—MISSES' BICYCLING COSTUME.—The pattern is cut in four sizes, ten to sixteen years, and in making in the fourteen-year size, as represented, four and three-quarters yards of dark

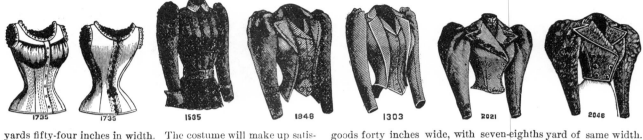

1735   1735   1535   1848   1303   2021   2046

yards fifty-four inches in width. The costume will make up satis-factorily in serge, cheviot, cravenette, cloth, etc. Price, 30 cents.

No. 2146.—LADIES' OUTING JACKET, WITH STRAPPED BACK.—The pattern is cut in eight sizes for ladies from thirty to

1981   1981

forty-four inches bust measure, and costs 25 cents. To make in the medium size it will re-quire three and three-quarters yards twenty-seven, two and one-quarter yards forty-four, or one and five-eighths yard of material fifty-four inches in width.

No. 2123.—LADIES' BI-CYCLING ZOUAVE TROUS-ERS.—The pattern is cut in six sizes, and costs 20 cents. To make in the medium size it will require four and three-eighths yards twenty-seven, three and one-quarter yards forty-four, or two and one-eighth yards of material fifty-four inches in width, with five-eighths yard of elastic braid, and eight buttons.

No. 2148 — LADIES' DIVIDED SKIRT BLOOM-ERS (*used for Mountain Climbing and Cross-saddle Riding*).—The pattern is

1894   1894

cut in six sizes for ladies from twenty to thirty inches waist measure, and costs 20 cents. To make in the medium size it will require six yards twenty seven, or three and five-eighths yards of material forty-four or fifty-four inches in width.

No. 2152. — MISSES' BICYCLING BLOOMERS.—The pattern is cut in four sizes for misses from ten to sixteen years of age, and costs 15 cents. To make in the fourteen-year size it will require three and one-half yards twenty-seven, two and one-eighth yards forty-four, or one and three-quarters yard of material fifty-four inches in width.

1806

No. 1735. — LADIES' CORSET WAIST.—Cut in eight sizes, twenty to thirty-four inches waist measure,

goods forty inches wide, with seven-eighths yard of same width. Price, 35 cents.

No. 1894.—MISSES' BLAZER JACKET (with Vest).—This pattern is cut in four sizes, ten to sixteen years. Fourteen-year size

requires two and one-quarter yards of forty inch, with five-eighths yard of thir-ty inch for vest. Price, 25 cents.

No. 1806.—GIRLS' AND MISSES' LEG-GING.—Three sizes, eleven to fifteen years. Price, 10 cents.

No. 1535. — LA-DIES' BOX PLEATED WAIST. — In eight sizes, thirty to forty-

1647   1647

four inches bust measure. Medium size three and three-eighths yards thirty-two to thirty-six inches. Price, 30 cents.

No. 1848.— LADIES' BASQUE — In eight sizes, thirty to forty-four inch-es bust meas-ure. For me-dium size, as represented, two and three-

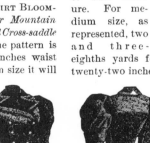

2114   2114

eighths yards forty inches, with one and three-eighths yard twenty-two inches goods for vest. Price, 30 cents.

No. 1303.—LADIES' BASQUE.—Cut in eight sizes, thirty to forty-four inches bust measure. Medium size one and one-half yards fifty to fifty-four inches. Price, 30 cents.

No. 2021.—LADIES' BASQUE.—In eight sizes, thirty to forty-four inches bust measure. Medium size requires four yards twenty-two, three yards thirty-two, two yards forty-four, or one and three-quarters yard fifty-four inch mate-rial. Price, 30 cents.

No. 1976.— LADIES' COS-TUME. — The pattern is cut in eight sizes,

869   869

thirty to forty-four inches bust measure, and to make in the medium size requires to make, as represented, five and one-quarter yards of forty-inch goods with seven-eighths yard of velvet twenty to twenty-two inches wide for vest, collar, etc., and four and one quarter yards of velvet ribbon to trim skirt will be sufficient. If one material is used alone in making, it will require four and three-quarters yards of fifty-four inch wide goods, five and five-eighths yards forty-four, seven and three-quarters yards thirty-two, or ten and three-quarters yards twenty-two. This dress will make up stylishly in novelty goods, tweed, serge, Panama cloth, sponged cloth, waterproof, cashmere. Price, 40 cents.

No. 2046.—LADIES' DOUBLE-BREASTED ETON JACKET.— This pattern is cut in eight sizes, from thirty to forty-four inches bust measure, medium size requires four yards twenty to twenty-two, three and one-eighth yards twenty-seven, two yards forty-four, or one and five-eighths yard fifty-four inches wide. Price, 20 cents.

No. 1647.—LADIES' SKIRT.—Cut in eight sizes, twenty to thirty-four inches waist, thirty-six to fifty inches hip measure. Medium size requires four and seven-eighths yards forty, eight

yards twenty-seven, or four yards fifty-four inches wide. Serge, hop-sacking, tweed, cloth, broadcloth, etc., may be used. Price, 30 cents.

No. 2114.—LADIES' JACKET BASQUE (suitable for riding, with close sleeves).—Cut in eight sizes, from thirty to forty-four inches bust measure. Medium size will require five and one-half yards twenty-two, three and five-eighths yards thirty-two, two and three-quarters yards forty-four, or two and one-eighth yards of material fifty-four inches inches in width. If made as represented it requires of plain material two and three-quarters yards forty inches wide, and one yard twenty-two, with one-quarter yard of velvet twenty inches wide for revers and collar facings. Small view for riding habit. Price, 30 cents.

No. 869.—LADIES' LEGGING AND OVERGAITER.—Requires for the medium size five-eighths of a yard for legging, or one-quarter of a yard for overgaiter. Price, 15 cents.

In making up skirts for bicycling they should be lined with silk or satin, as other linings are apt to cling uncomfortably to the underskirt or bloomers. No petticoats should be worn.

The Bicycle and Health.

WHAT PHYSICIANS AND RIDERS SAY IN ITS FAVOR.

WOMEN who have derived a great amount of benefit and health from cycling are prone to be much amused at the flimsy excuses for not doing so put forth by women who will not exert themselves to learn. We say *learn*, for when the first difficulties have been mastered few can resist the enthusiasm which at once pervades them, and riding "follows as the night the day."

The greatest obstacle for a sensible woman in this, as in all exercises, is an anxiety for the health. Some one has told her that bicycling and the running of a sewing machine are injurious, and, as she long since decided she could not sew, it seemed sheer madness to expose herself to a companion injury.

Experience alone can effectually explode this theory, yet it must be rational to a sensible thinker to deem the movements unlike when it is explained that on the wheel the action is distributed. When the right foot is at its lowest reach the left is highest, thus bringing an entirely different set of muscles into play and rest in each limb. With the sewing machine both feet fall and rise at the same time, thus extending all the muscles of the thigh and leg at the same time, and throwing them back into rest the next fraction of a second. Besides, the revolution of each pedal describes a circle of considerable dimensions, and thus makes the relaxation and extension of muscles easy and in better time. The wheel is propelled by pressing the balls of the foot to the pedals, and exerts the greatest stress upon the muscles in the calf of the leg, just as correct walking will do.

Others claim that nothing is so fatiguing as walking, and compare the up and down movement on the pedals to walking. This is true and yet not true, for although all the benefit and exercise which is derived from walking is present in wheeling, the wearying is obviated, as the weight of the body is supported upon the saddle.

Another feature of riding the wheel is that so many portions of the body are called into action. The arms, while extended and constantly in activity, are spared any pulling or reaching. This is a point in its favor, as few women can withstand the inroads upon the health caused by over-exertion in the arms. Heart trouble is one form of opposition to it. Cycling calls for activity, alertness, accuracy and grace in the upper portions of the body, but in no place is there an undue strain.

It is no wonder some women dread becoming round shouldered in view of the fact that some riders stoop so over their machines. This is a fact to be deplored, but it should in no way reflect upon

the exercise, as it is the fault of the individual, and does not accompany real skill. The straightest riders are the most expert, and, like bad walking, it is an unpardonable awkwardness.

There are so many physicians of both sexes riding to-day that it seems folly to quote them—their adoption of the wheel is its own argument—yet it may be well to state that, although several women who have hesitated at first because of their fear of physical injury, are now convinced by physicians that a wise decision may be made in favor of the wheel.

For stomach troubles—dyspepsia and the like—this exercise has no peer. Of course there are organic weaknesses which debar women from *any* exercise, even walking, and in our wide circuit of interviewing physicians the most adverse criticism was almost laughingly given in some such terms as—

"Well, you know, there is a saying that if consumptives can stand sea air it will benefit them, and so with this sport, which grows yearly more fascinating for women."

The head doctor of the New York Hospital on Fifteenth street states that no case has come under his notice where any organic weakness or derangement could be traced to bicycling. This is a sweeping assertion, considering the disinterested, conservative personality of the speaker, and the vast number of sufferers from every human ill who yearly come beneath his notice.

Moderation is the first rule for delicate riders, and new beginners are apt to let enthusiasm get the better of prudence. Use Dr. Johnson's rule for eating in the case of bicycling, and leave the feast while you yet have appetite for more, and next time you may extend your time a little longer.

Taking cold is to be guarded against, and is a likely result, unless an entire suit of wool is worn when riding, Winter and Summer.

This is kept of uniform weight in all seasons by some riders, there are others who wear it much lighter in Summer. With a complete suit of heavy wool you may, without fear, ride and exercise into a profuse perspiration and be safe from cold. Cotton or silk underwear will cause one to become thoroughly chilled as soon as the air strikes the dampened surface, and the heat of exercise is abated. Some women carry a sweater, and when taking long rides slip it on after dismounting from the wheel. In this case an inner vest of wool is not needed.

When the rider only goes out for light exercise it may be easily gauged just what weight of clothing is required.   C. M. H.

SPRING · & · SUMMER
1909

READY REFERENCE CATALOGUE

OF

McCALL PATTERNS

Compliments of

Louis Pine & Co.

Burlington, Vermont

Sole Agency for McCall Patterns

WHY McCALL PATTERNS ARE SIMPLE

This is a picture of McCall Pattern No. 2071—only 6 pieces, as shown below, the perforations few and distinct, the construction evident at a glance; yet the result, as shown by the finished waist, is a well-cut, well-planned, exquisitely simple and effective garment.

This pattern is not an exception, but illustrates our rule, which is to afford our customers the best style for the least labor.

McCall Pattern No. 2071—Ladies' Shirt Waist or Slip
Cut in 7 sizes, 32, 34, 36, 38, 40, 42 and 44 inches bust measure

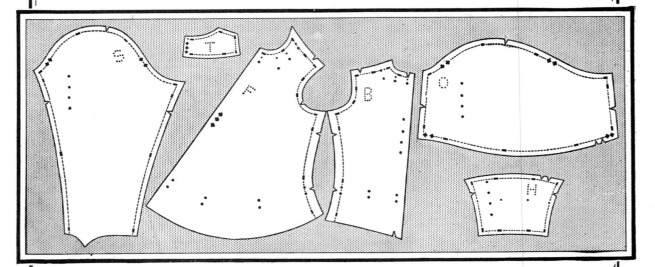

The following explanation of the marks used on the above pattern and in general use on all McCall Patterns shows the simplicity of our method

LETTERS mark the pieces: Front (F), Back (B), Collar (T), Puff Sleeve (O), Cuff (H) and Leg-o'-Mutton Sleeve (S).

LONG PERFORATIONS (▬) show the amount allowed for seams and the exact sewing line.

NOTCHES (>) show how the pattern goes together, mark the hems at back edges and indicate the waistline.

FOUR LARGE CIRCLES (●●●●) show the direction for straight of material in cutting.

THREE CROSSES (✚✚✚) show edges to be placed on a fold in cutting.

SMALL CIRCLES (●) mark line for cutting the round neck and shorter sleeve.

LARGE CIRCLES (●) mark line for cutting the square neck and lines for the waist shirrings.

DOUBLE CROSSES (✚✚) mark the sleeve gathers.

There are more McCall Patterns sold in the United States than of any other make because they are more stylish, more accurate and more simple than any other pattern. The name **McCall** stands for all that is **best** in paper patterns.

THE McCALL COMPANY

120

A Letter For You

DEAR MADAM:

This Catalogue contains over 300 designs of McCall Patterns, all of which are stylish and yet not hard to make up. All McCall Patterns are easy to use. There is no guesswork about them. The directions are easy to follow. All seams are allowed for, and every pleat, tuck, etc., is carefully shown on the pattern. Then, again, there is no waste of material, and if the directions are followed you are sure of a perfect fit. McCall Patterns have been on the market for 40 years, and are without a doubt the very best patterns made. **There are more McCall Patterns sold in the United States than of any other make.**

You can obtain any pattern in this Catalogue by sending your name and address, number, size and price to the address on the front cover.

THE McCALL COMPANY.

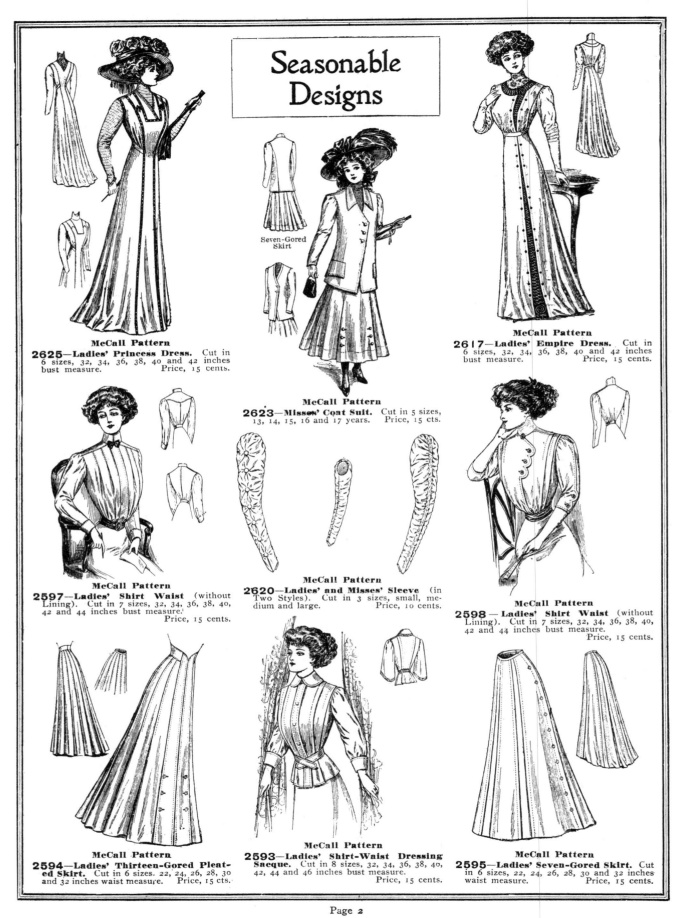

Seasonable Designs

McCall Pattern
2625—Ladies' Princess Dress. Cut in 6 sizes, 32, 34, 36, 38, 40 and 42 inches bust measure.   Price, 15 cents.

Seven-Gored Skirt

McCall Pattern
2623—Misses' Coat Suit. Cut in 5 sizes, 13, 14, 15, 16 and 17 years.   Price, 15 cts.

McCall Pattern
2617—Ladies' Empire Dress. Cut in 6 sizes, 32, 34, 36, 38, 40 and 42 inches bust measure.   Price, 15 cents.

McCall Pattern
2597—Ladies' Shirt Waist (without Lining). Cut in 7 sizes, 32, 34, 36, 38, 40, 42 and 44 inches bust measure.
Price, 15 cents.

McCall Pattern
2620—Ladies' and Misses' Sleeve (in Two Styles). Cut in 3 sizes, small, medium and large.   Price, 10 cents.

McCall Pattern
2598 — Ladies' Shirt Waist (without Lining). Cut in 7 sizes, 32, 34, 36, 38, 40, 42 and 44 inches bust measure.
Price, 15 cents.

McCall Pattern
2594—Ladies' Thirteen-Gored Pleated Skirt. Cut in 6 sizes, 22, 24, 26, 28, 30 and 32 inches waist measure.   Price, 15 cts.

McCall Pattern
2593—Ladies' Shirt-Waist Dressing Sacque. Cut in 8 sizes, 32, 34, 36, 38, 40, 42, 44 and 46 inches bust measure.
Price, 15 cents.

McCall Pattern
2595—Ladies' Seven-Gored Skirt. Cut in 6 sizes, 22, 24, 26, 28, 30 and 32 inches waist measure.   Price, 15 cents.

Page 2

Seven-Gored Skirt

McCall Pattern
2592—Ladies' Coat. Cut in 6 sizes, 32, 34, 36, 38, 40 and 42 inches bust measure.
Price, 15 cents.

McCall Pattern
2612—Ladies' Dress. Cut in 8 sizes, 32, 34, 36, 38, 40, 42, 44 and 46 inches bust measure. Price, 15 cents.

McCall Pattern
2606—Ladies' Coat. Cut in 6 sizes, 32, 34, 36, 38, 40 and 42 inches bust measure.
Price, 15 cents.

McCall Pattern
2611—Ladies' Shirt Waist (without Lining). Cut in 7 sizes, 32, 34, 36, 38, 40, 42 and 44 inches bust measure.
Price, 15 cents.

McCall Pattern
2607—Ladies' Shirt Waist (without Lining). Cut in 6 sizes, 32, 34, 36, 38, 40 and 42 inches bust measure. Price, 15 cts.

McCall Pattern
2588—Ladies' Blouse Waist (without Lining). Cut in 6 sizes, 32, 34, 36, 38, 40 and 42 inches bust measure. Price, 15 cts.

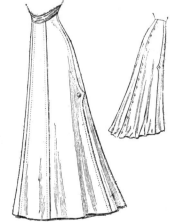

McCall Pattern
2586 — Ladies' Two - Piece Circular Skirt. Cut in 6 sizes, 22, 24, 26, 28, 30 and 32 inches waist measure. Price, 15 cts.

McCall Pattern
2624—Ladies' Five-Gored Skirt. Cut in 5 sizes, 22, 24, 26, 28 and 30 inches waist measure. Price, 15 cents.

McCall Pattern
2629—Ladies' Five-Gored Skirt. Cut in 6 sizes, 22, 24, 26, 28, 30 and 32 inches waist measure. Price, 15 cents.

Page 3

McCall Pattern
2602—Misses' Dress. Cut in 6 sizes, 13, 14, 15, 16, 17 and 18 years. Price, 15 cents.

Five-Gored Skirt

McCall Pattern
2622—Girls' Dress (to be worn over a Guimpe). Cut in 4 sizes, 6, 8, 10 and 12 years. Price, 15 cents.

Seven-Gored Side-Pleated Skirt

McCall Pattern
2614—Girls' Suit. Cut in 4 sizes, 6, 8, 10 and 12 years. Price, 15 cents.

Straight Side-Pleated Skirt

McCall Pattern
2581—Misses' Jumper Dress (with Guimpe). Cut in 6 sizes, 13, 14, 15, 16, 17 and 18 years. Price, 15 cents.

Circular Skirt

McCall Pattern
2585—Child's Dress. Cut in 4 sizes, 4, 6, 8 and 10 years. Price, 15 cents.

McCall Pattern
2603—Child's Dress (with Guimpe). Cut in 4 sizes, 2, 4, 6 and 8 years. Price, 15 cts.

Straight Pleated Skirt

McCall Pattern
2615—Child's Box-Pleated Dress (Closing at Front). Cut in 4 sizes, 2, 4, 6 and 8 years. Price, 15 cents.

McCall Pattern
2599—Girls' Dress (to be worn over a Guimpe). Cut in 4 sizes, 6, 8, 10 and 12 years. Price, 15 cents.

Seven-Gored Skirt

McCall Pattern
2610—Child's Skirt Rompers. Cut in 6 sizes, 1, 2, 3, 4, 5 and 6 years. Price, 10 cts.

McCall Pattern
2627—Child's Set of One-Piece Garments. Cut in 4 sizes, 6 months, 1, 2 and 3 years. Price, 15 cents.

McCall Pattern
2584—Boys' Blouse Suit (with Knickerbocker Trousers). Cut in 4 sizes, 4, 6, 8 and 10 years. Price, 15 cents.

Page 4

Ladies' Shirt Waists

McCall Pattern
2459—Ladies' Shirt Waist (without Lining). Cut in 7 sizes, 32, 34, 36, 38, 40, 42 and 44 inches bust measure. Price, 15 cents.

McCall Pattern
2395 — Ladies' Tucked Shirt Waist (without Lining). Cut in 7 sizes, 32, 34, 36, 38, 40, 42 and 44 inches bust measure. Price, 15 cents.

McCall Pattern
2534 — Ladies' Shirt Waist (without Lining). Cut in 8 sizes, 32, 34, 36, 38, 40, 42, 44 and 46 inches bust measure. Price, 15 cents.

McCall Pattern
2344—Ladies' Shirt Waist (without Lining). Cut in 6 sizes, 32, 34, 36, 38, 40 and 42 inches bust measure. Price, 15 cents.

McCall Pattern
2445 — Ladies' Shirt Waist (without Lining). Cut in 7 sizes, 32, 34, 36, 38, 40, 42 and 44 inches bust measure. Price, 15 cents.

McCall Pattern
2569 — Ladies' Shirt Waist (without Lining). Cut in 7 sizes, 32, 34, 36, 38, 40, 42 and 44 inches bust measure. Price, 15 cents.

McCall Pattern
2505 — Ladies' Shirt Waist (without Lining). Cut in 6 sizes, 32, 34, 36, 38, 40 and 42 inches bust measure. Price, 15 cents.

McCall Pattern
2492 — Ladies' Shirt Waist (without Lining). Cut in 7 sizes, 32, 34, 36, 38, 40, 42 and 44 inches bust measure. Price, 15 cents.

McCall Pattern
2253 — Ladies' Shirt Waist (without Lining). Cut in 5 sizes, 32, 34, 36, 38 and 40 inches bust measure. Price, 15 cents.

Page 5

Ladies' Shirt Waists

McCall Pattern
2444—Ladies' Blouse Waist (without Lining). Cut in 8 sizes, 32, 34, 36, 38, 40, 42, 44 and 46 inches bust measure.
Price, 15 cents.

McCall Pattern
2523—Ladies' Shirt Waist (without Lining). Cut in 7 sizes, 32, 34, 36, 38, 40, 42 and 44 inches bust measure.
Price, 15 cents.

McCall Pattern
2366—Ladies' Tucked Blouse Waist (without Lining). Cut in 6 sizes, 32, 34, 36, 38, 40 and 42 inches bust measure.
Price, 15 cents.

McCall Pattern
2543—Ladies' Shirt Waist (without Lining). Cut in 6 sizes, 32, 34, 36, 38, 40 and 42 inches bust measure. Price, 15 cents.

McCall Pattern
2086—Ladies' One-Piece Shirt Waist (without Lining). Cut in 6 sizes, 32, 34, 36, 38, 40 and 42 inches bust measure.
Price, 15 cents.

McCall Pattern
2495—Ladies' Shirt Waist (without Lining). Cut in 7 sizes, 32, 34, 36, 38, 40, 42 and 44 inches bust measure.
Price, 15 cents.

McCall Pattern
2406—Ladies' Shirt Waist (without Lining). Cut in 6 sizes, 32, 34, 36, 38, 40 and 42 inches bust measure.
Price, 15 cents.

McCall Pattern
2341—Ladies' Blouse Waist (without Lining). Cut in 6 sizes, 32, 34, 36, 38, 40 and 42 inches bust measure.
Price, 15 cents.

McCall Pattern
2393—Ladies' Surplice Waist (without Lining). Cut in 7 sizes, 32, 34, 36, 38, 40, 42 and 44 inches bust measure.
Price, 15 cents.

McCall Pattern
2397—Ladies' Shirt Waist (without Lining). Cut in 7 sizes, 32, 34, 36, 38, 40, 42 and 44 inches bust measure.
Price, 15 cents.

LADIES' WAISTS

McCall Pattern
2512—Ladies' Directoire Waist (with Lining). Cut in 6 sizes, 32, 34, 36, 38, 40 and 42 inches bust measure. Price, 15 cents.

McCall Pattern
2507—Ladies' Blouse Waist (with Lining). Cut in 6 sizes, 32, 34, 36, 38, 40 and 42 inches bust measure. Price, 15 cents.

McCall Pattern
2564—Ladies' Waist (with Lining). Cut in 6 sizes, 32, 34, 36, 38, 40 and 42 inches bust measure. Price, 15 cents.

McCall Pattern
1963—Ladies' Blouse Waist (High or Open Neck, Full-Length or Shorter Sleeves, and with or without Sleeve-Caps or Body Lining). Cut in 7 sizes, 32, 34, 36, 38, 40, 42 and 44 inches bust measure. Price, 15 cents.

McCall Pattern
2538—Ladies' Waist (without Lining). Cut in 6 sizes, 32, 34, 36, 38, 40 and 42 inches bust measure. Price, 15 cents.

McCall Pattern
2562—Ladies' Waist (without Lining). Cut in 6 sizes, 32, 34, 36, 38, 40 and 42 inches bust measure. Price, 15 cents.

McCall Pattern
2506—Ladies' Waist (without Body Lining). Cut in 5 sizes, 32, 34, 36, 38 and 40 inches bust measure. Price, 15 cents.

McCall Pattern
2494—Ladies' Blouse Waist (without Lining). Cut in 6 sizes, 32, 34, 36, 38, 40 and 42 inches bust measure. Price, 15 cents.

McCall Pattern
2457—Ladies' Blouse Waist (without Lining). Cut in 6 sizes, 32, 34, 36, 38, 40 and 42 inches bust measure. Price, 15 cents.

McCall Pattern
2102—Ladies' Blouse Waist (without Lining). Cut in 5 sizes, 32, 34, 36, 38 and 40 inches bust measure. Price, 15 cents.

Page 7

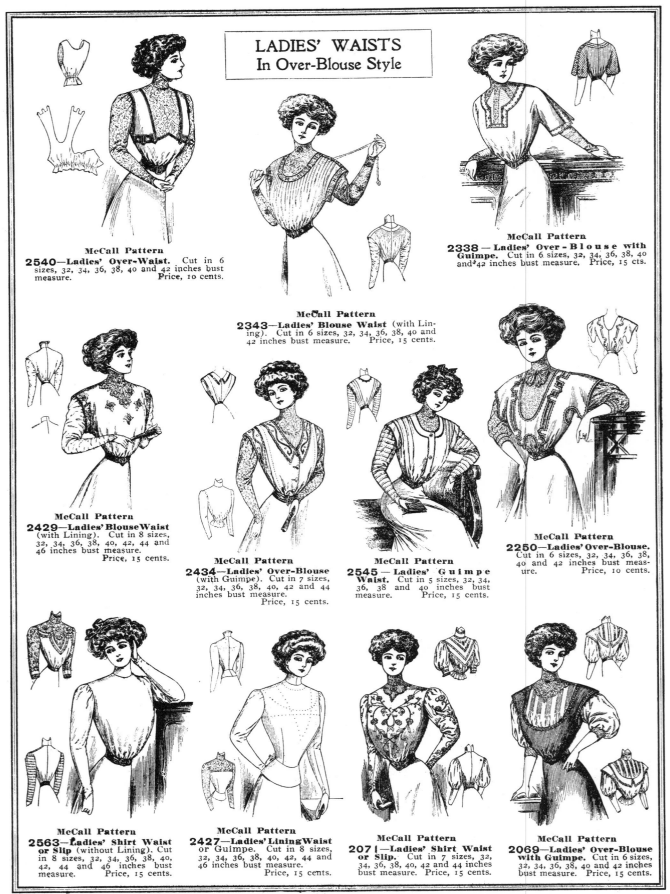

LADIES' WAISTS
In Over-Blouse Style

McCall Pattern
2540—Ladies' Over-Waist. Cut in 6 sizes, 32, 34, 36, 38, 40 and 42 inches bust measure. Price, 10 cents.

McCall Pattern
2343—Ladies' Blouse Waist (with Lining). Cut in 6 sizes, 32, 34, 36, 38, 40 and 42 inches bust measure. Price, 15 cents.

McCall Pattern
2338 — Ladies' Over-Blouse with Guimpe. Cut in 6 sizes, 32, 34, 36, 38, 40 and 42 inches bust measure. Price, 15 cts.

McCall Pattern
2429—Ladies' Blouse Waist (with Lining). Cut in 8 sizes, 32, 34, 36, 38, 40, 42, 44 and 46 inches bust measure. Price, 15 cents.

McCall Pattern
2434—Ladies' Over-Blouse (with Guimpe). Cut in 7 sizes, 32, 34, 36, 38, 40, 42 and 44 inches bust measure. Price, 15 cents.

McCall Pattern
2545 — Ladies' Guimpe Waist. Cut in 5 sizes, 32, 34, 36, 38 and 40 inches bust measure. Price, 15 cents.

McCall Pattern
2250—Ladies' Over-Blouse. Cut in 6 sizes, 32, 34, 36, 38, 40 and 42 inches bust measure. Price, 10 cents.

McCall Pattern
2563—Ladies' Shirt Waist or Slip (without Lining). Cut in 8 sizes, 32, 34, 36, 38, 40, 42, 44 and 46 inches bust measure. Price, 15 cents.

McCall Pattern
2427—Ladies' Lining Waist or Guimpe. Cut in 8 sizes, 32, 34, 36, 38, 40, 42, 44 and 46 inches bust measure. Price, 15 cents.

McCall Pattern
2071—Ladies' Shirt Waist or Slip. Cut in 7 sizes, 32, 34, 36, 38, 40, 42 and 44 inches bust measure. Price, 15 cents.

McCall Pattern
2069—Ladies' Over-Blouse with Guimpe. Cut in 6 sizes, 32, 34, 36, 38, 40 and 42 inches bust measure. Price, 15 cents.

Page 8

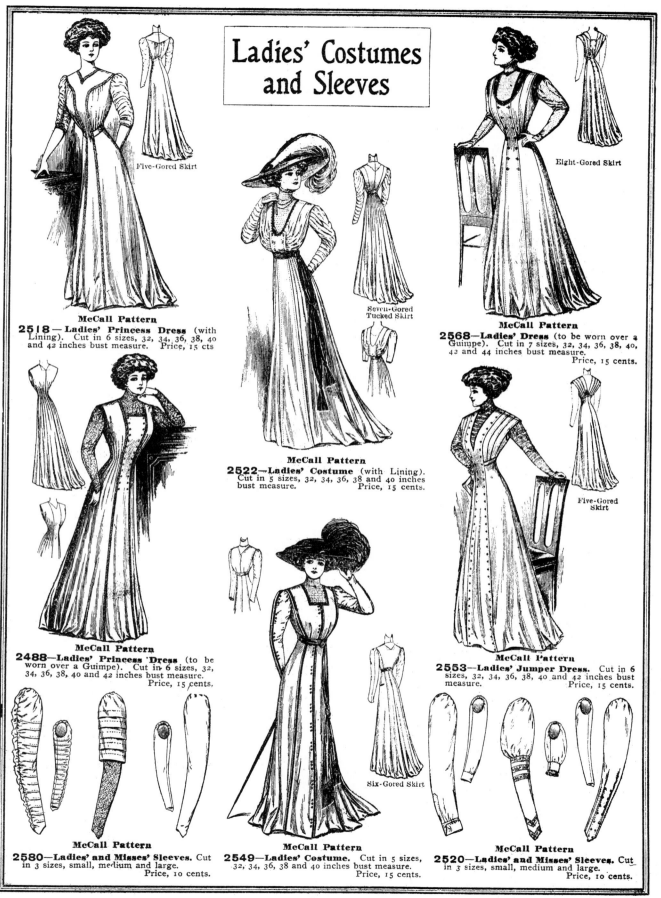

Ladies' Costumes and Sleeves

Five-Gored Skirt

McCall Pattern
2518—Ladies' Princess Dress (with Lining). Cut in 6 sizes, 32, 34, 36, 38, 40 and 42 inches bust measure. Price, 15 cts

Seven-Gored Tucked Skirt

McCall Pattern
2522—Ladies' Costume (with Lining). Cut in 5 sizes, 32, 34, 36, 38 and 40 inches bust measure. Price, 15 cents.

Eight-Gored Skirt

McCall Pattern
2568—Ladies' Dress (to be worn over a Guimpe). Cut in 7 sizes, 32, 34, 36, 38, 40, 42 and 44 inches bust measure. Price, 15 cents.

McCall Pattern
2488—Ladies' Princess Dress (to be worn over a Guimpe). Cut in 6 sizes, 32, 34, 36, 38, 40 and 42 inches bust measure. Price, 15 cents.

Five-Gored Skirt

McCall Pattern
2553—Ladies' Jumper Dress. Cut in 6 sizes, 32, 34, 36, 38, 40 and 42 inches bust measure. Price, 15 cents.

McCall Pattern
2580—Ladies' and Misses' Sleeves. Cut in 3 sizes, small, medium and large. Price, 10 cents.

Six-Gored Skirt

McCall Pattern
2549—Ladies' Costume. Cut in 5 sizes, 32, 34, 36, 38 and 40 inches bust measure. Price, 15 cents.

McCall Pattern
2520—Ladies' and Misses' Sleeves. Cut in 3 sizes, small, medium and large. Price, 10 cents.

Page 9

Ladies' Coats and Jackets

McCall Pattern
2105—Ladies' Sleeveless Jacket (with Deep Armholes). Cut in 6 sizes, 32, 34, 36, 38, 40 and 42 inches bust measure.
Price, 15 cents.

McCall Pattern
2557—Ladies' Eton Jacket. Cut in 6 sizes, 32, 34, 36, 38, 40 and 42 inches bust measure. Price, 15 cents.

McCall Pattern
2513—Ladies' Sleeveless Coat. Cut in 6 sizes, 32, 34, 36, 38, 40 and 42 inches bust measure. Price, 15 cents.

McCall Pattern
2206—Ladies' Coat (with Two Styles of Sleeves). Cut in 6 sizes, 32, 34, 36, 38, 40 and 42 inches bust measure. Price, 15 cts.

McCall Pattern
2533—Ladies' Coat. Cut in 7 sizes, 32, 34, 36, 38, 40, 42 and 44 inches bust measure. Price, 15 cents.

Six-Gored Skirt

McCall Pattern
2352—Ladies' Semi-Fitting Coat. Cut in 5 sizes, 32, 34, 36, 38 and 40 inches bust measure. Price, 15 cents.

McCall Pattern
2479—Ladies' Coat Suit. Cut in 6 sizes, 32, 34, 36, 38, 40 and 42 inches bust measure. Price, 15 cents.

McCall Pattern
1984—Ladies' Double-Breasted Jacket. Cut in 7 sizes, 32, 34, 36, 38, 40, 42 and 44 inches bust measure. Price, 15 cents.

Ladies' Coats and Jackets

McCall Pattern
2519—Ladies' Semi-Fitting Coat. Cut in 7 sizes, 32, 34, 36, 38, 40, 42 and 44 inches bust measure.   Price, 15 cents.

McCall Pattern
2092—Ladies' Coat (with Lapped Seams). Cut in 7 sizes, 32, 34, 36, 38, 40, 42 and 44 inches bust measure.   Price, 15 cents.

McCall Pattern
2555—Ladies' Directoire Coat. Cut in 5 sizes, 32, 34, 36, 38 and 40 inches bust measure.   Price, 15 cents.

McCall Pattern
2478—Ladies' Coat. Cut in 6 sizes, 32, 34, 36, 38, 40 and 42 inches bust measure.   Price, 15 cents.

McCall Pattern
2004—Ladies' Single-Breasted Jacket. Cut in 8 sizes, 32, 34, 36, 38, 40, 42, 44 and 46 inches bust measure.   Price, 15 cents.

McCall Pattern
2353—Ladies' Semi-Fitting Coat. Cut in 8 sizes, 32, 34, 36, 38, 40, 42, 44 and 46 inches bust measure.   Price, 15 cents.

McCall Pattern
2376—Ladies' Semi-Fitting Coat. Cut in 6 sizes, 32, 34, 36, 38, 40 and 42 inches bust measure.   Price, 15 cents.

McCall Pattern
2318—Ladies' Jacket (with Full-Length or Shorter Sleeves). Cut in 6 sizes, 32, 34, 36, 38, 40 and 42 inches bust measure.   Price, 15 cents.

Page 11

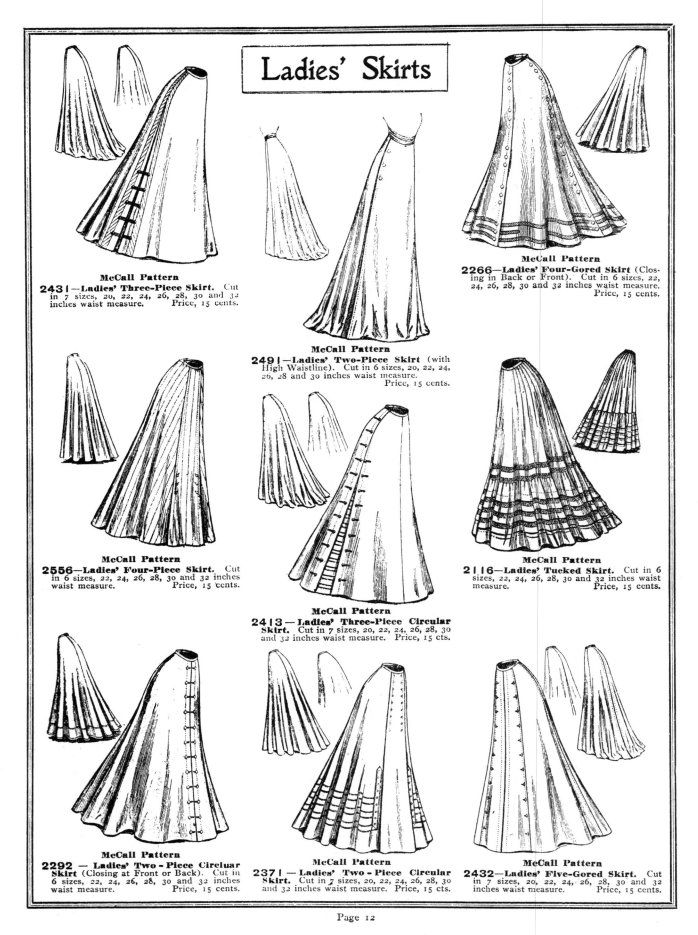

Ladies' Skirts

McCall Pattern
2431—Ladies' Three-Piece Skirt. Cut in 7 sizes, 20, 22, 24, 26, 28, 30 and 32 inches waist measure. Price, 15 cents.

McCall Pattern
2491—Ladies' Two-Piece Skirt (with High Waistline). Cut in 6 sizes, 20, 22, 24, 26, 28 and 30 inches waist measure. Price, 15 cents.

McCall Pattern
2266—Ladies' Four-Gored Skirt (Closing in Back or Front). Cut in 6 sizes, 22, 24, 26, 28, 30 and 32 inches waist measure. Price, 15 cents.

McCall Pattern
2556—Ladies' Four-Piece Skirt. Cut in 6 sizes, 22, 24, 26, 28, 30 and 32 inches waist measure. Price, 15 cents.

McCall Pattern
2413—Ladies' Three-Piece Circular Skirt. Cut in 7 sizes, 20, 22, 24, 26, 28, 30 and 32 inches waist measure. Price, 15 cts.

McCall Pattern
2116—Ladies' Tucked Skirt. Cut in 6 sizes, 22, 24, 26, 28, 30 and 32 inches waist measure. Price, 15 cents.

McCall Pattern
2292 — Ladies' Two - Piece Circular Skirt (Closing at Front or Back). Cut in 6 sizes, 22, 24, 26, 28, 30 and 32 inches waist measure. Price, 15 cents.

McCall Pattern
2371 — Ladies' Two - Piece Circular Skirt. Cut in 7 sizes, 20, 22, 24, 26, 28, 30 and 32 inches waist measure. Price, 15 cts.

McCall Pattern
2432—Ladies' Five-Gored Skirt. Cut in 7 sizes, 20, 22, 24, 26, 28, 30 and 32 inches waist measure. Price, 15 cents.

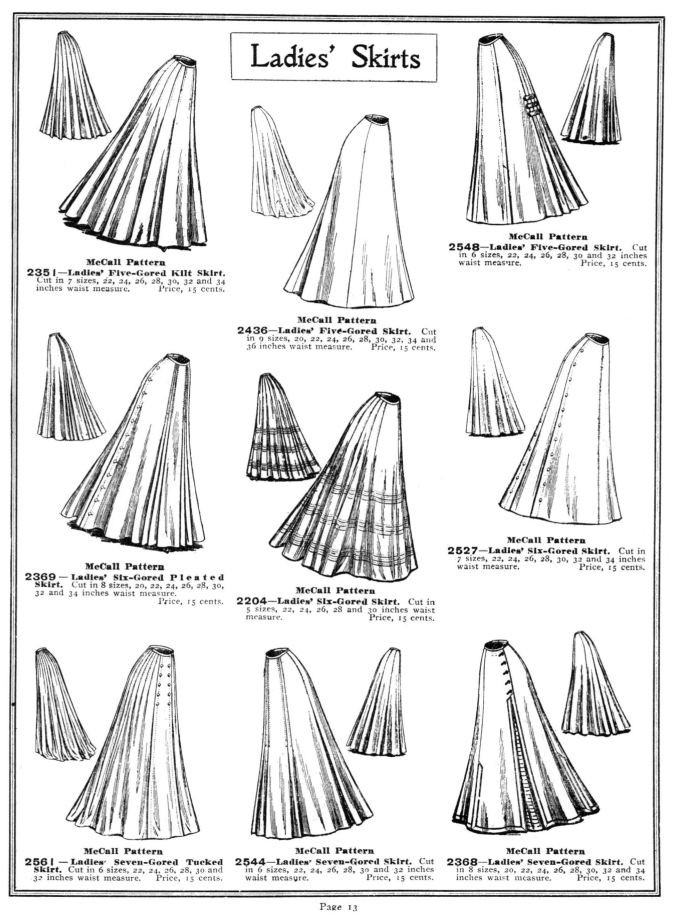

Ladies' Skirts

McCall Pattern
2351—Ladies' Five-Gored Kilt Skirt.
Cut in 7 sizes, 22, 24, 26, 28, 30, 32 and 34 inches waist measure.   Price, 15 cents.

McCall Pattern
2436—Ladies' Five-Gored Skirt. Cut in 9 sizes, 20, 22, 24, 26, 28, 30, 32, 34 and 36 inches waist measure.   Price, 15 cents.

McCall Pattern
2548—Ladies' Five-Gored Skirt. Cut in 6 sizes, 22, 24, 26, 28, 30 and 32 inches waist measure.   Price, 15 cents.

McCall Pattern
2369—Ladies' Six-Gored Pleated Skirt. Cut in 8 sizes, 20, 22, 24, 26, 28, 30, 32 and 34 inches waist measure.
Price, 15 cents.

McCall Pattern
2204—Ladies' Six-Gored Skirt. Cut in 5 sizes, 22, 24, 26, 28 and 30 inches waist measure.   Price, 15 cents.

McCall Pattern
2527—Ladies' Six-Gored Skirt. Cut in 7 sizes, 22, 24, 26, 28, 30, 32 and 34 inches waist measure.   Price, 15 cents.

McCall Pattern
2561—Ladies' Seven-Gored Tucked Skirt. Cut in 6 sizes, 22, 24, 26, 28, 30 and 32 inches waist measure.   Price, 15 cents.

McCall Pattern
2544—Ladies' Seven-Gored Skirt. Cut in 6 sizes, 22, 24, 26, 28, 30 and 32 inches waist measure.   Price, 15 cents.

McCall Pattern
2368—Ladies' Seven-Gored Skirt. Cut in 8 sizes, 20, 22, 24, 26, 28, 30, 32 and 34 inches waist measure.   Price, 15 cents.

Page 13

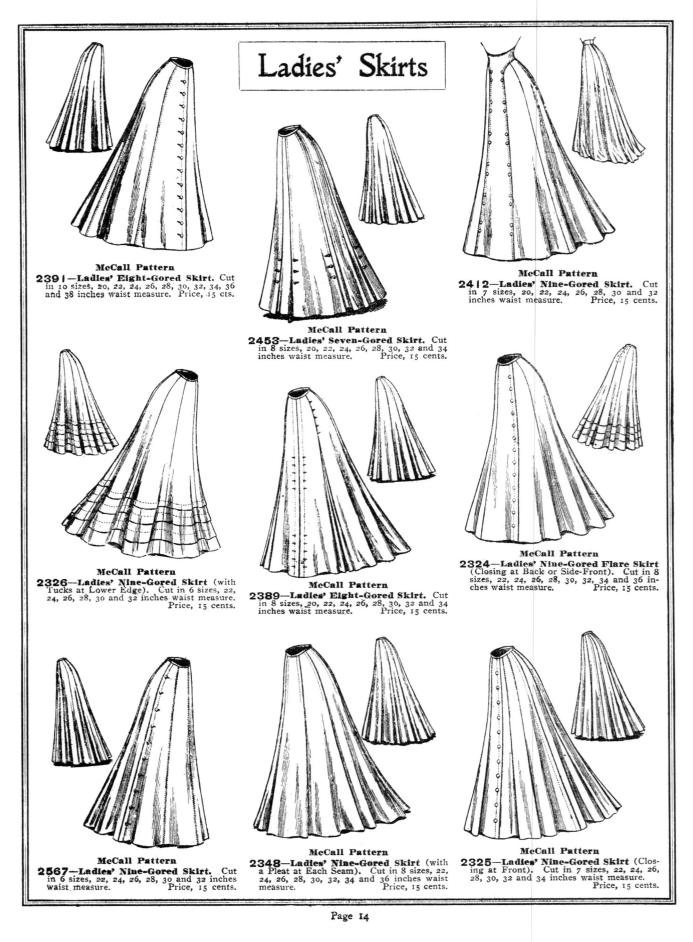

Ladies' Skirts

McCall Pattern
2391—Ladies' Eight-Gored Skirt. Cut in 10 sizes, 20, 22, 24, 26, 28, 30, 32, 34, 36 and 38 inches waist measure. Price, 15 cts.

McCall Pattern
2453—Ladies' Seven-Gored Skirt. Cut in 8 sizes, 20, 22, 24, 26, 28, 30, 32 and 34 inches waist measure. Price, 15 cents.

McCall Pattern
2412—Ladies' Nine-Gored Skirt. Cut in 7 sizes, 20, 22, 24, 26, 28, 30 and 32 inches waist measure. Price, 15 cents.

McCall Pattern
2326—Ladies' Nine-Gored Skirt (with Tucks at Lower Edge). Cut in 6 sizes, 22, 24, 26, 28, 30 and 32 inches waist measure. Price, 15 cents.

McCall Pattern
2389—Ladies' Eight-Gored Skirt. Cut in 8 sizes, 20, 22, 24, 26, 28, 30, 32 and 34 inches waist measure. Price, 15 cents.

McCall Pattern
2324—Ladies' Nine-Gored Flare Skirt (Closing at Back or Side-Front). Cut in 8 sizes, 22, 24, 26, 28, 30, 32, 34 and 36 inches waist measure. Price, 15 cents.

McCall Pattern
2567—Ladies' Nine-Gored Skirt. Cut in 6 sizes, 22, 24, 26, 28, 30 and 32 inches waist measure. Price, 15 cents.

McCall Pattern
2348—Ladies' Nine-Gored Skirt (with a Pleat at Each Seam). Cut in 8 sizes, 22, 24, 26, 28, 30, 32, 34 and 36 inches waist measure. Price, 15 cents.

McCall Pattern
2325—Ladies' Nine-Gored Skirt (Closing at Front). Cut in 7 sizes, 22, 24, 26, 28, 30, 32 and 34 inches waist measure. Price, 15 cents.

Page 14

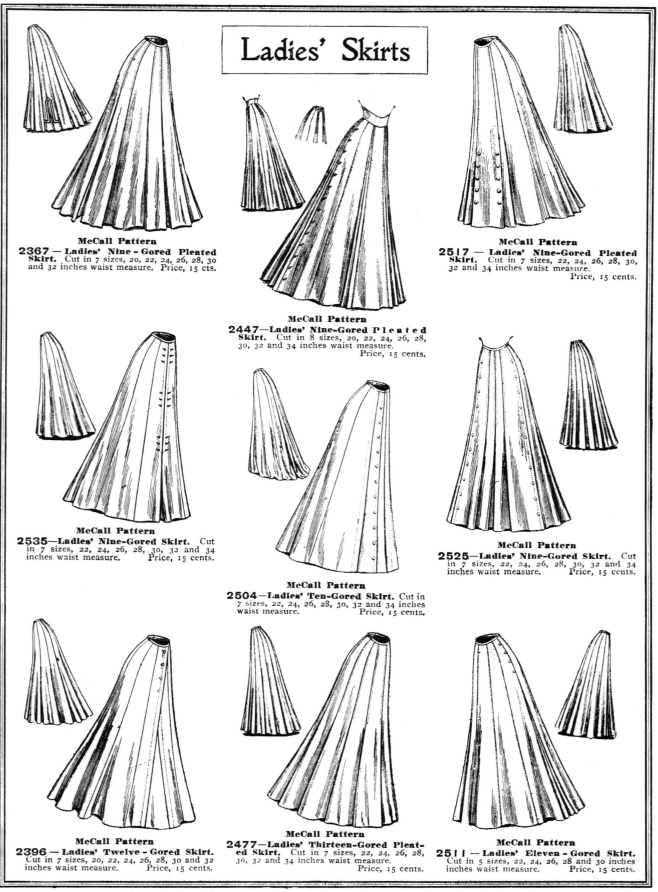

Ladies' Skirts

McCall Pattern

2367—Ladies' Nine-Gored Pleated Skirt. Cut in 7 sizes, 20, 22, 24, 26, 28, 30 and 32 inches waist measure. Price, 15 cts.

McCall Pattern

2447—Ladies' Nine-Gored Pleated Skirt. Cut in 8 sizes, 20, 22, 24, 26, 28, 30, 32 and 34 inches waist measure. Price, 15 cents.

McCall Pattern

2517—Ladies' Nine-Gored Pleated Skirt. Cut in 7 sizes, 22, 24, 26, 28, 30, 32 and 34 inches waist measure. Price, 15 cents.

McCall Pattern

2535—Ladies' Nine-Gored Skirt. Cut in 7 sizes, 22, 24, 26, 28, 30, 32 and 34 inches waist measure. Price, 15 cents.

McCall Pattern

2504—Ladies' Ten-Gored Skirt. Cut in 7 sizes, 22, 24, 26, 28, 30, 32 and 34 inches waist measure. Price, 15 cents.

McCall Pattern

2525—Ladies' Nine-Gored Skirt. Cut in 7 sizes, 22, 24, 26, 28, 30, 32 and 34 inches waist measure. Price, 15 cents.

McCall Pattern

2396—Ladies' Twelve-Gored Skirt. Cut in 7 sizes, 20, 22, 24, 26, 28, 30 and 32 inches waist measure. Price, 15 cents.

McCall Pattern

2477—Ladies' Thirteen-Gored Pleated Skirt. Cut in 7 sizes, 22, 24, 26, 28, 30, 32 and 34 inches waist measure. Price, 15 cents.

McCall Pattern

2511—Ladies' Eleven-Gored Skirt. Cut in 5 sizes, 22, 24, 26, 28 and 30 inches waist measure. Price, 15 cents.

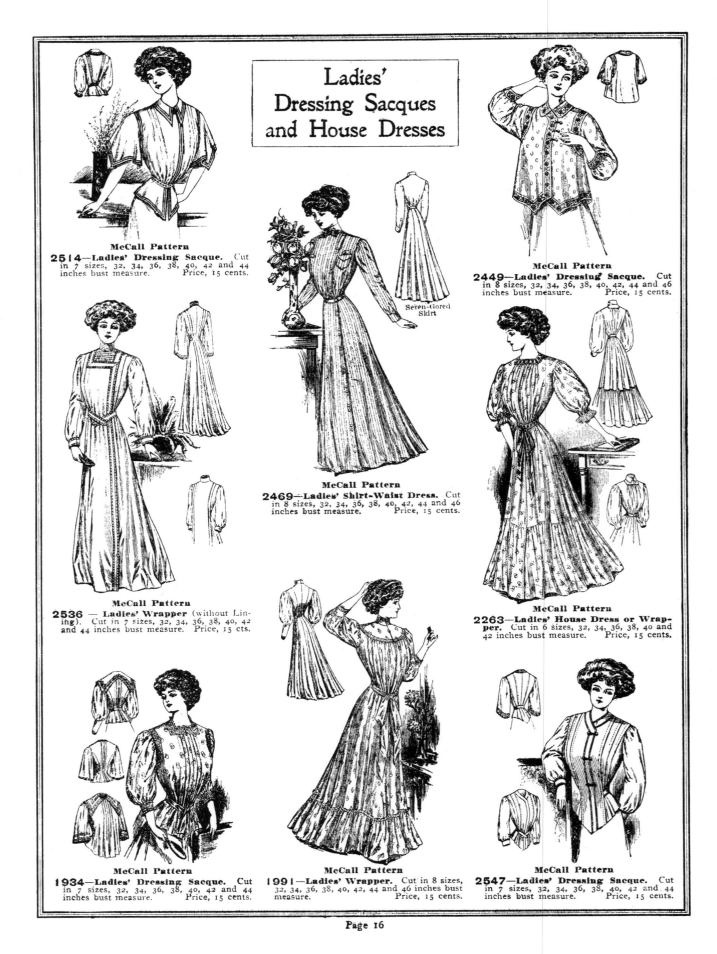

Ladies' Dressing Sacques and House Dresses

McCall Pattern
2514—Ladies' Dressing Sacque. Cut in 7 sizes, 32, 34, 36, 38, 40, 42 and 44 inches bust measure. Price, 15 cents.

McCall Pattern
2449—Ladies' Dressing Sacque. Cut in 8 sizes, 32, 34, 36, 38, 40, 42, 44 and 46 inches bust measure. Price, 15 cents.

Seven-Gored Skirt

McCall Pattern
2469—Ladies' Shirt-Waist Dress. Cut in 8 sizes, 32, 34, 36, 38, 40, 42, 44 and 46 inches bust measure. Price, 15 cents.

McCall Pattern
2536 — Ladies' Wrapper (without Lining). Cut in 7 sizes, 32, 34, 36, 38, 40, 42 and 44 inches bust measure. Price, 15 cts.

McCall Pattern
2263—Ladies' House Dress or Wrapper. Cut in 6 sizes, 32, 34, 36, 38, 40 and 42 inches bust measure. Price, 15 cents.

McCall Pattern
1934—Ladies' Dressing Sacque. Cut in 7 sizes, 32, 34, 36, 38, 40, 42 and 44 inches bust measure. Price, 15 cents.

McCall Pattern
1991—Ladies' Wrapper. Cut in 8 sizes, 32, 34, 36, 38, 40, 42, 44 and 46 inches bust measure. Price, 15 cents.

McCall Pattern
2547—Ladies' Dressing Sacque. Cut in 7 sizes, 32, 34, 36, 38, 40, 42 and 44 inches bust measure. Price, 15 cents.

McCall Pattern

2411—Ladies' Dressing Sacque (with Body and Sleeves in One). Cut in 8 sizes, 32, 34, 36, 38, 40, 42, 44 and 46 inches bust measure. Price, 15 cents.

McCall Pattern

2372—Ladies' Dressing Sacque. Cut in 7 sizes, 32, 34, 36, 38, 40, 42 and 44 inches bust measure. Price, 15 cents.

McCall Pattern

2355—Ladies' Dressing Sacque. Cut in 8 sizes, 32, 34, 36, 38, 40, 42, 44 and 46 inches bust measure. Price, 15 cents.

McCall Pattern

8632—Ladies' Tucked Kimono. Cut in 7 sizes, 32, 34, 36, 38, 40, 42 and 44 inches bust measure. Price, 15 cents.

McCall Pattern

9364—Ladies' Dressing Sacque (Tucked or Gathered, with Two Styles of Sleeves and Collars). Cut in 7 sizes, 32, 34, 36, 38, 40, 42 and 44 inches bust measure.

McCall Pattern

2187—Ladies' Dressing Sacque (with Body and Sleeves in One). Cut in 7 sizes, 32, 34, 36, 38, 40, 42 and 44 inches bust measure. Price, 15 cents.

McCall Pattern

2554—Ladies Kimono. Cut in 6 sizes, 32, 34, 36, 38, 40 and 42 inches bust measure. Price, 15 cents.

McCall Pattern

1329—Ladies' Dressing Sacque (High or Low Neck, Full-Length or Three-Quarter Sleeves in Either of Two Styles). Cut in 6 sizes, 32, 34, 36, 38, 40 and 42 inches bust measure. Price, 15 cents.

McCall Pattern

2521—Ladies' Wrapper. Cut in 7 sizes, 32, 34, 36, 38, 40, 42 and 44 inches bust measure. Price, 15 cents.

Misses' Costumes

McCall Pattern
2552—Misses' Dress with Bloomers. Cut in 6 sizes, 13, 14, 15, 16, 17 and 18 years. Price, 10 cents.

Thirteen-Gored Pleated Skirt

McCall Pattern
2531—Misses' Thirteen-Gored Skirt. Cut in 6 sizes, 13, 14, 15, 16, 17 and 18 years. Price, 15 cents.

Seven-Gored Skirt

McCall Pattern
2208—Misses' Jumper Dress (to be worn over a Guimpe, and having a Seven-Gored Skirt). Cut in 5 sizes, 13, 14, 15, 16 and 17 years. Price, 15 cents.

Five-Gored Skirt

McCall Pattern
2461—Misses' Dress. Cut in 5 sizes, 13, 14, 15, 16 and 17 years. Price, 15 cents.

McCall Pattern
2404—Misses' Dress (without Lining). Cut in 5 sizes, 13, 14, 15, 16 and 17 years. Price, 15 cents.

Seven-Gored Skirt

McCall Pattern
2476—Misses' Box-Pleated Dress (with Lining). Cut in 5 sizes, 13, 14, 15, 16 and 17 years. Price, 15 cents.

Eleven-Gored Skirt

McCall Pattern
2083—Misses' Princess Dress. Cut in 5 sizes, 13, 14, 15, 16 and 17 years. Price, 15 cents.

McCall Pattern
1229—Misses' Straight Kilt-Pleated Skirt. Cut in 5 sizes, 13, 14, 15, 16 and 17 years. Price, 15 cents.

McCall Pattern
2176—Misses' Jumper Dress (to be worn over a Guimpe). Cut in 5 sizes, 13, 14, 15, 16 and 17 years. Price, 15 cents.

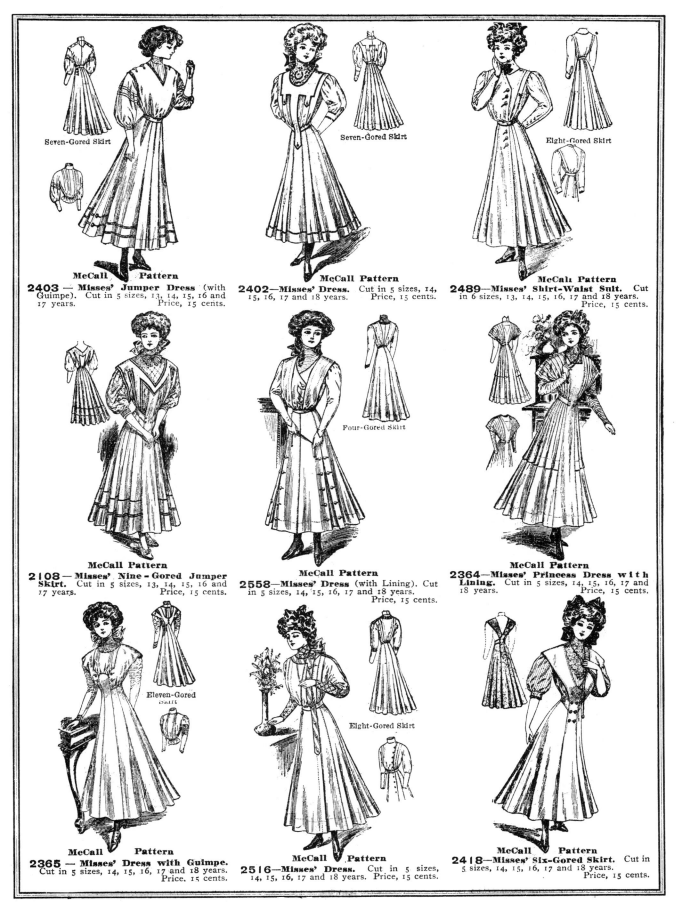

McCall Pattern
2403 — Misses' Jumper Dress (with Guimpe). Cut in 5 sizes, 13, 14, 15, 16 and 17 years.　　Price, 15 cents.

Seven-Gored Skirt

McCall Pattern
2402 — Misses' Dress. Cut in 5 sizes, 14, 15, 16, 17 and 18 years.　　Price, 15 cents.

Seven-Gored Skirt

McCall Pattern
2489 — Misses' Shirt-Waist Suit. Cut in 6 sizes, 13, 14, 15, 16, 17 and 18 years.　　Price, 15 cents.

Eight-Gored Skirt

McCall Pattern
2108 — Misses' Nine-Gored Jumper Skirt. Cut in 5 sizes, 13, 14, 15, 16 and 17 years.　　Price, 15 cents.

McCall Pattern
2558 — Misses' Dress (with Lining). Cut in 5 sizes, 14, 15, 16, 17 and 18 years.　　Price, 15 cents.

Four-Gored Skirt

McCall Pattern
2364 — Misses' Princess Dress with Lining. Cut in 5 sizes, 14, 15, 16, 17 and 18 years.　　Price, 15 cents.

McCall Pattern
2365 — Misses' Dress with Guimpe. Cut in 5 sizes, 14, 15, 16, 17 and 18 years.　　Price, 15 cents.

Eleven-Gored Skirt

McCall Pattern
2516 — Misses' Dress. Cut in 5 sizes, 14, 15, 16, 17 and 18 years. Price, 15 cents.

Eight-Gored Skirt

McCall Pattern
2418 — Misses' Six-Gored Skirt. Cut in 5 sizes, 14, 15, 16, 17 and 18 years.　　Price, 15 cents.

Page 19

Misses' Costumes

McCall Pattern
2321—Misses' Dress (Closing at Front).
Cut in 5 sizes, 13, 14, 15, 16 and 17 years.
Price, 15 cents.

Four-Gored Skirt

McCall Pattern
2439—Misses' Russian Dress. Cut in 5 sizes, 13, 14, 15, 16 and 17 years.
Price, 15 cents.

Eight-Gored Skirt

Straight Box-Pleated Skirt

McCall Pattern
2487 — Misses' Coat Suit. Cut in 5 sizes, 14, 15, 16, 17 and 18 years.
Price, 15 cents.

McCALL PATTERNS 10c AND 15c NONE HIGHER

Nine-Gored Pleated Skirt

McCall Pattern
2539—Misses' Shirt-Waist Suit. Cut in 6 sizes, 13, 14, 15, 16, 17 and 18 years.
Price, 15 cents.

McCall Pattern
2017—Misses' Costume. Cut in 4 sizes, 14, 15, 16 and 17 years. Price, 15 cents.

Seven-Gored Skirt

Six-Gored Skirt

McCall Pattern
2571—Misses' Coat Suit. Cut in 5 sizes, 14, 15, 16, 17 and 18 years. Price, 15 cents.

Nine-Gored Pleated Skirt

2419—Misses' Coat Suit. Cut in 5 sizes, 14, 15, 16, 17 and 18 years.
Price, 15 cents.

Seven-Gored Box-Pleated Skirt

McCall Pattern
2526 — Misses' Coat Suit. Cut in 5 sizes, 13, 14, 15, 16 and 17 years.
Price, 15 cents.

Page 20

Girls' Dresses

Straight Gathered Skirt

McCall Pattern
2565 — Girls' Bretelle Dress (with Guimpe). Cut in 5 sizes, 4, 6, 8, 10 and 12 years. Price, 15 cents.

Two-Piece Skirt

McCall Pattern
2319—Girls' Surplice Dress with Guimpe (Dress Front-Closing). Cut in 4 sizes, 6, 8, 10 and 12 years. Price, 15 cts.

Six-Gored Skirt

McCall Pattern
2524—Girls' Dress (to be worn over a Guimpe). Cut in 5 sizes, 4, 6, 8, 10 and 12 years. Price, 15 cents.

Eight-Gored Box-Pleated Skirt

McCall Pattern
2416—Girls' Dress (with Lining). Cut in 4 sizes, 6, 8, 10 and 12 years. Price, 15 cents.

Nine-Gored Pleated Skirt

McCall Pattern
2405—Girls' Dress. Cut in 4 sizes, 6, 8, 10 and 12 years. Price, 15 cents.

Five-Gored Pleated Skirt

McCall Pattern
2438—Girls' Dress. Cut in 4 sizes, 6, 8, 10 and 12 years. Price, 15 cents.

Five-Gored Skirt

McCall Pattern
2483—Girls' Box-Pleated Dress. Cut in 4 sizes, 6, 8, 10 and 12 years. Price, 15 cents.

McCall Pattern
2574 — Girls' Dress with Bloomers. Cut in 4 sizes, 6, 8, 10 and 12 years. Price, 15 cents.

Straight Pleated Skirt

McCall Pattern
2502—Girls' Sailor Dress Cut in 4 sizes, 6, 8, 10 and 12 years. Price, 15 cents.

Page 21

Girls' Dresses

Five-Gored Skirt

McCall Pattern
2462—Girls' Dress. Cut in 4 sizes, 6, 8, 10 and 12 years.   Price, 15 cents.

Straight Gathered Skirt

McCall Pattern
2384—Girls' Dress (with Guimpe). Cut in 4 sizes, 6, 8, 10 and 12 years. - Price, 15 cents.

Straight Gathered Skirt

McCall Pattern
2454—Girls' Dress (with Guimpe). Cut in 4 sizes, 6, 8, 10 and 12 years.   Price, 15 cents.

McCall Pattern
2398—Girls' Box-Pleated Dress. Cut in 5 sizes, 4, 6, 8, 10 and 12 years.   Price, 15 cents.

Straight Gathered Skirt

McCall Pattern
1607—Girls' Jumper Dress. Cut in 5 sizes, 4, 6, 8, 10 and 12 years. Price, 15 cts.

Thirteen-Gored Side-Pleated Skirt

McCall Pattern
2335—Girls' Dress (to be worn over a Guimpe). Cut in 4 sizes, 6, 8, 10 and 12 years.   Price, 15 cents.

McCall Pattern
2471—Girls' Russian Dress. Cut in 4 sizes, 6, 8, 10 and 12 years. Price, 15 cts.

Thirteen-Gored

McCall Pattern
2328—Girls' Dress with Shield. Cut in 4 sizes, 6, 8, 10 and 12 years.   Price, 15 cents.

Straight Gathered Skirt

McCall Pattern
2501—Girls' Surplice Dress (with Guimpe). Cut in 4 sizes, 6, 8, 10 and 12 years.   Price, 15 cents.

Girls' Dresses

Straight Skirt

McCall Pattern
2273—Girls' Dress with Guimpe. Cut in 4 sizes, 6, 8, 10 and 12 years.
Price, 15 cents.

Straight Skirt

McCall Pattern
2186—Girls' Dress (having Full-Length or Shorter Sleeves, and a Straight Skirt, and with or without Bretelles). Cut in 4 sizes, 6, 8, 10 and 12 years. Price, 15 cts.

Straight Skirt

McCall Pattern
2289—Girls' Dress (Body and Sleeves in One). Cut in 4 sizes, 6, 8, 10 and 12 years. Price, 15 cents.

Five-Gored Pleated Skirt

McCall Pattern
1956—Girls' Dress (to be worn over a Guimpe). Cut in 4 sizes, 6, 8, 10 and 12 years. Price, 15 cents.

Straight Pleated Skirt

McCall Pattern
2551—Girls' Dress (to be worn over a Guimpe). Cut in 4 sizes, 6, 8, 10 and 12 years. Price, 15 cents.

Straight Side-Pleated Skirt

McCall Pattern
1921—Girls' Dress (to be worn over a Guimpe). Cut in 4 sizes, 6, 8, 10 and 12 years. Price, 15 cents.

McCall Pattern
2291—Girls' Princess Dress. Cut in 5 sizes, 4, 6, 8, 10 and 12 years.
Price, 15 cents.

Straight Gathered Skirt

McCall Pattern
2559—Child's Dress. Cut in 4 sizes, 4, 6, 8 and 10 years.
Price, 15 cents.

Straight Skirt

McCall Pattern
1978—Child's Dress with Guimpe. Cut in 4 sizes, 4, 6, 8 and 10 years.
Price, 15 cents.

Three-Piece Skirt

McCall Pattern
2485—Child's Dress (with Lining). Cut in 4 sizes, 4, 6, 8 and 10 years.
Price, 15 cents.

Straight Gathered Skirt

McCall Pattern
2415—Child's Three-Piece Suit. Cut in 5 sizes, 4, 6 8, 10 and 12 years.
Price, 15 cents.

McCall Pattern
2219—Child's Dress with Guimpe having Full-Length or Shorter Sleeves). Cut in 4 sizes, 4, 6, 8 and 10 years.
Price, 15 cents.

Five-Gored Tucked Skirt

McCall Pattern
9181—Girls' Jacket Costume. Cut in 5 sizes, 6, 8, 10, 12 and 14 years.
Price, 15 cents.

Seven-Gored Pleated Skirt

McCall Pattern
2573—Girls' Three-Piece Suit. Cut in 4 sizes, 6, 8, 10 and 12 years. Price, 15 cts.

Nine-Gored Box-Pleated Skirt

McCall Pattern
2401—Girls' Coat Suit (with Skirt and Suspenders). Cut in 4 sizes, 6, 8, 10 and 12 years.
Price, 15 cents.

McCall Pattern
2347—Girls' Coat. Cut in 6 sizes, 2, 4, 6, 8, 10 and 12 years.
Price, 15 cents.

McCall Pattern
2532—Child's Coat. Cut in 5 sizes, 2, 4, 6, 8 and 10 years.
Price, 15 cents.

McCall Pattern
1575—Child's Double-Breasted Coat (in Three-Quarter or Reefer Length). Cut in 4 sizes, 2, 4, 6 and 8 years.
Price, 15 cents.

McCall Pattern
2576—Child's Coat. Cut in 4 sizes, 1, 2, 3 and 4 years.
Price, 15 cents.

Page 24

CHILDREN'S DRESSES

McCall Pattern

2575 — Child's Dress with Bloomers. Cut in 3 sizes, 2, 4 and 6 years. Price, 15 cents.

McCall Pattern

2150 — Child's One - Piece Dress. Cut in 3 sizes, 2, 4 and 6 years. Price, 10 cents.

McCall Pattern

1545 — Child's One - Piece Dress (to be Slipped on over the Head). Cut in 3 sizes, 2, 4 and 6 years. Price, 10 cents.

2572 — Child's Dress (with Shield). Cut in 4 sizes, 4, 6, 8 and 10 years. Price, 15 cents.

McCall Pattern

2330 — Child's Dress (having a Straight Lower Edge). Cut in 5 sizes, 2, 3, 4, 5 and 6 years. Price, 10 cents.

McCall Pattern

2455 — Child's Pleated Dress (with Underbody and Bloomers). Cut in 4 sizes, 4, 6, 8 and 10 years. Price, 15 cents.

McCall Pattern

2079 — Child's Dress with Guimpe. Cut in 4 sizes, 2, 4, 6 and 8 years. Price, 15 cents.

McCall Pattern

2498 — Child's Dress. Cut in 4 sizes, 2, 4, 6 and 8 years. Price, 15 cents.

McCall Pattern

2200 — Child's Dress (having a Straight Gathered Skirt). Cut in 5 sizes, 2, 4, 6, 8 and 10 years. Price, 10 cents.

McCall Pattern

2400 — Child's Dress (Closed at Side-Front). Cut in 4 sizes, 2, 4, 6 and 8 years. Price, 10 cents.

McCall Pattern

2333 — Child's Dress (with Shield). Cut in 4 sizes, 2, 4, 6 and 8 years. Price, 15 cents.

McCall Pattern

1485 — Child's Dress (to be worn over a Guimpe). Cut in 6 sizes, 1, 2, 3, 4, 5 and 6 years. Price, 10 cents.

McCall Pattern

1870 — Child's Dress. Cut in 5 sizes, 6 months, 1, 2, 3 and 4 years. Price, 10 cents.

McCall Pattern

1826 — Child's Dress. Cut in 4 sizes, 2, 4, 6 and 8 years. Price, 15 cents.

Page 25

CHILDREN'S DRESSES

McCall Pattern
Straight Skirt
2234—Child's Dress. Cut in 4 sizes, 2, 4, 6 and 8 years. Price, 15 cents.

McCall Pattern
2410—Child's One-Piece Dress. Cut in 4 sizes, 2, 4, 6 and 8 years. Price, 10 cts.

McCall Pattern
2399—Girls' Dress with Guimpe. Cut in 4 sizes, 2, 4, 6 and 8 years. Price, 15 cents.

Two-Piece Skirt

McCall Pattern
2070 — Child's One - Piece Dress (to be Slipped on over the Head and worn over a Guimpe). Cut in 4 sizes, 2, 4, 6 and 8 years. Price, 10 cents.

McCall Pattern
2570—Child's Dress. Cut in 7 sizes, 6 months, 1, 2, 3, 4, 5 and 6 years. Price, 10 cents.

McCall Pattern
2515—Child's Dress. Cut in 6 sizes, 1, 2, 3, 4, 5 and 6 years. Price, 15 cents.

McCall Pattern
2509—Child's Dress. Cut in 4 sizes, 2, 4, 6 and 8 years. Price, 15 cents.

Straight Gathered Skirt

McCall Pattern
2196—Child's Dress with Guimpe. Cut in 3 sizes, 2, 4 and 6 years. Price, 15 cents.

Straight Skirt

McCall Pattern
2510 — Child's Dress or Slip. Cut in 7 sizes, 6 months, 1, 2, 3, 4, 5 and 6 years. Price, 10 cents.

McCall Pattern
2421—Child's Dress. Cut in 3 sizes, 2, 4 and 6 years. Price, 15 cents.

McCall Pattern
2385 — Child's One - Piece Dress (with Guimpe). Cut in 3 sizes, 2, 4 and 6 years. Price, 15 cents.

Infants' and Children's Sets

McCall Pattern
2265—Infants' Princess Set. Cut in one size.   Price, 15 cents.

McCall Pattern
1291—Child's Set of Short Clothes (consisting of a Coat with or without the Cape, and a Dress with Full-Length or Elbow Sleeves and with or without the Bretelles). Cut in 4 sizes, 6 months, 1, 2 and 3 years.   Price, 15 cents.

McCall Pattern
8508—Infants' Set (consisting of Dress, Kimono perforated for Short Length, Slip or Nightgown, Skirt, Pinning Blanket, Diaper Drawers and Band). Cut in one size.   Price, 15 cents.

McCall Pattern
2566—Infants' Set. Cut in one size.   Price, 15 cents.

SHAPE OF ONE-PIECE CAP

McCall Pattern
2220—Infants' Set (One-Piece Cape, Bib, Bootees and Pillow-Case). Cut in one size.   Price, 10 cents.

McCall Pattern
8525 — Child's Set of Short Clothes (consisting of Dress with High or Dutch Neck and Full or Three-Quarter Length Sleeves, a Petticoat, Drawers and House Sacque). Cut in 4 sizes, 6 months, 1, 2 and 3 years.   Price, 15 cents.

McCall Pattern
8818 — Child's Set of Short Clothes (consisting of a Box-Coat with or without the Cape or Cuffs, a Dress with High or Dutch Neck and Full or Three-Quarter Length Sleeves, and a Petticoat). Cut in 4 sizes, 6 months, 1, 2 and 3 years.   Price, 15 cents.

McCall Pattern
1497—Infants' Set (having Dress, Kimono and Nightgown) Cut in one size.   Price, 15 cents.

McCall Pattern
1547—Infants' Set (Sacque, Cloak and Cap). Cut in one size.   Price, 15 cents.

Page 27

BOYS' SUITS

McCall Pattern
2336—Boys' Russian Suit with Knickerbockers. Cut in 5 sizes, 2, 3, 4, 5 and 6 years.   Price, 15 cents.

McCall Pattern
2167—Little Boys' Russian Suit (with Knickerbocker Trousers). Cut in 3 sizes, 2, 4 and 6 years.   Price, 15 cents.

McCall Pattern
2422—Boys' Russian Suit. Cut in 3 sizes, 2, 4 and 6 years.   Price, 15 cents.

McCall Pattern
2577—Boys' Russian Suit. Cut in 5 sizes, 2, 3, 4, 5 and 6 years.   Price, 15 cents.

McCall Pattern
2210—Boys' Blouse (in Regulation Naval Style, with or without Yoke Facing). Cut in 6 sizes, 4, 6, 8, 10, 12 and 14 years.   Price, 10 cents.

McCall Pattern
2508—Boys' Shirt Waist Suit. Cut in 4 sizes, 4, 6, 8 and 10 years.   Price, 15 cts.

McCall Pattern
9065—Boys' Suit (consisting of a Double Breasted Blouse with Removable Eton Collar, and Knickerbocker Trousers). Cut in 6 sizes, 3, 4, 5, 6, 7 and 8 years.   Price, 15 cents.

McCall Pattern
2542—Little Boys' Russian Suit. Cut in 5 sizes, 2, 3, 4, 5 and 6 years.   Price, 15 cents.

McCall Pattern
2486—Little Boys' Russian Suit. Cut in 4 sizes, 3, 4, 5 and 6 years.   Price, 15 cents.

McCall Pattern
2475—Little Boys' Russian Suit. Cut in 3 sizes, 2, 4 and 6 years.   Price, 15 cents.

McCall Pattern
2499—Boys' Suit. Cut in 5 sizes, 2, 3, 4, 5 and 6 years.   Price, 15 cents.

Page 28

Men's and Boys' Garments

McCall Pattern
2541—Men's Negligee Shirt (with Coat Closing). Cut in 9 sizes, 14, 14½, 15, 15½, 16, 16½, 17, 17½ and 18 inches neck measure. Price, 15 cents.

McCall Pattern
7496—Boys' Pajamas. Cut in 7 sizes, 4, 6, 8, 10, 12, 14 and 16 years. Price, 10c.

McCall Pattern
8384—Boys' Negligee Shirt (with Attached Collar, or with Neckband and Detachable Collar). Cut in 4 sizes, 10, 12, 14 and 16 years. Price, 15 cents.

McCall Pattern
2300—Boys' Shirt Waist (with or without Back Yoke). Cut in 5 sizes, 4, 6, 8, 10 and 12 years. Price, 10 cents.

McCall Pattern
8808—Boys' Knee Trousers without a Fly. Cut in 6 sizes, 3, 4, 5, 6, 7 and 8 years.

McCall Pattern
8734—Men's Pajamas (with Collar or Band Facing). Cut in 6 sizes, 34, 36, 38, 40, 42 and 44 inches breast measure. Price, 15 cents.

McCall Pattern
2529—Men's Sack Coat. Cut in 6 sizes, 34, 36, 38, 40, 42 and 44 inches breast measure. Price, 15 cents.

McCall Pattern
8489—Boys' Overalls. Cut in 8 sizes, 2, 4, 6, 8, 10, 12, 14 and 16 years. Price, 10 cents.

McCall Pattern
9144—Men's Night Shirt. Cut in 7 sizes, 36, 38, 40, 42, 44, 46 and 48 inches breast measure. Price, 15 cents.

McCall Pattern
9259—Boys' Night Shirt. Cut in 6 sizes, 6, 8, 10, 12, 14 and 16 years. Price, 10 cts.

McCall Pattern
8840—Boys' Norfolk Suit. Cut in 8 sizes, 5, 6, 7, 8, 9, 10, 11 and 12 years. Price, 15 cents.

McCall Pattern
9767—Boys' Knickerbocker Trousers. Cut in 6 sizes, 2, 3, 4, 5, 6 and 7 years. Price, 10 cents.

Page 29

McCall Pattern
1776—Ladies' One-Piece Nightgown.
Cut in 7 sizes, 32, 34, 36, 38, 40, 42 and 44 inches bust measure.   Price, 15 cents.

McCall Pattern
1980—Ladies' and Misses' One-Piece Corset Cover (having Straight Upper Edge). Cut in 7 sizes, 30, 32, 34, 36, 38, 40 and 42 inches bust measure. Price, 10 cts.

McCall Pattern
1880—Ladies' Corset Cover. Cut in 7 sizes, 32, 34, 36, 38, 40, 42 and 44 inches bust measures.   Price, 10 cents.

McCall Pattern
2383—Ladies' Empire Night Dress.
Cut in 8 sizes, 32, 34, 36, 38, 40, 42, 44 and 46 inches bust measure.   Price, 15 cents.

McCall Pattern
1492—Ladies' Corset Cover. Cut in 6 sizes, 32, 34, 36, 38, 40 and 42 inches bust measure.   Price, 10 cents.

McCall Pattern
9370—Ladies' French Open Drawers (Pleated or Gathered at the Back). Cut in 6 sizes, 22, 24, 26, 28, 30 and 32 inches waist measure.   Price, 10 cents.

McCall Pattern
2350 — Ladies' Chemise (having Deep Armholes). Cut in 8 sizes, 32, 34, 36, 38, 40, 42, 44 and 46 inches bust measure.
Price, 10 cents.

McCall Pattern
1990—Ladies' One-Piece Drawers. Cut in 6 sizes, 22, 24, 26, 28, 30 and 32 inches waist measure.   Price, 10 cents.

McCall Pattern
2528—Ladies' Combination Corset Cover and Open Drawers. Cut in 7 sizes, 32, 34, 36, 38, 40, 42 and 44 inches bust measure.   Price, 15 cents.

McCall Pattern
1278—Ladies' Seven-Gored Petticoat (with an Inverted Pleat or Gathers at the Back). Cut in 5 sizes, 22, 24, 26, 28 and 30 inches waist measure.   Price, 15 cents.

McCall Pattern
8839 — Ladies' Open Drawers with Yoke (with Inverted Pleat or Gathers at the Back). Cut in 7 sizes, 22, 24, 26, 28, 30, 32 and 34 inches waist measure.
Price, 10 cents.

Page 30

McCall Pattern

2490—Ladies' Corset Cover. Cut in 8 sizes, 32, 34, 36, 38, 40, 42, 44 and 46 inches bust measure. Price, 10 cents.

McCall Pattern

9465 — Misses' Work Apron (with or without Sleeves, and with Yoke perforated for Low Neck). Cut in 4 sizes, 12, 14, 16 and 18 years. Price, 10 cents.

McCall Pattern

8601 — Child's One-Piece Drawers. Cut in 5 sizes, 1, 2, 3, 4 and 5 years. Price, 10 cents.

McCall Pattern

7560—Ladies' Work Apron. Cut in 3 sizes, small, medium and large. Price, 10 cents.

McCall Pattern

2340—Ladies' and Misses' Apron. Cut in 3 sizes, small, medium and large. Price, 10 cents.

McCall Pattern

8513 — Misses' and Girls' Drawers. Cut in 5 sizes, 8, 10, 12, 14 and 16 years. Price, 10 cents.

McCall Pattern

2550—Ladies' One-Piece Work Apron. Cut in 3 sizes, small, medium and large. Price, 10 cents.

McCall Pattern

2450—Ladies' Corset Cover. Cut in 6 sizes, 32, 34, 36, 38, 40 and 42 inches bust measure. Price, 10 cents.

McCall Pattern

1005—Child's Nightgown (High or Low Neck, Full or Three-Quarter Length Sleeves). Cut in 4 sizes, 6 months, 2, 4 and 6 years. Price, 10 cents.

McCall Pattern

8709—Ladies' Tucked Nightgown (with High or Dutch Neck, and Full or Three-Quarter Length Sleeve). Cut in 7 sizes, 32, 34, 36, 38, 40, 42 and 44 inches bust measure. Price, 15 cents.

McCall Pattern

9183—Misses' and Girls' Square-Yoke Nightgown (High or Low Neck, Full-Length or Shorter Bishop Sleeves). Cut in 6 sizes, 6, 8, 10, 12, 14 and 16 years. Price, 10 cents.

Page 31

APRONS, ETC.

McCall Pattern
9403 — **Child's Apron** (High or Low Neck, with or without Sleeves and Collar). Cut in 6 sizes, 2, 4, 6, 8, 10 and 12 years.
Price, 10 cents.

McCall Pattern
2530 — **Child's Combination Undergarment.** Cut in 4 sizes, 2, 4, 6 and 8 years.
Price, 10 cents.

McCall Pattern
1529 — **Child's Play Suit or Paddlers** (with Detachable Sleeves). Cut in 5 sizes, 1, 2, 3, 4 and 5 years. Price, 10 cents.

McCall Pattern
2380 — **Dolls' Dress, Coat and Bonnet.** Cut in 4 sizes, 18, 20, 22 and 24 inches long. Price, 10 cents.

McCall Pattern
2560 — **Child's One-Piece Apron.** Cut in 5 sizes, 2, 4, 6, 8 and 10 years.
Price, 10 cents.

McCall Pattern
7574 — **Child's Night Drawers** (with Bishop or Plain Sleeves, with or without Collar). Cut in 10 sizes, 2, 3, 4, 5, 6, 7, 8, 9, 10 and 11 years. Price, 10 cents.

McCall Pattern
2500 — **Ladies' Open Knickerbocker Drawers** (with Yoke). Cut in 7 sizes, 22, 24, 26, 28, 30, 32 and 34 inches waist measure. Price, 10 cents.

McCall Pattern
2060 — **Ladies' and Misses Collar and Cuff Set** (for Shirt Waists and Coats). Cut in 3 sizes, small, medium and large.
Price, 10 cents.

McCall Pattern
9759 — **Child's Sack Apron** (with or without the Sash or Strap). Cut in 7 sizes, 1, 2, 3, 4, 5, 6 and 7 years.
Price, 10 cents.

McCall Pattern
9198 — **Ladies' Sack Apron** (perforated for Round or Square Neck). Cut in 7 sizes, 32, 34, 36, 38, 40, 42 and 44 inches bust measure. Price, 15 cents.

McCall Pattern
9453 — **Children's Rompers.** Cut in 3 sizes, 2, 4 and 6 years. Price, 10 cents.

Page 32

152

HOW TO TAKE MEASUREMENTS
FOR McCALL PATTERNS

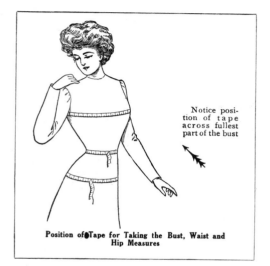

Notice position of tape across fullest part of the bust

Position of Tape for Taking the Bust, Waist and Hip Measures

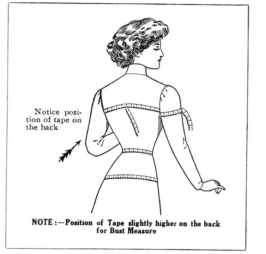

Notice position of tape on the back

NOTE:—Position of Tape slightly higher on the back for Bust Measure

LADIES

Bust—Pass the tape around the body over the fullest part of the bust—a little higher in the back—and draw close but not tight.

Waist—Draw the tape tight around the waist.

Hip—Adjust the tape over the hips 6 inches below the waistline and draw moderately close.

Sleeve—Measure around muscular part of the arm, about 1 inch below the armhole.

MISSES, GIRLS AND CHILDREN

Breast—Pass the tape around the body close up under the arm. Give both age and breast measure.

Waist—Draw the tape straight around the waist.

Head—Adjust the tape around the head, across middle of forehead. The following are corresponding head and cap measures:

Age,	. .	½	2	4	6	8	10	12 years.
Head,	. .	17	18⅞	19⅝	20⅜	20¾	20¾	21⅛ ins.
Cap,	. .	5¼	5⅞	6⅛	6⅜	6½	6½	6⅝

MEN AND BOYS

Breast—For shirts, coats, overcoats, vests, etc.—pass the tape around the body about 1 inch below the armhole and across fullest part of the breast.

Waist—For trousers—pass the tape around the waist and draw moderately close.

Neck—For neckband—pass the tape around the neck for exact size and then add 1 inch.

DOLLS

Height—Measure from top of head to sole.

YOU CAN HAVE ANY McCALL PATTERN
FREE

McCALL'S MAGAZINE HAS MORE SUBSCRIBERS THAN ANY OTHER LADIES' MAGAZINE IN THE WORLD

You can have any McCall Pattern FREE by subscribing for McCall's Magazine (The Queen of Fashion) for one year. McCall's is exclusively a Woman's Magazine. It tells all about the very latest styles in garments and millinery; how to be well dressed; how to do plain and fancy needlework; how to cook delicious dishes; how to dress and take care of the hair, and many other things that a woman wants to know about. For the small sum of fifty cents, this delightful magazine—the most popular ladies' magazine published in the world—will be mailed to your home regularly every month for 12 months. Select the pattern you want, and subscribe now through the merchant who supplied you with this Catalogue. Do not put it off. There are over one million women in the United States who pay to receive McCall's Magazine regularly every month. They think it worth the money, and you will too. Only fifty cents a year with one McCall Pattern free to every subscriber.

Subscribe at the store from which you received this Catalogue of Fashion.

THE McCALL COMPANY